Rethinking Public Governance

RETHINKING POLITICAL SCIENCE AND INTERNATIONAL STUDIES

This series is a forum for innovative scholarly writing from across all substantive fields of political science and international studies. The series aims to enrich the study of these fields by promoting a cutting-edge approach to thought and analysis. Academic scrutiny and challenge is an essential component in the development of political science and international studies as fields of study, and the act of re-thinking and re-examining principles and precepts that may have been long-held is imperative.

Rethinking Political Science and International Studies showcases authored books that address the field from a new angle, expose the weaknesses of existing concepts and arguments, or 're-frame' the topic in some way. This might be through the introduction of radical ideas, through the integration of perspectives from other fields or even disciplines, through challenging existing paradigms, or simply through a level of analysis that elevates or sharpens our understanding of a subject.

For a full list of Edward Elgar published titles, including the titles in this series, visit our website at www.e-elgar.com.

Rethinking Public Governance

Jacob Torfing

Professor of Politics and Institutions, Department of Social Sciences and Business, Roskilde University, Denmark and Professor, Faculty of Social Sciences, Nord University, Norway

RETHINKING POLITICAL SCIENCE AND INTERNATIONAL STUDIES

Edward Elgar
PUBLISHING

Cheltenham, UK • Northampton, MA, USA

Published by
Edward Elgar Publishing Limited
The Lypiatts
15 Lansdown Road
Cheltenham
Glos GL50 2JA
UK

Edward Elgar Publishing, Inc.
William Pratt House
9 Dewey Court
Northampton
Massachusetts 01060
USA

A catalogue record for this book
is available from the British Library

Library of Congress Control Number: 2023937061

This book is available electronically in the **Elgar**online
Political Science and Public Policy subject collection
http://dx.doi.org/10.4337/9781789909777

MIX
Paper from
responsible sources
FSC
www.fsc.org   FSC® C013056

ISBN 978 1 78990 976 0 (cased)
ISBN 978 1 78990 977 7 (eBook)

Printed and bound in Great Britain by TJ Books Limited, Padstow, Cornwall

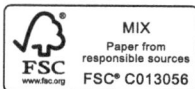

Contents

1. Introduction

This book argues that public governance is changing so rapidly and profoundly that public administration research is struggling to keep up and to keep track of the changes and their various implications. A broad range of well-established principles, perceptions and forms of governing in the public sector are being challenged by new ideas, concepts and practices that, when taken together, are transforming the *modus operandi* of public governance. Hence, new and emerging forms of political leadership, public management, public organization, administrative steering, cross-boundary collaboration, public regulation and societal problem-solving are being combined with new digital technologies and a novel focus on the production of innovative public value outcomes.

The pace of governance changes has accelerated in recent decades. After half a century of an almost undisputed reign of liberal democracy and public bureaucracy, New Public Management (NPM) reforms swept the world beginning in the late 1970s. Despite their positive impact and results, these NPM practices soon gave rise to an array of criticisms that, in the subsequent decades, spurred the proliferation of several new governance paradigms. Hence, public administration researchers started talking about the Neo-Weberian State (Pollitt & Bouckaert 2011), Digital Era Governance (Dunleavy 2006), Public Value Management (Benington & Moore 2010) and New Public Governance (Osborne 2010). In many cases, the new ideas about public governance triggered reforms, resulting in new practices. While it is difficult to explain the growing pace of public governance reforms, globalization, new technologies, growing citizen demands and the recognition of the planetary limits seem to have disrupted the established forms of public governance and have engaged elected politicians, public managers and an army of private consultants in experimentation, learning and innovation diffusion. In other words, changes in the public sector reflect both external societal change and internal agency-based learning and entrepreneurship.

The COVID-19 pandemic has further accelerated the transformation of public governance. Against a tragic background of illness, death and economic hardship, public sectors around the world have produced numerous innovations in response to the immense pressures from the pandemic, lockdowns and the new health regulations. These crisis-induced innovations have transformed both the form and function of administrative systems and the provision of services to citizens (Torfing et al. 2022). Some of them might vanish with the return to normalcy, but proactive efforts to learn from the catastrophic health crisis and retain new and better practices will help to produce a lasting impact on public governance.

What is perceived as "new" and "changed" is often more a matter of poor memory, as it merely reactivates, recycles and repackages old ideas and practices as part of repetitive pendulum swings. While this is true, we should be careful not to adopt a circular view of history that precludes disruptive change. Hence, we seldom solve new and emerging problems by returning to the past. Instead, we engage in what Schumpeter (1942) once termed "creative destruction." As such, there is little doubt that much of the current change is "real" in the sense of taking us in new directions that challenge the *public governance orthodoxy*, which combines national forms of representative democracy and public bureaucracy with NPM elements.

The foundation of the public governance orthodoxy in the Western world was established following the Second World War, when public bureaucracy expanded under the aegis of democratically elected governments. In response to mounting criticisms in the 1970s, the democratic and bureaucratic nation-state gradually integrated core elements from NPM, such as an increased reliance on competitive markets and systematic use of performance management (Hood 1991). The result was a new public governance system that, at least in theory, could deliver democratic accountability, bureaucratic compliance and economic efficiency. It is this public governance orthodoxy that is now being challenged by new trends and developments that are triggered by a combination of organizational learning, chance discoveries, emerging challenges, new possibilities and changing administrative fads and fashions. Yet it is clear that the tried-and-true forms of politics and administration associated with the public governance orthodoxy are neither disappearing overnight nor rendered obsolete by the new and promising forms of public governance. We usually find ourselves stuck in the middle between old and new forms of governance. This pinch tends to make us feel as though we must choose between adhering to the past or embracing the future, when we should rather be searching for ways to combine and balance new and old ideas and practices. Perhaps we should be rearticulating both as part of a robust and future-oriented public governance system aimed at combining the best from the past with the best of the new and emerging forms of public governance, while being prepared to flexibly adapt the combination of disparate public governance tools to changing conditions and new challenges.

THEORIES OF PUBLIC GOVERNANCE CHANGE

This book defines public governance as the more or less institutionalized processes through which political, administrative and societal actors formulate and achieve common objectives (Torfing et al. 2019). This broad definition makes public governance inseparable from democracy, public administration and the exercise of leadership. It also tends to perceive government as a particular form of governance that is characterized by being both formal and unicentric. Public governance can in fact assume different forms, since common objectives may be formulated and achieved by political and administrative leaders of hierarchical government, quasi-markets involving private firms in state-regulated competition for public service contracts, or relevant and affected actors engaged in collaborative forms of governance in networks and partnerships.

Public governance is constantly changing as new forms of governance emerge and combine with existing forms of governance. To understand the changing forms of governance, public administration research has developed several change theories. The first group of theories is *rational reform theories*, which basically argue that public organizations monitor their performance and regularly identify problems and challenges that trigger the search for alternative solutions, along with the calculation of the costs and benefits of each available solution, and finally select and implement the most promising solution. There are several modifications of the theories of rational reform. Some researchers point to the absence of full information about alternative solutions and the limited decision-making capacity that forces decision-makers to adopt satisfactory rather than optimal solutions (Simon 1996). Others have stressed the political opposition and conflicts that tend to prevent the top-down implementation of public reform initiatives (Peters 2002). Finally, some scholars claim that the rational change agents are not found at the apex of public organizations but rather at the agency level, where public managers and employees are engaged in budget maximizing (Niskanen 1968) and bureau-shaping (Dunleavy 1998).

A second group of change theories is associated with *historical institutionalism*, which claims that the institutional density in the field of public governance tends to lock public policy and administration into stable paths that are almost inescapable, even in the face of feasible alternatives that could potentially enhance efficiency (Pierson 2000; Torfing 2009). A stable path is created through a mixture of accidental events and the codification of compromises between conflicting actors, and it tends to govern the thinking and doing in a particular field for long periods of time with only small, incremental changes (Hall 1993; Mahoney 2000; True et al. 2019). A combination of sunk costs and the uncertainty and risks associated with reform prevents rational reform, so the stable path will endure until a major crisis destabilizes and disrupts it, thus opening the window of opportunity for reform.

A third group of *incremental change theories* questions the sharp division between stable institutionalized paths and rational intentional reforms, arguing that even stable paths may be subject to gradual change. Stable paths may defy radical reform attempts but be susceptible to incremental change through the continuous replacement of old rules with new ones, the layering of new rules and values on top of old changes in the environment that alter the meaning and significance of established rules and norms, and strategic changes in the application of existing rules (Streeck & Thelen 2005; Mahoney & Thelen 2009). Echoing earlier theories of muddling through (Lindblom 1959), this incremental change theory complements the historical institutionalist theory of path-dependent lock-ins by accounting for the possibility of change *in* rather than *of* a particular path. The gradual changes in a particular path may be completely uncoordinated and thus go in different directions. Hence, we are still far away from the assumptions of hierarchically controlled strategic change found in rational reform theory.

What all of these change theories lack is a clear understanding of the driver of change in public governance. Fortunately, Powell and DiMaggio (1983) come to our rescue as they convincingly show how public organizations tend to adopt the latest fad and fashion in order to appear legitimate in the eyes of external actors. Apparently, legitimacy is more important than efficiency for the long-term survival of public governance institutions. If a public organization is doing either what the government prescribes, what other similar organizations are doing or what their new employees say is the "new black," the organization is likely to be forgiven for being somewhat inefficient. An important modification to this theory is that public organizations rarely buy the whole package of prescriptions for governance reform, tending instead to use a mix-and-match strategy when adopting new fashionable ideas and practice. New organizational templates are disaggregated and subsequently translated and adapted before particular parts of them are adopted (Røvik 2016).

The role of "magic concepts" in spurring change in public governance has been highlighted by Pollitt and Hupe (2011), who also recognize the limits to theories about the pressures from shifting fashions. What becomes fashionable has a certain bearing on the problems and challenges encountered by leading political and administrative actors. Hence, as famously suggested by Kingdon (1984), innovation is a result of the contingent alignment of separate streams of problems and solutions with favorable political forces that are driven by new ideas, perceptions and discourses. The successful alignment of problems, solutions and discursive contexts is most likely in situations characterized by crisis and disruption and tends to be carried out by skillful policy entrepreneurs (Birkmann et al. 2010). The latter might be found at the apex of government institutions, at lower organizational levels or among private stakeholders. Hence, collaboration and coalition-building are crucial to fostering change.

In Kingdon's multiple-stream framework, problems and solutions are floating around in the "primeval soup" before policy entrepreneurs seize the right moment and exploit a particular occasion to join them and show how they fit the discourse they are trying to advance. Hence, we are still in the realm of temporal sorting where solutions may precede problems and vice versa, meaning that traditional means–end rationality is limited (March & Olsen 1989).

This book eclectically combines all of the above-mentioned change theories in arguing that public decision-makers often see themselves as drivers of rational reform, but quickly realize the political barriers and the inertia of highly institutionalized paths, which may be subject to incremental change until they are shattered by disruptive events. These open the window of opportunity and create a terrain for policy entrepreneurs to create what might become a new stable path through the alignment of problems and solutions with new fashionable ideas and discourses (Torfing 1999).

FIND AND ENLARGE

This book is about rethinking public governance. Rather than engaging in a critical and constructive reading of existing theories of public governance (see Ansell 2023) however, it has an empirical starting point. Hence, the present attempt to rethink public governance is prompted by observations of new, interesting and promising trends detectable in some but not all Western countries. The identification of these trends relies on subjective interpretations of emerging ideas and practices backed by empirical accounts and scholarly discussions.

Looking back on my own research, I realize that I tend to use the same method of inquiry over and over again. This method could be called "find and enlarge," and it begins by looking for new and promising solutions to pressing problems. When a solution is found and positively evaluated, it is time to go back to the drawing board to properly conceptualize, theorize and scrutinize the new promising finding based on existing concepts and theories—and perhaps the invention of new ones that better capture what is happening. This endeavor is crucial to avoid falling into the trap of impressionistic descriptivism and premature diffusion of new fads and fashions. The final step is to enlarge the newly conceptualized promising finding by looking for empirical manifestations in different places, conducting systematic studies of its conditions, forms and impact, and experimenting with its usage to pave the way for its future extension and robust application. The find-and-enlarge method is basically an abductive method aiming to posit a solution to relevant societal problems while alternately drawing on empirical and theoretical resources in a back-and-forth movement (Glynos & Howarth 2007).

To illustrate, the COVID-19 pandemic serves as a magnifying glass revealing how the public sector is expected to solve not only simple and complex problems but also turbulent problems characterized by unpredictability, uncertainty, inconsistency and instability. Looking at the attempts to deal with the pandemic, which has stretched the public sector to its limits, it is interesting and encouraging to see how public organizations have produced an array of agile responses that are flexibly adapted to changing conditions and seek to exploit new opportunities to produce innovative solutions. To capture this promising way of responding to the health crisis, cutting-edge research has started exploring robust solutions to turbulent problems. Robustness is conceptualized as a dynamic resilience aimed at exploiting the crisis situation to foster adaptive and innovative solutions that, instead of aiming to restore a pre-crisis equilibrium, seek to take us to a new and better place (Ansell et al. 2020). Hence, robust solutions aim to bounce forward instead of bouncing back. The concept of policy and governance robustness provides a new strategy for maintaining key functions, goals and values in the public sector in times of crisis-induced turbulence by means of flexible adaptation and proactive innovation (Capano & Woo 2018).

The find-and-enlarge method is a way of rethinking public governance based on a theoretical and practical interrogation of pressing problems and promising solutions. It aims to describe and advance possible solutions, some of which might sweep the world, while others appear to be dead ends or survive in new and unexpected forms. The method informs all of the chapters in this book, each of which explores a particular aspect of public governance and aims to identify problems and promising solutions that are conceptualized and theorized in order to enlarge their impact.

The method clearly has a normative foundation since it aims to identify promising solutions to pressing problems. This begs the question: What is a "promising" solution? It is certainly neither an ideal or optimal solution, nor is it a proven and well-documented solution. It is a solution that offers an attractive yet feasible solution to an urgent governance problem, thus promising to contribute to the production of a contextually defined value. Hence, the ultimate normative yardstick is the production of public value defined as what has value for society at large and what different publics value (Moore 1995). It goes without saying that there will often be a conflict between what has value for society at large and what has value for particular groups in society, and that the final negotiation of such conflicts is highly contingent and inherently political.

AIM AND CONTENT

This book aims to identify, explain and critically evaluate new and emerging ideas, practices and institutions that are transforming how public governance is perceived and conducted in practice. It focuses on cutting-edge developments in public governance and analyzes how they are framed and theorized. The hope is that the book will inspire graduate students, established researchers, and engaged practitioners to rethink how public governance and public administration may be functioning, operating, and organized in the future.

The next chapter will paint a broad picture of the public governance orthodoxy that, in recent decades, has combined representative democracy and public bureaucracy with NPM elements. The book then devotes a full chapter to each of the ten most significant transformations that have occurred in the field of public governance and discusses how the new and old forms of governance can be combined in a pragmatic and constructive manner to align the quest for accountability, compliance, and efficiency with the ability to mobilize the knowledge and resources of a broad range of actors in the pursuit of innovative solutions to pressing societal problems. The concluding chapter reflects on how students of public governance can best comprehend, study, and take advantage of the current transformations in public governance.

REFERENCES

Ansell, C., Sørensen, E. & Torfing, J. (2020). When Governance Meets Political Sociology: Reflections on the Social Embedding of Generic Governance Instruments. In Meek, J. (Ed.), *Handbook on Collaborative Public Management* (405–24). Cheltenham: Edward Elgar.

Benington, J. & Moore, M. H. (Eds.) (2010). *Public Value: Theory and Practice.* Basingstoke: Palgrave Macmillan.

Birkmann, J., Buckle, P., Jaeger, J., Pelling, M., Setiadi, N., Garschagen, M., Fernando, N. & Kropp, J. (2010). Extreme Events and Disasters: A Window of Opportunity for Change? *Natural Hazards*, *55*(3), 637–55.

Capano, G. & Woo, J. J. (2018). Designing Policy Robustness: Outputs and Processes. *Policy and Society*, *37*(4), 422–40.

Dunleavy, P. (1998). The Bureau-Shaping Model. In Hill, M. (Ed.), *The Policy Process: A Reader*. New York: Routledge.

Dunleavy, P. (2006). *The Westminster Model and the Distinctiveness of British Politics*. Basingstoke: Palgrave Macmillan.

Glynos, J. & Howarth, D. (2007). Logics of Critical Explanation in Social and Political Theory. In Howarth, D. & Glynos, J. (Eds.), *Logics of Critical Explanation in Social and Political Theory* (1–109). London: Routledge.

Hall, P. A. (1993). Policy Paradigms, Social Learning, and the State: The Case of Economic Policymaking in Britain. *Comparative Politics, 25*(3), 275–96.

Hood, C. (1991). A Public Management for All Seasons? *Public Administration, 69*(1), 3–19.

Kingdon, J. (1984). *Agendas, Alternatives and Public Policies*. New York: Harper Collins College Publishers.

Lindblom, C. (1959). The Science of "Muddling Through." *Public Administration Review*, *19*(2), 79–88.

Mahoney, J. (2000). Path Dependence in Historical Sociology. *Theory and Society*, *29*(4), 507–48.

Mahoney, J. & Thelen, K. (2009). *Explaining Institutional Change: Ambiguity, Agency and Power*. Cambridge: Cambridge University Press.

March, J. G. & Olsen, J. P. (1989). *Rediscovering Institutions*. New York: The Free Press.

Moore, M. H. (1995). *Creating Public Value*. Cambridge, MA: Harvard University Press.

Niskanen, W. A. (1968). The Peculiar Economics of Bureaucracy. *The American Economic Review*, *58*(2), 293–305.

Osborne, S. P. (Ed.) (2010). *New Public Governance*. London: Routledge.

Peters, B. G. (2002). *Politics of Bureaucracy*. London: Routledge.

Pierson, P. (2000). Increasing Returns, Path Dependence, and the Study of Politics. *American Political Science Review*, *94*(2), 251–67.

Pollitt, C. & Bouckaert, G. (2011). *Continuity and Change in Public Policy and Management*. Cheltenham: Edward Elgar.

Pollitt, C. & Hupe, P. (2011). Talking about Government: The Role of Magic Concepts. *Public Management Review*, *13*(5), 641–58.

Powell, W. W. & DiMaggio, P. J. (1983). The Iron Cage Revisited: Institutional Isomorphism and Collective Rationality in Organizational Fields. *American Sociological Review*, *48*(2), 147–60.

Røvik, K. A. (2016). Knowledge Transfer as Translation: Review and Elements of an Instrumental Theory—Knowledge Transfer as Translation. *International Journal of Management Reviews*, *18*(3), 290–310.

Schumpeter, J. A. (1942). *Capitalism, Socialism and Democracy*. New York: Harper & Brothers.

Simon, H. A. (1996). *The Sciences of the Artificial*. Cambridge, MA: MIT Press.

Streeck, W. & Thelen, K. (Eds.) (2005). *Beyond Continuity: Institutional Change in Advanced Political Economies*. Oxford: Oxford University Press.

Torfing, J. (1999). Towards a Schumpeterian Workfare Postnational Regime: Path-Shaping and Path-Dependency in Danish Welfare State Reform. *Economy and Society*, *28*(3), 369–402.

Torfing, J. (2009). Rethinking Path-Dependence in Public Policy Research. *Critical Policy Studies*, *3*(1), 70–83.

Torfing, J., Bentzen, T. Ø. & Jensen, D. C. (2022). COVID-19 som Kriseinduceret Styringslaboratorium. *Politica*, *54*(3), 254–76.

Torfing, J., Sørensen, E. & Røiseland, A. (2019). Transforming the Public Sector into an Arena for Co-Creation: Barriers, Drivers, Benefits, and Ways Forward. *Administration & Society*, *51*(5), 795–825.

True, J., Jones, B. & Baumgartner, F. (2019). Punctuated-Equilibrium Theory. In Sabatier, P. A. (Ed.), *Theories of the Policy Process* (155–87). New York: Routledge.

2.   The public governance orthodoxy

This chapter aims to establish the baseline against which to measure and discuss the current changes in public governance. It sets out the general features of liberal representative democracy and public bureaucracy, showing how these classical forms of government have been supplemented with key elements drawn from New Public Management (NPM) (Hood 1991) to produce a new orthodoxy that forms the backbone of public governance in most Western countries and even in some non-Western ones.

Talking about public governance as an "orthodoxy" serves to highlight the discursive embeddedness of how governance is practiced in a particular period of time. An orthodoxy is often perceived as a set of generally accepted ideas and practices aspiring to become a totalizing discourse that enjoys widespread support in the face of actual transgressions, deviations, and violations. Hence, a public governance orthodoxy can be defined as a relatively institutionalized discourse about how to govern and be governed that has acquired a hegemonic status in a certain time period. The "public governance orthodoxy" concept shares much in common with Foucault's notion of "governmentality," as it is imbued with power and knowledge and describes an art of governing that seems to condition particular acts of governing (Foucault 1991). However, the argument advanced in this book has no need to enter the labyrinth of Foucauldian thinking, which, despite its constructive originality, tends to indulge in (over-)complexification.

As we shall see, the current public governance orthodoxy is founded on the central notion of government defined as the collection of formal political and administrative institutions that exercise public authority, provide a general direction to society, and make collectively binding and bureaucratically enforced decisions while being indirectly controlled by the people through its elected representatives. The government-centric view is evidenced by the fact that most people associate governance with the acts of formal government institutions (the cabinet, elected assembly, public courts). They call on government to take action when society and the economy are hit by crisis, and they blame elected government when things go wrong. The role and size of government have grown steadily, but its form and function have also been subject to change. To capture the contemporary forms of government, which have enjoyed strong support from elected politicians, public managers, media commentators and international organizations over the last fifty years, this chapter

takes a closer look at liberal democracy, public bureaucracy, and some key
elements of NPM, which together constitute the public governance orthodoxy.

The public governance orthodoxy has a certain affinity with the notion of
good governance promoted by the World Bank, the International Monetary
Fund, and the United Nations, which tends to stress respect for human rights
and the rule of law, transparent and accountable government, administrative
effectiveness and efficiency, the absence of corruption, and democratic inclusion of all parts of the population (Rothstein 2012). While this vision of "good
governance" clearly supports the wish for developing countries in the Global
South to adopt a combination of liberal democracy and public bureaucracy, it
fails to capture the elements of marketization and performance management
that most Western societies have introduced in the wake of the bleak diagnosis
provided by the Trilateral Commission that described many decades ago how
the Western welfare states based on a large public sector are suffering from
"government overload" and "societal ungovernability" (Crozier et al. 1975).

THE RISE OF LIBERAL DEMOCRACY

Liberal democracy can be defined as the ability of citizens to effectively influence the public political decisions that affect their lives through free and equal
participation based on civic, political, and social rights and a certain level of
government transparency that enables critical public scrutiny of government
actions and inactions. In ancient Greek societies, affluent males gathered in
a public square to discuss and decide on public issues, but this direct democracy model was untenable in modern mass societies, where growing sections
of the populace became enfranchised and participated in free and fair elections
that authorize a group of political representatives to govern on behalf of the
population until they are held to account at the next election. The ancient
Greek democracy and modern forms of liberal democracy in Europe were
separated by a lengthy period in which the fall of the Roman Empire gave way
to political rivalry and societal turbulence and a subsequent reorganization of
the social order around the Catholic Church and, finally, the establishment
of a system of sovereign nation-states with the Westphalian Peace in 1648.
Around that time, the formation of absolutist states started to demolish the
aristocratic privilege system and to centralize power in the hands of a king. As
the intellectual transition from Hobbes to Locke indicates, this development
paved the way for the democratization of state power and the creation of a capitalist market economy based on a legal system protecting private property and
ensuring contractual compliance.

The rise of liberal democracy was based on civil and political rights heralded
by the American (1775–83) and French (1789–99) revolutions. Civil rights
include the right to free thought, speech, religion, and press, together with legal

protection against discrimination based on gender, race, age, faith, and so on. Political rights include the right to fair trial, freedom of association, the right to assemble, and the right to vote. The growing economic inequalities in the capitalist economy tend to undermine the free and equal right to influence political decisions (MacPherson 1977). In response, many Western European societies developed a set of social rights to employment and a minimum standard of living that were tied to a social citizenship (Marshall 1959) and translated these rights into a more or less elaborate system of welfare services and benefits financed by taxes, insurance, and/or charity (Esping-Andersen 1990).

Looking back at the history of liberal democracy in Europe, North America, and the Antipodes, it is remarkable how long it took to create relatively well-functioning liberal democracies based on universal suffrage and how many hard-won political battles it took (and continues to take) to ensure basic civil, political, and social rights and to protect democratic principles and institutions. Recent events in the US, such as the January 6, 2021, storming of Capitol Hill and white-on-black police violence, further attest to this. On an even grander scale, we see how the expansion and consolidation of liberal democracy in Europe developed through three consecutive waves: a first wave beginning in 1848, a second wave in some southern European countries in the 1970s, and a third wave in eastern and central Europe after the fall of the Berlin Wall in 1989 (Weyland 2014). Today, there is more focus on the "wave-breakers." Hence, we have numerous reports describing democratic backsliding and the development of illiberal democracy in some of the new European democracies (Cianetti et al. 2018), and there is no way of taking liberal democracy for granted, despite the sentiment that "we should continue to support democracy because it's the least bad form of government."

Liberal democracy prescribes a series of institutional procedures for supporting the formation and political role of political parties, carrying out regular elections, organizing the work of the legislative assembly, appointing and dismissing governments, providing judicial review, securing transparency, and so on. Rather than seeking to eliminate power, the democratic system in liberal societies is designed to secure the distribution and constant circulation of power so that nobody can usurp power and use it in the pursuit of their own interests (Lefort 1988). Shifting governments exercise political power by making laws and regulating society and the economy, but the politicians tend to leave the implementation of political decisions to civil servants, who play a kind of "transmission belt" role: connecting political leaders to the citizens in their capacity as service users, benefit recipients, and subjects to public decisions.

The textbook description of the chain of government in liberal democracy is based on principal–agency theory and shows how voters use the ballot box to delegate power to and subsequently control an elected assembly, which in turn controls and constrains a government that drives majoritarian or consensual lawmaking, instructs public bureaucracy to provide services and undertake societal regulation, and deploys different means to ensure the compliance of the administrative agents in charge of implementing legislative decisions (Rose 1974; Olsen 1983). On the receiver's end, we find citizens as well as social and economic actors who may use different forms of voice and exit to provide feedback to elected governments (Hirschman 1970).

The chain of government has considerable prescriptive power, and many researchers tend to think that it also provides a good, fair, and realistic description of the interactions between voters, elected politicians, and civil servants (Strøm et al. 2003; Christiansen & Togeby 2006). However, the Scandinavian research-based evaluations of power and democracy have all raised concerns about the robustness of the chain of government in the face of globalization, mediatization and the countervailing power of big business, and assertive citizens. No matter their different conclusions about its current state (Gullbrandsen et al. 2002; Togeby et al. 2003; Engelstad et al. 2003), the chain of government provides the yardstick for assessing the exercise of power and democracy.

The chain of government provides an organizing perspective telling us how politics and power in liberal democracy are supposed to function. It holds sway over experts, politicians, public managers, and lay actors, despite numerous obvious problems. Declining party membership and voter turnout problematize the link between the voters and political parties (Mair 2013). The growing power of prime ministers and cabinets tends to leave parliaments as mere rubber stamps for political executives (Poguntke & Webb 2007). And last but not least, civil servants are recognized to have their own agendas, to exercise real political power, to be much less obedient than Weber prescribed and to be engaged in sabotage and shirking on the frontline of the public sector (Brehm & Gates 1999; Peters 2002; but see Pierre & Peters 2017). Despite these objections, we continue to act as if the democratic chain of government is largely unchallenged—and therein lies the totalizing gesture that makes it a part of the public governance orthodoxy.

To the above problems regarding the democratic chain of government, we may add a series of inner tensions in liberal democracy; a basic tension exists between the pluralism associated with "liberal" and the idea of the will of the people associated with "democracy." Hence, a pluralist logic of difference that celebrates diversity wrestles with a democratic logic of equivalence that assumes the near homogeneity of the people. In modern forms of democracy, political leaders therefore aim to speak in the name of the people, but in liberal societies we recognize the presence of different ideas, opinions, interests, and identities that divide the people into a babble of voice (Mouffe 2000). To cope with this basic tension, we draw on different procedures for the aggregation

and integration of preferences (March & Olsen 1995) and combine majoritarian decision-making with consensual models (Lijphart 2002). As such,
we attempt to contingently construct the will of the people based on myriad
different interests and preferences.

Another tension exists between the electoral delegation of power to competing political elites and the idea that democracy distributes power equally
among the members of the demos (Kane & Patapan 2012). The democratic
revolution was thus founded on the idea of free and equal influence of collective political decisions, but the end result was a model of representative
government empowering political leaders with a particular set of resources and
competences to lead based on their own ideas and conscience. The political
leaders often end up constituting an elevated elite that exercise power over the
people rather than power from and for the people. This tension is mediated by
attempts of political leaders to acquire some sort of mandate from the people
during the election campaign and the subsequent demand for elected politicians to deliver on their promises and to be responsive to popular demands
(Naurin et al. 2019).

A final tension in liberal democracy is between the building of strong state
capacities to carry out democratic decisions and the democratic attempt to
ensure transparency and accountability (Bovens et al. 2014). Strong state
capacities bolstered by the creation of autonomous public agencies and
reliance of secrecy acts may hamper accountability, and the expansion of
accountability mechanisms may weaken government to the point where it
cannot secure the implementation of government policy. One way of coping
with this dilemma and holding public authorities to account without undermining their capacity to act is to follow Montesquieu's call for a separation
of powers between different branches of the state and the parallel introduction
of a system of checks and balances (Vile 2012). Free and independent mass
media may also help to ensure accountability if there is sufficient access to
information about government action and inaction.

More tensions could be mentioned, but the basic point remains the same:
liberal democracy owes its broad support in the Western world to its ability
to cope with its inner tensions and offer a credible model for how popular
sovereignty is transformed into the effective governing of society and the
economy by linking elected politicians, public administrators, and societal
actors, including organizations and citizens.

PUBLIC BUREAUCRACY CUM PROFESSIONAL RULE

Bureaucracy is both an everyday word used by lay actors and an analytical
concept used by public governance and administration researchers. In its
everyday meaning, bureaucracy is associated with rigid formal rules and

complex and time-consuming decision-making. To say that something sounds "bureaucratic" indicates that some kind of red tape makes a process overly cumbersome and dysfunctional. Everyday scorn about bureaucracy is frequently reflected in contemporary politics, where we have seen a good deal of "bureaucracy bashing," especially in the USA, where several presidents (Ronald Reagan in particular) have declared public bureaucracy to be more a problem than a solution. This political denigration of bureaucracy may explain the staunch defense of bureaucracy in North America among certain public administration scholars who insist that there is something inherently good about bureaucracy (Wamsley et al. 1990; Goodsell 2004, 2015; Durant 2012).

European researchers have also contributed to the defense of bureaucracy (du Gay 2000, 2005; Olsen 2006), and for good reason: the introduction of bureaucracy as a governance model complementing liberal democracy constitutes a clear advantage compared to the previous forms of public governance, which were often associated with an unfortunate combination of political and administrative power, lack of organizational structure and coherence, incompetent staff, the transfer of positions in the public sector from father to son (patrimony), the exchange of public services for support (political patronage), and arbitrary and illegitimate decisions. None of this is compatible with the rationalism of modern society and the introduction of bureaucracy, with its emphasis on the separation of politics and administration, means–end rationality, centralized hierarchical rule, horizontal specialization, governance based on compliance with written rules, and the recruitment of well-paid and professionally trained civil servants based on their merits.

Bureaucracy as a hierarchical, rule-based form of governance can be traced back to the Chinese system of mandarins and Bismarckian Prussia, but the modern Weberian and Wilsonian forms of bureaucracy have been seen as important additions to liberal democracy (although bureaucracy has also revealed its efficiency in non-democratic dictatorships associated with communism, fascism and Nazism, where lower-level perpetrators of crimes against humanity have defended themselves with claims that they were just following orders). Nevertheless, Weber and Wilson both saw liberal democracy and bureaucracy as two sides of the same coin; the political processes in liberal democracy define the overall political goals and set the direction for the development of society and the economy, while the task of bureaucracy is to find and deploy the means that ensure an efficient, effective, and professional implementation of democratic decisions. In line with this, Waldo (1948: 200) would later claim that "democracy, if it were to survive, could not afford to ignore the lessons of centralization, hierarchy and discipline." In his view, democracy and bureaucracy are intrinsically linked.

Despite the close relation between liberal democracy and bureaucracy, Wilson worried that a bureaucratic state, regardless of its effectiveness, would undermine democracy by concentrating power in the hands of a centralized state apparatus, which would tend to prioritize technocratic matters over the public interest. In contrast, Weber saw bureaucracy as a precondition for democracy for exactly the same reason: the concentration of power at the top of the hierarchical bureaucratic organization helped to ensure that representative government could control the state apparatus by relying on the chain of government. At the same time, Weber feared that state bureaucracy together with Western capitalism could easily develop into a rationalistic iron cage that leaves very little space for human empathy, social morals, and individual freedom. Hence, modern society was a victim of its own success and had to cultivate and protect the social lifeworld (Habermas) or civil society (Giddens), which was not ruled by a systemic rationality based on power and money.

Looking inside bureaucracy, the role and position of professional frontline staff (e.g., doctors, nurses, schoolteachers, police officers, college professors) may appear slightly ambiguous. On the one hand, they are strictly controlled by hierarchical command structures and prescriptive rules that clearly place public professionals in a subordinate role with limited discretion and maneuverability. On the other, public employees are described as well trained, competent, politically neutral and motivated by public interests—a description that makes them highly trustworthy and capable of acting on their own with minimal supervision (Torfing et al. 2020). This inherent ambiguity in bureaucracy has been exploited in the development of a system of professional rule within well-established bureaucracies (Laffin 1986). Professional rule delegates particular tasks to relatively autonomous and powerful groups of professionally trained public employees who draw on their specialized knowledge and norms when producing public services. The public professionals are expected to update their knowledge, regulate themselves and sanction members of their profession who neglect professional expertise and norms. Professional rule is particularly strong in the decentralized Scandinavian welfare states and some Anglophone countries, where the professions are represented by private practitioners. It is less strong in central European countries such as Germany and France, where professions are well developed but subjected to intense bureaucratic regulation.

The rise of professional rule has been supported by the so-called "scientific management" movement, which discovered how an organizational division of labor and enhanced autonomy for employees with specialized competences may boost efficiency (Knott & Miller 1987), but it goes against the grain of neo-Weberian profession theory, which worries that professional groups will encapsulate themselves socially, cognitively and professionally, using their expertise and monopoly power to get what they want (i.e., money, status and more power) (Roberts & Dietrich 1999). Based on these insights, it is hardly surprising that the advancement of professional rule from the 1960s onwards was based on a tacit "regulatory bargain" (Byrkjeflot 2011) according to which elected politicians and public managers gave professional groups bounded autonomy in return for their professional commitment to delivering high-quality welfare services based on their professional knowledge, norms, and methods. Professional rule enhances the autonomy of professional front-line staff within a centrally defined framework of goals, rules, and standards, and much depends on the balance between central control and local professional autonomy. Imbalances in favor of the professional groups may result in an explosive expansion of service production costs in a particular area and the development of self-glorifying professions that ignore both the political signals from their principals and the needs and demands of service users (Le Grand 2010). An imbalance in favor of the political and administrative principals and their work to regulate the behavior of professional public employees may lead to the downsizing of the production of welfare services in a particular area, growing mistrust in public employees and the development of elaborate control systems that demotivate the public professionals and take time from service production. Fortunately, the expectation is that a near-symbiotic balance between bureaucratic control and professional autonomy will emerge as a result of negotiations in which different groups of welfare professionals are either delegated or struggle to acquire some degree of professional autonomy.

To fully understand the widespread support for the bureaucratic model of government, we must consider its normative foundation in a broad range of public values (Jørgensen & Bozeman 2007). Bureaucracy is founded on a long list of values aiming to secure legality, fairness, and legitimacy. Cherished values, such as the rule of law, equal rights, predictability, reliability, neutrality, factuality, transparency, accountability, responsiveness, reason, and orientation toward the common good, therefore undergird public bureaucracy to the extent that deviations from bureaucracy will often be seen as an attack on the fundamental principles of liberal democracy.

Together, liberal democracy and bureaucracy provide a strong public governance package that provides ways of letting citizens influence and control government action (input legitimacy), a fair and square way to translate societal inputs into policy outputs (throughput legitimacy), and effective governance that solves societal problems and delivers high-quality services to citizens (output legitimacy). Supported by its promise to deliver the responsible and efficient governance of modern mass societies, the potent coupling of liberal democracy and public bureaucracy provides seemingly unbeatable public governance orthodoxy, at least in the postwar period, which was fueled by faith in the expansion of a rights-based democracy and an effective bureaucracy engaged in social engineering for the common good.

NPM: THE NEW PUBLIC MANAGEMENT REFORM MOVEMENT

Liberal democracy, public bureaucracy and some degree of professional rule are a good fit; and in the postwar era, the three forms of governance became increasingly integrated in most Western societies. In the early 1970s, North American advocates of New Public Administration called for a revival of classical public sector values associated with democracy, bureaucracy, and professional values (Marini 1971; Waldo 1971; Wamsley & Zald 1973). At the time, however, public choice theorists had already begun criticizing the failure of liberal democracy to properly aggregate individual preferences into a collective preference (Arrow 1950), the growing ossification of public bureaucracy (Downs 1967) and the ever-rising public budgets (Niskanen 1971). These and other, similar criticisms were taken up and popularized by neoliberal and neoconservative governments pledging to roll back the welfare state and replace the bureaucratic state with competitive markets. However, the ideological crusade against public bureaucracy failed to dismantle the modern welfare state because of its inherent path-dependency (Pierson 1994). Instead of a direct assault on the public sector, we saw the rise of a more modest NPM reform movement aimed at making public bureaucracies more economic, effective, and efficient. This reform movement had its epicenter in Anglophone countries but soon swept the world (Pollitt & Bouckaert 2004).

NPM criticized the political detail-steering of the public sector, which often succumbs to demands from pressure groups or the short-sighted concerns of political representatives to win the next election (Rosenberg 1992). It bemoaned the tendency for the bureaucratic focus on control-based rule compliance to overshadow the concern for the production of measurable results and to contribute to making public services inflexible, poor, and expensive (Barzelay & Armajani 1992). Finally, it criticized public employees for exploiting their principals' lack of performance information to pursue their narrow self-interest in less work and more pay (Lane 2006). These criticisms required radical reforms and could not be tackled by minor technical and organizational adjustments. However, despite dramatic book titles such as *Reinventing Government* (Osborne & Gaebler 1992) and *Banishing Bureaucracy* (Osborne & Plastrik 1997), NPM did not intend to replace bureaucracy with a new model of governance. Even Osborne and Gaebler (1992: 15–16) admitted that "if the environment is stable, the task is relatively simple, every customer wants the same service, and the quality of performance is not critical, a traditional public bureaucracy can do the job."

The NPM reform movement called for elected politicians to focus their attention on defining the overall goals and budget frames, thus leaving it to professional public managers to improve bureaucratic efficiency and deliver measurable results. Public organizations should be disaggregated into smaller units, compete with each other and with private companies for service contracts and customers, and use incentives to make managers manage and make frontline staff improve their performance (Dunleavy et al. 2006). While the clarification of the political and administrative roles in the vertical chain of government and the emphasis on leadership, management and performance measurement were compatible with the traditional ideas of public bureaucracy, the introduction of horizontal market competition as a way of incentivizing the public sector appears to be an enemy of top-down bureaucratic control (Hood 1991). However, the NPM-inspired creation of quasi-markets based on a purchaser–provider split maintained a considerable degree of public sector control as the decision to "make or buy," the orchestration of the bidding process, and the completion and enforcement of service contracts were tasks assigned to public managers. Nevertheless, a real tension has emerged between the primacy of politics inherent to liberal democracy and the proliferation of quasi-autonomous public and private agencies operating at arm's length (Christensen & Lægreid 2006). The growing distance between elected government and the increasing number of special-purpose public and private agencies limits the opportunities available to elected politicians to control what is going on in the public sector and to hold failing agencies to account (Egeberg & Trondal 2009). This problem initially spurred on the development of new forms of regulation, but we have since seen a wave of de-agentification (Randma-Liiv et al. 2011; Elston 2013).

Not all Western countries have followed the NPM recipe; for instance, the Scandinavian countries have been keen to strengthen public management and performance management but reluctant to embrace the marketization agenda and turn citizens into customers (Dunn & Miller 2007; Greve et al. 2016; Pollitt & Bouckaert 2017). Nevertheless, most public bureaucracies adopted some key elements of NPM that appeared to make the public sector more professional, efficient and responsive, and supplemented the political participation of citizens as "voters" in democratic elections with the ability of citizens in their new role as "customers" to vote with their feet and penalize poor service providers based on a free service choice. Hence, although NPM has not really delivered on its promise to make the public sector work better and cost less (Hood & Dixon 2015; Petersen et al. 2017), it has reformed and curtailed bureaucracy and professional rule in ways that seem to have enhanced public governance legitimacy.

THE PUBLIC GOVERNANCE ORTHODOXY

Liberal democracy accounts for how citizens can influence the political decisions affecting their lives by joining political parties and voting in regular elections and how elected assemblies appoint and control government. This account is complemented by public bureaucracy, which describes how political decisions are fairly and efficiently implemented. If, over time, the resulting chain of government appeared slightly too top-heavy, ossified and inefficient, and to be failing to provide needs-based solutions to the increasingly affluent and demanding middle classes, NPM helped to distribute decision-making competence downwards to local agencies, strengthen the transformative power of entrepreneurial public managers, and enhance efficiency through a combination of performance management and competition. NPM also sought to empower citizens as customers in the newly created quasi-markets, and the new exit options provided by free service choice are sometimes supplemented with new voice options through the formation of elected user boards overseeing local service production (Pierre & Røiseland 2016).

The combination of liberal democracy and public bureaucracy with varying degrees of marketization and performance management enjoys considerable support from political and administrative elites in Western countries, although we also find considerable path-dependent variation (Pollitt et al. 2007). Despite key elements of NPM (e.g., privatization, contracting out, agentification) appearing to have lost their appeal (Hammerschmidt et al. 2016), there has been widespread support for using strategic management, performance measurement and incentives to make bureaucracy more economic, efficient, and effective, thus ensuring that the decisions of elected politicians are properly executed. The actual performance of public bureaucracy may vary, but at least until the mid-2010s, there were few practitioners entertaining ideas about deviating substantially from the public governance orthodoxy that appeared to be capable of meeting most expectations through minor adjustments and incremental changes.

The public governance orthodoxy that emerged in the postwar period and partially integrated elements associated with NPM into bureaucratic forms of liberal democracy reached its zenith at the beginning of the twenty-first century. As a discursive horizon for thinking about and organizing public governance, it has been quite stable. As we shall see, however, all three of its basic components have been challenged and supplemented by different, alternative and even opposing forms of governance.

Liberal representative democracy has been challenged by direct democracy in the form of referendums that either allow the people to make authoritative decisions (binding referendums) or recommend a particular solution to the political representatives, who then make the final decision (non-binding referendums). Referendums tend to undermine the political responsibility and democratic accountability of the elected politicians, since they are forced to govern based on decisions that they may not support themselves (Setälä & Schiller 2009). In addition, representative democracy has been supplemented by participatory and deliberative forms of democracy, although this tends to happen in small pockets of classrooms, workplaces and local communities that are capable of self-government within a broader legislative framework (Pateman 1970). Here, people participate directly and actively in discussions about decisions and issues that are central to their daily lives. Since the members of the self-governing community make their own decisions, there is no need for political representatives, although some form of political leadership may still be required to set the overall course of society and frame local discussions.

While direct, participatory, and deliberative democracy all represent attempts at strengthening democracy by introducing alternatives to regular elections and parliamentary control with government, we also see examples of liberal democracy being undermined by the weakening of civic and political rights. Zakaria (1997) has dubbed this phenomenon "illiberal democracy." In illiberal democracies, there might still be democratic elections, but the right to organize freely, express one's opinion and vote may be suppressed by the government, and the elected rulers may ignore or bypass constitutional constraints on their exercise of power. Hungary, Poland, and Turkey are European examples of illiberal democracies in which liberal rights are curtailed.

Public bureaucracy has not reigned uncontested either. Bureaucracy is based on norms about impartiality and equal treatment, but there are several examples of bureaucratic clientelism where bureaucrats—more or less explicitly supported by the political principals—have favored particular groups of citizens (Lyrintzis 1984). Bureaucrats have also been described as self-interested maximizers (Dunleavy 1991) and as policymakers pursuing their own private or professional interests (Egeberg 1995). Moreover, the hierarchical and compartmentalized bureaucratic organizations frequently seem to co-exist with forms of cross-cutting adhocracy (Mintzberg 1979; Mintzberg & McHugh 1985). When a crisis emerges, bureaucratic organizations often create a flexible and informal task force, bringing together expertise from different parts of the organization to create an agile, strategic response to the problems at hand, which short-circuits the standard decision-making procedures in a bureaucracy. Finally, the political and administrative leadership of central public organizations (e.g., ministries, regulatory agencies) has frequently invited peak interest organizations to participate in both the formulation and implementation of public policy. Countries such as Austria, France, Germany, the Netherlands, and the Scandinavian countries have long and strong traditions for corporatist involvement (Schmitter 1985; Cawson 1985), although the role of tripartite consultations seems to have declined since the 1980s (Rommetvedt 2017).

Finally, NPM has been challenged by new developments emerging in response to its inherent shortcomings. First, the new managerialism was based on transactional leadership aimed at using conditional rewards and punishment (sticks and carrots) to enhance the performance of public employees, who were supposed to be motivated by the fear of rebuke and an interest in rewards (Burns 1978; Bass 1985). The problem with transactional leadership is that it tends to strengthen the extrinsic motivation of public employees while crowding out their intrinsic task motivation as well as their public service motivation, which are crucial forms of motivation with professional public employees. This problem has been remedied by adopting a more transformational leadership style that seeks to formulate and communicate the vision, goals, and values of the organization in order to make public employees transcend their personal and professional self-interests (Jensen et al. 2019). While this strategic move may help to strengthen the capacity of public managers to lead and manage their employees in line with NPM recommendations, it breaks with its motivational "economic man" theory, which sees preferences as exogenous and behavior as shaped by the rational pursuit of self-interest (Torfing et al. 2020: 20).

Second, the creation of quasi-autonomous special-purpose agencies and the increasing use of key performance indicators to measure the performance of each bureau have led to an increasing fragmentation within the public sector, which in turn has increased the need for cross-cutting coordination and collaboration. In response, we have seen the rise of joined-up government aimed at bringing together public agencies in a joint effort to solve overlapping problems and tasks (Pollitt 2003; Bogdanor 2005). Joined-up government is closely connected with the new "whole of government" approach that encourages public service agencies to work across portfolio boundaries to achieve a shared goal and produce an integrated government response to societal problems and challenges (Christensen & Lægreid 2007).

Lastly, yet importantly, the problems with monitoring and regulating private contractors who seek to maximize their payment while taking any shortcut they possibly can have stimulated the formation of public–private partnerships (PPPs), which internalize the risk of opportunistic behavior and sub-optimization, thus enhancing the overall performance of infrastructure projects or service delivery systems (Broadbent & Laughlin 2003). PPPs represent an innovative extension of NPM that introduces collaboration in the midst of competition, and this deviates from the core tenets of NPM.

All of these problematizing challenges and alternatives to the core features of the public governance orthodoxy seem to suggest that the orthodoxy has been crumbling and losing momentum. However, this is not how an orthodoxy works. Transgressions, deviations, and even momentary losses of faith are met with a strengthening of the core faith in the key tenets. As such, orthodoxies are ideological fantasies that enable people to continue to act as if liberal democracy, public bureaucracy and the necessary and well-integrated adjustments associated with NPM remain intact and worthy of praise and unflinching support. We are gripped by such ideological fantasies about how public governance should be carried out, either because the fantasies promise an ideal imaginary fullness or because we fear the alternative that appears to be messy, disorderly, or even horrific. The fantasy structures the interests of its supporters, who strive to realize it but are forced to accept that the object of desire is elusive and bound to disappear (Glynos 2008). In sum, the public governance orthodoxy described above appears to be relatively robust in the face of problems and challenges, and it will therefore take a good deal of disruption and the development of promising practical alternatives to destabilize and change it.

THE CURRENT UNRAVELING OF THE PUBLIC GOVERNANCE ORTHODOXY

We tend to stick to the shared governance narratives that we see as attractive from a practical and normative point of view and that have withstood pressure from problematizing challenges and alternatives. As the historical institutionalists have stressed over and over again, considerable societal turbulence and ideational disruption together with a number of major agenda-setting events are required to change a stable path of governance—and even when the window of opportunity opens, we are only gradually and stubbornly changing our perceptions, which often seem to lag behind the real events.

Just as the limits to the uncontested rule of the bureaucratic model were revealed in the 1960s and 1970s and paved the way for the integration of key elements associated with NPM, we are now witnessing several disruptive societal developments, ideational trends and turbulent events that seem to unravel the predominant public governance orthodoxy and open a discursive and practical space for renewal. The result of the potential re-articulation of the public governance orthodoxy is unpredictable, but this book will seek to take stock of some of the most interesting and promising transformations in order to determine their direction and potential impact.

The question is whether the current disruption of the public governance orthodoxy is large enough to produce significant changes. To answer this question, let's take a closer look at some of the societal developments, ideational trends, and turbulent events that seem to question the public governance orthodoxy.

Societal Developments

The first of a series of ongoing societal developments that have been questioning the public governance orthodoxy is *globalization*. Globalization involves the expansion of global capitalism, but it cannot be reduced to its economic dimension. Globalization also involves an accelerated global diffusion and consumption of cultural products, images, and identities, leading to a growing dissociation of cultural practices and locality. Finally, globalization has a political dimension that reveals the formation of global demands for human rights, the formation of global political agendas (e.g., the UN Sustainable Development Goals), the growing power of transnational economic and civil society actors, and the formation of a post-national, polycentric world of political conflict and collaboration (Beck 2018). In terms of governance, globalization means that the nation-state is no longer the privileged site for making and implementing authoritative decisions and regulating social and economic life. Governance takes place at multiple levels and is subject to processes of upscaling and downscaling. At each level of governance and across all of the different levels, multiple actors from the state, economy, and civil society are involved in interactive governance processes, which at the global level involve threats, diplomacy, and collaboration in the shadow of superpower rivalries and in the absence of a world government.

Globalization is supported by digitalization and the accelerated growth of new digital technologies that are revolutionizing social and public communication by cutting transaction costs, as well as changing the daily practices of buying and selling services and commodities, how large organizations store and retrieve information, how wars are fought and military operations are conducted, and how government operates. In much the same way as social and economic life are disrupted by the advance of new digital technologies, governance practices are thoroughly transformed. Digital technologies are used as a tool to reduce administrative costs, to provide needs-based online services to citizens, to solve societal problems such as the climate crisis by building smart cities, to surveille public spaces and monitor the population, and to create platforms for collaborative interaction between government officials and relevant stakeholders, including citizens, communities, and civil society organizations. The new social media (e.g., Facebook, Twitter) were initially invented to facilitate communication between citizens but are increasingly used by elected politicians to communicate directly to their various constituencies without the press asking critical questions about facts and consequences. Former US President Donald Trump at times seemed to believe that he could govern the entire country and whole world via Twitter. Social media can also be used by citizens who want to raise an issue or comment on political issues, but the algorithms governing social media tend to create a risk of confirmation bias within echo chambers in which people share the same core beliefs.

There are many citizens who want to speak and make their point, and they generally seem to be becoming less allegiant and more assertive (Dalton & Welzel 2014). The educational revolution has enhanced the competences of large segments of the population, and the anti-authoritarian cultural movement has enhanced the self-confidence of citizens who think that they are entitled to be heard about the decisions that affect their lives. Demands for active participation are further enhanced by positive and empowering experiences with participation in local planning processes, school boards, voluntary associations, and social movements (Nabatchi & Leighninger 2015). The democratic role of being a voter participating in an election every fourth year or so appears to be insufficient, at least to those who want to participate more directly and actively in public governance. At the same time, there are others who feel that the technocratic political elites are not listening when they speak and therefore become disempowered, lose confidence in democratic participation altogether, and turn their back on the political establishment. The latter group of citizens may end up supporting authoritarian populist movements led by charismatic personalities such as Trump, who promised to "drain the swamp" and replace corrupted elites with an effective and determined leadership based on a politics of redemption (Stoker 2019).

The last of the disruptive societal developments that demands our attention is the pervasiveness of complex and turbulent problems. Rittel and Webber (1973) discovered complex and allegedly "wicked" problems in the field of planning and environmental regulations, where problems are often ill-defined, causalities are multiple and tangled, goal conflicts are clearly visible, and standard solutions are absent. Although we should be careful not to perceive all public problems as wicked (Alford & Head 2017; Peters 2017), those that are pose a real challenge to public bureaucracy, which is accustomed to solving rather simple problems in the field of health, education, and social affairs through the provision of mass-produced standard solutions delivered based on established administrative routines. Wicked problems require new, collaborative governance procedures and more innovative solutions.

However, this is not the full story of the challenges to the public sector, since the COVID-19 pandemic has drawn our attention to the heightened societal turbulence and the pervasiveness of a new type of turbulent problem. Turbulent problems are not only complex in a cognitive sense but also unpredictable, partly unknown, uncertain, inconsistent, and changing. Several turbulent problems other than the COVID-19 pandemic also warrant mention, including the opioid crisis, fiscal crisis, refugee crisis, climate crisis, energy crisis, inflation crisis, and the many identity-related conflicts caused by the presumed lack of fair, impartial, and non-discriminatory governance that tends to stir the antagonistic clashes that divide the population into a growing number of oppositional camps. The design of robust solutions to turbulent problems calls for cross-boundary collaboration but also for agile and distributed experimentation based on exchanges between different perspectives (Ferraro et al. 2015).

Ideational Challenges

Partly inspired by the disruptive societal developments and the detection of problems within established forms of public governance, we have seen a number of ideational re-orientations and breakthroughs that are currently challenging the public governance orthodoxy. The first of these ideational challenges takes issue with the harsh criticisms of public bureaucracy launched by NPM advocates. The rise of NPM was founded on a major assault on public bureaucracy, which was portrayed as an inefficient parasite on the private sector that extracted and squandered value produced by private firms and hard-working laborers. From this highly skeptical, neoliberal account of the public sector, it followed that the ossified public bureaucracy should be replaced by competitive markets capable of generating and distributing private value. Against this radical critique of the public sector, Moore (1995) maintained that the public sector cannot be reduced to an unproductive parasite, as it produces its own distinctive form of "public value." Instead of bringing us back to the normative foundation of public bureaucracy emphasizing the need for legality, impartiality, equity, transparency, and so on, Moore's notion of public value draws attention to the outcome of public governance. Through its services, regulations and interventions, the public sector produces value for citizens and society at large.

Moore goes on to explain how public managers are constantly searching for new ways of enhancing public value production, as well as exploring how their ideas and propositions are authorized by elected politicians and relevant stakeholders and how public organizations are trimmed to be able to deliver new and improved solutions. While this argument answers much of the critique of public bureaucracy, Moore seems to subscribe to the managerialism inherent to NPM, as public managers are seen as the drivers of public value production. As we shall see, new research extends the list of actors who can contribute to public value production. Still, there is little doubt that the public value perspective has promoted a new agenda that perceives the public sector as a vehicle for problem-solving and the advancement of a good, just, and well-functioning society.

The focus on public value production resonates with the development of an innovative, mission-driven public sector. For many years, however, the public sector was associated with hierarchy and red tape combined with a profound lack of competition and economic incentives, the conventional wisdom being that the public sector was largely incapable of producing innovation. By contrast, the private market economy was depicted as the epicenter of innovation. Unlike public organizations, which tend to survive despite flagrant inefficiencies, no private business can survive in a cut-throat market if it fails to innovate its technology, product, and marketing strategy. The sharp contrast between the innovative private sector and the ossified public sector meant that there was hardly any research on public innovation. Even when research on how to spur innovation in large organizations boomed in the 1970s, there was hardly any attempt to distinguish between public and private sector innovation (Kattel et al. 2013). Fortunately, this all changed with the publication of the path-breaking *The Entrepreneurial State* by Mazzucato (2013), which clearly demonstrated the strong innovative capacity of the public sector and thus legitimized new and exciting research focused on public innovation that has spurred the formation of public innovation agencies (Ansell & Torfing 2014). The new public innovation agenda gained widespread support in the face of the cross-pressure between rising political and societal expectations to the public sector and the continued scarcity of public finance. It seemed to be a widespread experience that neither classical bureaucracy nor NPM were capable of cutting costs through stronger controls and incentive-driven management; it was not enough to work harder, as it had become necessary to find ways of working smarter.

Collaboration is a key driver of innovation and public value production (Stoker 2006; Torfing 2016), but in fact there has been a new and growing embrace of the idea of cross-boundary collaboration in and around the public sector. Hence, we have learned in recent decades to count to three and more. Bureaucracy was initially taken to be solely responsible for public governance—and thus to blame when things went wrong. When NPM questioned the public monopoly on service production, it resulted in an enhanced focus on "make or buy" decisions that created a new competition between public and private service providers. Together with the growing agentification of the public sector as a tool for reducing complexity and ensuring compliance with performance demands, the contracting out of public services increased the institutional fragmentation of the public sector. In response, the formation of cross-cutting networks helps to enhance coordination and allows the mobilization of private actors from civil society, which can often contribute valuable knowledge and resources to public value production. This development was well captured by the booming literature on collaborative governance (Ansell & Gash 2008; Sirianni 2010; Emerson & Nabatchi 2015), which has swept public administration research and seems to inform public governance reforms around the world. The net effect is that unicentric bureaucracy is not only supplemented with public–private competition but also with pluricentric forms of collaboration that are scaffolded by new institutional platforms (Ansell & Gash 2018).

Whereas the Weberian model of bureaucracy relied on civil servants being driven by good and noble intentions to pursue the public interest and forsake temptations to act opportunistically, NPM took the opposite view, insisting that public employees are rational, self-interested actors who are bound to slack if not properly managed with the right combination of conditional punishment and rewards. As mentioned above, however, the hard power associated with public managers using sticks and carrots has a tendency to stir conflict and opposition and prevent the creation of a thriving working environment. Moreover, it appears as though public employees are driven by motives other than individual self-interests. These insights have paved the way for a growing appreciation of the mixed-motive model that assumes that people are motivated by varying degrees of self-interests and other-interests (Ritz 2015; Ritz et al. 2016; Amendola et al. 2020). The balancing of altruistic and egotistical motivations is not only sound and realistic but also calls for more managerial use of soft power, which speaks to the professional identity and prosocial motivation of public employees. Control can at least partially be replaced with trust, thus inviting a shift from principal–agent theory to the new stewardship theory (Schillemans 2008; Torfing & Bentzen 2020). Hence, trust-based leadership is gaining ground and the new challenge is how to combine trust in the competences and motivations of public employees with legitimate control with their overall performance and contribution to public value production.

As we shall see, there are many other ideational shifts that are challenging the conventional ways of thinking and doing public governance, but the above-mentioned redirections provide sufficient evidence of the troubles that the public governance orthodoxy is facing and the reasons why it is crumbling.

Challenging Events

The final nail in the coffin is the many different crises that have hit the public sector and revealed the inadequacy of the established way of governing society and the economy. First, the 2007 financial crisis revealed the limitations of the fiscal policy straitjacket in the Eurozone that proved to be an obstacle to growth stimulation and resulted in massive popular protests (Ongaro 2014). The long-lasting socioeconomic impact of the crisis in large parts of southern and central-eastern Europe has also questioned the capacity of governments to steer the economy and prompted the need for multilateral policy coordination (Schirm 2011). Finally, yet importantly, the economic downswing placed massive pressure on public finances, leading to cutbacks (Randma-Liiv & Kickert 2017) but also to growing support for new agendas focusing on spurring public innovation and mobilizing societal resources through the co-production of services and co-creation of public value outcomes (Ansell & Torfing 2021).

The recent refugee crisis in Europe and elsewhere has further revealed the need for local resource mobilization and the co-creation of both emergency assistance and integration. It has also problematized the idea of a well-functioning and well-integrated system of multi-level governance and not least exposed the lack of supranational coordination and initiatives, thus leaving countries such as Greece and Italy to fend for themselves without adequate support from the European Union (Campomori & Ambrosini 2020). Moreover, the refugee crisis and the large and sudden influx of immigrants has fueled the formation and mobilization of strong anti-immigration movements, which in many countries consist of people who feel alienated from the political system and the traditional political parties and thus tend to support authoritarian populist movements and leaders who question the rules of the game in liberal democracy (Wodak et al. 2013). Finally, the political salience of immigration policy has revealed a gulf separating the political elites from large segments of the population and thus pointed out the need for reconnecting the people and governing elites.

The climate crisis, with its alternating problems of heatwaves and torrential downpours, has fully demonstrated the lack of political will and courage to address the really big questions that require solutions that will forever change our energy production, transport systems, and daily living. Despite years of scientific evidence and warnings and scores of international meetings and agreements, it took a young Swedish schoolgirl and some European-wide school strikes before the popular momentum was strong enough to convince elected politicians that action was strictly required. While the new, more or less ambitious climate goals can be reached partly through regulation and public investment, the current lesson is that governments cannot achieve the goals singlehandedly but must create alliances, partnerships and networks with a broad range of relevant and affected actors in order to create the innovative solutions that are needed and to develop widespread support for their implementation (Hofstad & Torfing 2017; Sørensen & Torfing 2020). Citizen engagement also appears necessary to reach out and change the daily behavior of people at home, in the workplace, and in travel and leisure activities.

Finally, as explained above, the COVID-19 pandemic has revealed the limitations of forecasting and preparedness and demonstrated the need for robustness in the face of turbulence. The design of robust solutions requires a much more agile public sector that flexibly and pragmatically combines elements from a broad range of public governance paradigms. So perhaps the time of shifting orthodoxies is running out in favor of a new form of bricolage in which we use and combine all the possible ideas, means, and resources at our disposal to provide new, tentative solutions that we can modify through rapid-learning processes.

Summing up, decades of intentional reform and less intentional trial and error bolstered by professional and scholarly discourses have created a public governance orthodoxy combining liberal democracy, public bureaucracy (involving varying degrees of professional rule) and certain elements of NPM. The orthodoxy has shaped actual forms and acts of governance in most countries in Europe, the Americas, and the Antipodes—and even beyond these countries. However, the last fifteen years have seen an intensified discussion of the continued viability of this orthodoxy that is currently being stretched to cope with new, challenging developments, ideas, and events, but is increasingly dislocated, thus opening up new spaces for imagining and experimenting with new forms of public governance. This book takes a closer look at this experimentation.

REFERENCES

Alford, J. & Head, B. W. (2017). Wicked and Less Wicked Problems: A Typology and a Contingency Framework. *Policy and Society*, *36*(3), 397–413.

Amendola, F., Boccia, M. & Troisi, R. (2020). Motivation of Public Servants in Europe: A Proposal for a "Mixed Motives" Approach. *European Journal of Economics, Finance and Administrative Sciences*, *105*, 121–33.

Ansell, C. & Gash, A. (2008). Collaborative Governance in Theory and Practice. *Journal of Public Administration Research and Theory*, *18*(4), 543–71.

Ansell, C. & Gash, A. (2018). Collaborative Platforms as a Governance Strategy. *Journal of Public Administration Research and Theory*, *28*(1), 16–32.

Ansell, C. & Torfing, J. (Eds.) (2014). *Public Innovation through Collaboration and Design*. New York: Routledge.

Ansell, C. & Torfing, J. (2021). *Public Governance as Co-Creation: A Strategy for Revitalizing the Public Sector and Rejuvenating Democracy*. Cambridge: Cambridge University Press.

Arrow, K. J. (1950). A Difficulty in the Concept of Social Welfare. *The Journal of Political Economy*, *58*(4), 328–46.

Barzelay, M. & Armajani, B. J. (1992). *Breaking through Bureaucracy: A New Vision for Managing in Government*. Chicago, IL: University of Chicago Press.

Bass, B. M. (1985). *Leadership and Performance beyond Expectations*. New York: The Free Press.

Beck, U. (2018). *What Is Globalization?* Cambridge: Polity Press.

Bogdanor, V. (Ed.) (2005). *Joined-Up Government*. Oxford: Oxford University Press.

Bovens, M., Goodin, R. E. & Schillemans, T. (2014). *The Oxford Handbook of Public Accountability*. Oxford: Oxford University Press.

Brehm, J. & Gates, S. (1999). *Working, Shirking, and Sabotage: Bureaucratic Response to a Democratic Public*. Ann Arbor, MI: University of Michigan Press.

Broadbent, J. & Laughlin, R. (2003). Public Private Partnerships: An Introduction. *Accounting, Auditing, & Accountability*, *16*(3), 332–41.

Burns, J. M. (1978). *Leadership*. New York: Harper & Row.

Byrkjeflot, H. (2011). Healthcare States and Medical Professions: The Challenges from NPM. In Christensen, T. & Lægreid, P. (Eds.), *The Ashgate Research Companion to New Public Management* (147–60). London: Routledge.

Campomori, F. & Ambrosini, M. (2020). Multilevel Governance in Trouble: The Implementation of Asylum Seekers' Reception in Italy as a Battleground. *Comparative Migration Studies*, *8*(1), 1–19.

Cawson, A. (1985). *Organized Interests and the State: Studies in Meso-Corporatism.* London: Sage Publications.

Christensen, T. & Lægreid, P. (Eds.) (2006). *Autonomy and Regulation: Coping with Agencies in the Modern State.* Cheltenham, UK: Edward Elgar Publishing.

Christensen, T. & Lægreid, P. (2007). *Transcending New Public Management: The Transformation of Public Sector Reforms.* Farnham: Ashgate Publishing.

Christiansen, P. M. & Togeby, L. (2006). Power and Democracy in Denmark: Still a Viable Democracy. *Scandinavian Political Studies*, *29*(1), 1–24.

Cianetti, L., Dawson, J. & Hanley, S. (2018). Rethinking "Democratic Backsliding" in Central and Eastern Europe: Looking beyond Hungary and Poland. *East European Politics*, *34*(3), 243–56.

Crozier, M., Huntington, S. & Watanuki, J. (1975). *The Crisis of Democracy: Report on the Governability of Democracies in the Trilateral Commission.* New York: New York University Press.

Dalton, R. J. & Welzel, C. (Eds.) (2014). *The Civic Culture Transformed: From Allegiant to Assertive Citizens.* New York: Cambridge University Press.

Downs, A. (1967). *Inside Bureaucracy.* Boston, MA: Little, Brown and Company.

Du Gay, P. (2000). *In Praise of Bureaucracy.* London: Sage Publications.

Du Gay, P. (Ed.) (2005). *The Values of Bureaucracy.* Oxford: Oxford University Press.

Dunleavy, P. (1991). *Democracy, Bureaucracy and Public Choice: Economic Approaches in Political Science.* Florence: Taylor & Francis.

Dunleavy, P., Margetts, H., Bastow, S. & Tinkler, J. (2006). New Public Management Is Dead: Long Live Digital-Era Governance. *Journal of Public Administration Research and Theory*, *16*(3), 467–94.

Dunn, W. N. & Miller, D. Y. (2007). A Critique of the New Public Management and the Neo-Weberian State: Advancing a Critical Theory of Administrative Reform. *Public Organization Review*, *7*(4), 345–58.

Durant, R. (2012). *The Oxford Handbook of the American Bureaucracy.* Oxford: Oxford University Press.

Egeberg, M. (1995). Bureaucrats as Public Policy-Makers and Their Self-Interests. *Journal of Theoretical Politics*, *7*(2), 157–67.

Egeberg, M. & Trondal, J. (2009). Political Leadership and Bureaucratic Autonomy: Effects of Agencification. *Governance*, *22*(4), 673–88.

Elston, T. (2013). Developments in UK Executive Agencies: Re-Examining the "Disaggregation–Reaggregation" Thesis. *Public Policy and Administration*, *28*(1), 66–89.

Emerson, K. & Nabatchi, T. (2015). *Collaborative Governance Regimes.* Washington, DC: Georgetown University Press.

Engelstad, F., Selle, P. & Østerrud, Ø. (2003). *Makten og demokratiet. En sluttrapport fra Makt- og demokratiutredningen.* Oslo: Gyldendal Akademisk.

Esping-Andersen, G. (1990). *The Three Worlds of Welfare Capitalism.* Princeton, NJ: Princeton University Press.

Ferraro, F., Etzion, D. & Gehman, J. (2015). Tackling Grand Challenges Pragmatically: Robust Action Revisited. *Organization Studies*, *36*(3), 363–90.

Foucault, M. (1991). Governmentality. In Burchell, G., Gordon, C. & Miller, P. (Eds.), *The Foucault Effect* (87–104). Hemel Hempstead: Harvester Wheatsheaf.

Glynos, J. (2008). Ideological Fantasy at Work. *Journal of Political Ideologies, 13*(3), 275–96.

Goodsell, C. (2004). *The Case for Bureaucracy*. Washington, DC: CQ Press.

Goodsell, C. (2015). *The New Case for Bureaucracy*. Washington, DC: Sage Publications.

Greve, C., Lægreid, P. & Rykkja, L. (2016). The Nordic Model Revisited: Active Reformers and High Performing Public Administrations. In Greve, C., Lægreid, P. & Rykkja, L. (Eds.), *Nordic Administrative Reforms: Public Sector Organizations* (189–212). London: Palgrave Macmillan.

Gullbrandsen, T., Engelstad, F., Klausen, T. B., Skjeie, H., Teigen, M. & Østerud, Ø. (2002). *Norske makteliter*. Oslo: Gyldendal.

Hammerschmidt, G., van de Walle, S., Andrews, R. & Bezes, P. (Eds.) (2016). *Public Administration Reforms in Europe: The View from the Top*. Cheltenham: Edward Elgar Publishing.

Hirschman, A. O. (1970). *Exit, Voice and Loyalty: Responses to Decline in Firms, Organizations and States*. Cambridge, MA: Harvard University Press.

Hofstad, H. & Torfing, J. (2017). Towards a Climate-Resilient City: Collaborative Innovation for a "Green Shift." In Fernandez, R. A., Zubelzu, S. & Martínez, R. (Eds.), *Oslo Carbon Footprint and the Industrial Life Cycle* (221–42). Cham: Springer.

Hood, C. (1991). A Public Management for All Seasons? *Public Administration, 69*(1), 3–19.

Hood, C. & Dixon, R. (2015). *A Government that Works Better and Costs Less?* Oxford: Oxford University Press.

Jensen, U. T., Andersen, L. B., Bro, L. L., Bøllingtoft, A., Eriksen, T. L. M., Holten, A. L., … & Westergård-Nielsen, N. (2019). Conceptualizing and Measuring Transformational and Transactional Leadership. *Administration & Society, 51*(1), 3–33.

Jørgensen, T. B. & Bozeman, B. (2007). Public Values: An Inventory. *Administration & Society, 39*(3), 354–81.

Kane, J. & Patapan, H. (2012). *The Democratic Leader: How Democracy Defines, Empowers, and Limits Its Leaders*. Oxford: Oxford University Press.

Kattel, R., Cepilovs, A., Drechsler, W., Kalvet, T., Lember, V. & Tõnurist, P. (2013). Can We Measure Public Sector Innovation? A Literature Review. *LIPSE Working Papers* (2). Rotterdam: Erasmus University.

Knott, J. H. & Miller, G. J. (1987). *Reforming Bureaucracy: The Politics of Institutional Change*. Englewood Cliffs, NJ: Prentice Hall.

Laffin, M. (1986). *Professionalism and Policy: The Role of the Professions in the Central-Local Government Relationship*. Aldershot: Gower.

Lane, J. E. (2006). *Public Administration and Public Management: The Principal–Agent Perspective*. London: Routledge.

Lefort, C. (1988). *Democracy and Political Theory*. Cambridge: Polity Press.

Le Grand, J. (2010). Knights and Knaves Return: Public Service Motivation and the Delivery of Public Services. *International Public Management Journal, 13*(1), 56–71.

Lijphart, A. (2002). Negotiation Democracy versus Consensus Democracy: Parallel Conclusions and Recommendations. *European Journal of Political Research, 41*(1), 107–13.

Lyrintzis, C. (1984). Political Parties in Post–Junta Greece: A Case of "Bureaucratic Clientelism"? *West European Politics*, *7*(2), 99–118.

MacPherson, C. B. (1977). *The Life and Times of Liberal Democracy*. Oxford: Oxford University Press.

Mair, P. (2013). *Ruling the Void: The Hollowing of Western Democracy*. London: Verso.

March, J. G. & Olsen, J. P. (1995). *Democratic Governance*. New York: Free Press.

Marini, F. (Ed.) (1971). *Toward a New Public Administration: The Minnowbrook Perspective*. Scranton, PA: Chandler Publishing.

Marshall, T. H. (1959). *Citizenship and Social Class*. Cambridge: Cambridge University Press.

Mazzucato, M. (2013). *The Entrepreneurial State*. London: Anthem Press.

Mintzberg, H. (1979). An Emerging Strategy of "Direct" Research. *Administrative Science Quarterly*, *24*(4), 582–9.

Mintzberg, H. & McHugh, A. (1985). Strategy Formation in an Adhocracy. *Administrative Science Quarterly*, *30*(2), 160–97.

Moore, M. H. (1995). *Creating Public Value: Strategic Management in Government*. Cambridge, MA: Harvard University Press.

Mouffe, C. (2000). *The Democratic Paradox*. London: Verso.

Nabatchi, T. & Leighninger, M. (2015*). Public Participation for 21st Century Democracy*. San Francisco, CA: Jossey-Bass.

Naurin, E., Royed, T. J. & Thomson, R. (Eds.) (2019). *Party Mandates and Democracy: Making, Breaking, and Keeping Election Pledges in Twelve Countries*. Ann Arbor, MI: University of Michigan Press.

Niskanen, W. A. (1971). *Bureaucracy and Representative Government*. Chicago, IL: Aldine Atherton.

Olsen, F. E. (1983). The Family and the Market: A Study of Ideology and Legal Reform. *Harvard Law Review*, *96*(7), 1497–578.

Olsen, J. P. (2006). Maybe It Is Time to Rediscover Bureaucracy. *Journal of Public Administration Research and Theory*, *16*(1), 1–24.

Ongaro, E. (2014). The Changed EU Governance and Administrative Reforms in Member States under Fiscal Stress: Making the Case for Learning from Similar Countries. EGPA Policy Paper.

Osborne, D. E. & Gaebler, T. (1992). *Reinventing Government: How the Entrepreneurial Spirit Is Transforming the Public Sector*. Reading, MA: Addison-Wesley Publishing.

Osborne, D. & Plastrik, P. (1997). *Banishing Bureaucracy: The Five Strategies for Reinventing Government*. Reading, MA: Addison-Wesley Publishing.

Pateman, C. (1970). *Participation and Democratic Theory*. Cambridge: Cambridge University Press.

Peters, B. G. (2002). *Politics of Bureaucracy*. London: Routledge.

Peters, B. G. (2017). What Is So Wicked about Wicked Problems? A Conceptual Analysis and a Research Program. *Policy and Society*, *36*(3), 385–96.

Petersen, O. H., Hjelmar, U. & Vrangbæk, K. (2017). Is Contracting Out Still the Great Panacea? A Systematic Review of Studies on Economic and Quality Effects from 2000–2014. *Social Policy and Administration*, *51*(2), 130–57.

Pierre, J. & Peters, B. G. (2017). The Shirking Bureaucrat: A Theory in Search of Evidence? *Policy & Politics*, *45*(2), 157–72.

Pierre, J. & Røiseland, A. (2016). Exit and Voice in Local Government Reconsidered: A "Choice Revolution"? *Public Administration*, *94*(3), 738–53.

Pierson, P. (1994). *Dismantling the Welfare State?* Cambridge: Cambridge University Press.

Poguntke, T. & Webb, P. (Eds.) (2007). *The Presidentialization of Politics: A Comparative Study of Modern Democracies.* Oxford: Oxford University Press.

Pollitt, C. (2003). Joined-Up Government: A Survey. *Political Studies Review, 1*(1), 34–49.

Pollitt, C. & Bouckaert, G. (2004). *Public Management Reform: A Comparative Analysis.* Oxford: Oxford University Press.

Pollitt, C. & Bouckaert, G. (2017). *Public Management Reform: A Comparative Analysis into the Age of Austerity.* Oxford: Oxford University Press.

Pollitt, C., Van Thiel, S. & Homburg, V. (Eds.) (2007). *New Public Management in Europe.* Basingstoke: Palgrave Macmillan.

Randma-Liiv, T. & Kickert, W. (2017). The Impact of the Fiscal Crisis on Public Administration Reforms: Comparison of 14 European Countries. *Journal of Comparative Policy Analysis: Research and Practice, 19*(2), 155–72.

Randma-Liiv, T., Nakrošis, V. & Hajnal, G. (2011). Public Sector Organization in Central and Eastern Europe: From Agencification to De-Agencification. *Transylvanian Review of Administrative Sciences, 7*(SI), 160–75.

Rittel, H. W. & Webber, M. M. (1973). Dilemmas in a General Theory of Planning. *Policy Sciences, 4*(2), 155–69.

Ritz, A. (2015). Public Service Motivation and Politics: Behavioral Consequences among Local Councillors in Switzerland. *Public Administration, 93*(4), 1121–37.

Ritz, A., Brewer, G. A. & Neumann, O. (2016). Public Service Motivation: A Systematic Literature Review and Outlook. *Public Administration Review, 76*, 414–26.

Roberts, J. & Dietrich, M. (1999). Conceptualizing Professionalism: Why Economics Needs Sociology. *American Journal of Economics and Sociology, 58*(4), 977–98.

Rommetvedt, H. (2017). Scandinavian Corporatism in Decline. In Knutsen, O. (Ed.), *The Nordic Models in Political Science* (171–92). Bergen: Fagbokforlaget.

Rose, R. (1974). *The Problem of Party Government.* London: Palgrave Macmillan.

Rosenberg, J. (1992). Rationality and the Political Business Cycle: The Case of Local Government. *Public Choice, 73*(1), 71–81.

Rothstein, B. (2012). Good Governance. In Levi-Faur, D. (Ed.), *The Oxford Handbook of Governance.* Oxford: Oxford University Press.

Schillemans, T. (2008). Accountability in the Shadow of Hierarchy: The Horizontal Accountability of Agencies. *Public Organization Review, 8*(2), 175–94.

Schirm, S. A. (2011). Varieties of Strategies: Societal Influences on British and German Responses to the Global Economic Crisis. *Journal of Contemporary European Studies, 19*(1), 47–62.

Schmitter, P. C. (1985). Neo-Corporatism and the State. In Grant, W. (Ed.), *The Political Economy of Corporatism* (32–62). London: Macmillan Publishers.

Setälä, M. & Schiller, T. (Eds.) (2009). *Referendums and Representative Democracy: Responsiveness, Accountability and Deliberation.* London: Routledge.

Sirianni, C. (2010). *Investing in Democracy: Engaging Citizens in Collaborative Governance.* Washington, DC: Brookings Institution Press.

Sørensen, E. & Torfing, J. (2020). Radical and Disruptive Answers to Downstream Problems in Collaborative Governance? *Public Management Review, 23*(11), 1590–611.

Stoker, G. (2006). Public Value Management: A New Narrative for Networked Governance? *The American Review of Public Administration, 36*(1), 41–57.

Stoker, G. (2019). Can the Governance Paradigm Survive the Rise of Populism? *Policy & Politics*, *47*(1), 3–18.

Strøm, K., Müller, W. C. & Bergman, T. (2003). Challenges to Parliamentary Democracy. In Müller, W. C. (Ed.), *Delegation and Accountability in Parliamentary Democracies* (705–46). Oxford: Oxford University Press.

Togeby, L., Andersen, J. G., Christiansen, P. M., Valgårda, S. & Jørgensen, T. B. (2003). *Demokratiske udfordringer: kort udgave af Magudredningens hovedresultater*. Aarhus: Aarhus University Press.

Torfing, J. (2016). *Collaborative Innovation in the Public Sector*. Washington, DC: Georgetown University Press.

Torfing, J. & Bentzen, T. Ø. (2020). Does Stewardship Theory Provide a Viable Alternative to Control-Fixated Performance Management? *Administrative Sciences*, *10*(4), 86.

Torfing, J., Andersen, L. B., Greve, C. & Klausen, K. K. (2020). *Public Governance Paradigms: Competing and Co-existing*. Cheltenham: Edward Elgar Publishing.

Torfing, J., Cristofoli, D., Gloor, P. A., Meijer, A. J. & Trivellato, B. (2020). Taming the Snake in Paradise: Combining Institutional Design and Leadership to Enhance Collaborative Innovation. *Policy and Society*, *39*(4), 592–616.

Vile, M. J. C. (2012). *Constitutionalism and the Separation of Powers*. Indianapolis, IN: Liberty Fund.

Waldo, D. (1948). *The Administrative State: A Study of the Political Theory of American Public Administration*. New York: Ronald Press.

Waldo, D. (Ed.) (1971). *Public Administration in a Time of Turbulence*. Scranton, PA: Chandler Publishing.

Wamsley, G. L. & Zald, M. N. (1973). *The Political Economy of Public Administration: A Critique and Approach to the Study of Public Administration*. Lexington, MA: Lexington Books.

Wamsley, G. L., Bacher, R. N., Goodsell, C. T., Kronenberg, P. S., Rohr, J. A., Stivers, C. M., White, O. F. & Wolf, J. F. (1990). *Refounding Public Administration*. Newbury Park, CA: Sage.

Weyland, K. (2014). *Making Waves: Democratic Contention in Europe and Latin America since the Revolutions of 1848*. Cambridge: Cambridge University Press.

Wodak, R., Khosravinik, M. & Mral, B. (Eds.) (2013). *Right-Wing Populism in Europe: Politics and Discourse*. London: Bloomsbury Academic.

Zakaria, F. (1997). The Rise of Illiberal Democracy. *Foreign Affairs*, *76*(6), 22–43.

3. From sovereign to interactive political leadership

There has been an explosion in the number of journal articles on public leadership in the last four decades (Van Wart 2013), but in the tsunami of new leadership literature there is a dearth of books and articles focusing on political leadership (but see Blondel 1987; Burns 1978; Tucker 1995). A major exception is the biographical and historical books about specific political leaders who are typically heads of state, such as Thatcher, Bush, and Obama, or leaders of social movements, such as Gandhi and Mandela. The scant regard for political leadership in current leadership research is surprising given the importance of political leadership in democratic societies (Hartley & Benington 2010), the recent challenges to the exercise of political leadership (Helms 2012) and the current crisis of democratic political leadership evidenced by the dramatic events before, during, and after the Trump administration (Fraser 2020).

To compensate for this benign neglect, this chapter studies the crisis and possible transformation of political leadership in Western democracies in which elected politicians assume the main responsibility for lawmaking, the provision or commissioning of public services, the regulation of society and the economy, and public problem-solving. It argues that the traditional ways of thinking about and organizing the exercise of political leadership are challenged by political and social developments that undermine the ability of elected politicians to play the role they are supposed to play. It explores the new and tentative forms of interactive political leadership that aim to bring elected politicians and citizens together in ongoing, problem-focused discussions aiming to create new and innovative solutions with a broad-based ownership. It assesses the gains and barriers of interactive political leadership and discusses how it can be advanced by the construction of collaborative platforms and arenas. Finally, it looks at how interactive political leadership can be combined with more traditional forms of sovereign political leadership that place the ultimate power for political decision-making in the hands of elected politicians.

DEMOCRATIC GOVERNMENT AND THE ROLE OF POLITICAL LEADERSHIP

The horizontal division of power between the legislative, executive, and judicial branches of government, which forms the basis of the democratic system of checks and balances aimed at preventing the usurpation of political power by a singular actor, cannot hide the fact that democratic government tends to be hierarchically organized. Hence, in their capacity as voters, citizens elect a representative assembly that controls and constrains the government leaders (and in some countries a directly elected president), who in turn controls the administrative apparatus that delivers services and solutions to citizens who may hold the responsible politicians to account in the next election. The hierarchy is less pronounced in presidential systems and clearer in countries subscribing to the Westminster model of parliamentary democracy, but even presidential systems have a chain of government based on delegation and control that links citizens to representative institutions, government leaders, and administrative agencies.

Political leadership and political leaders play a pivotal role both inside and outside the legislative and executive branches of government, where they aspire to perform three key functions: (1) setting the political agenda by means of defining problems that call for political action; (2) giving direction to and proposing and promoting relevant policy solutions; and (3) generating support for their realization (Tucker 1995). When performing these three functions in a democracy, political leaders contribute to transforming the manifold wants and interests of the people into joint solutions that enjoy widespread support. As such, political leaders are centrally involved in aggregating and integrating preferences as part of democratic will formation and subsequently turning them into policy outputs that voters can evaluate in the next election.

If leadership in its most generic form involves an attempt by leaders to achieve goals with or through other actors, *political* leadership is a particular form of leadership that seeks to win the acceptance of a particular problem diagnosis and mobilize support for specific goals and actions from a significant number of followers in a context of competition and conflict (Burns 1978: 425). Compared to administrative leadership, political leadership faces a much higher degree of horizontal competition and much stronger demands for downward accountability toward the voting population. While administrative leaders compete on their merits to land a top job and may be rewarded based on their administrative performance, political leaders are constantly involved in fierce party-political competition for voters, office, and issue ownership. Some would go so far as to see competition between political elites as the defining characteristic of liberal democracy (Schumpeter 2010 [1942]). By the same token, the administrative leaders of public service organizations may be subjected to critical scrutiny of their professional performance by the citizens that their organization is serving, but they are not put on trial in regular elections in the same way as political leaders, who may be ousted from office if they have performed poorly or failed to justify their actions.

That said, we should bear in mind that political leadership is not only exercised by leaders situated within formal political institutions but also by the leaders of social and political movements who are also involved in interpreting pressing problems, developing visionary, yet feasible solutions, and mobilizing support for their implementation. However, it is important to note that while leaders of social and political movements can exercise soft power based on ideology, symbolism, rituals, and storytelling, they do not have the same privileged access as the formal political leaders to coercive and inducing forms of hard power based on state apparatus resources (Masciulli et al. 2016: 6).

The advent of modern mass society meant that democracy had to build on representation, since it was impossible for all of the citizens in the newly created nation-states to meet face to face and make authoritative decisions based on all-inclusive deliberation (Sartori 1987). Hence, the people had to delegate their sovereign power to elected politicians, who were supposed to govern on their behalf until Election Day, when the electorate would hold them to account for their (mis)deeds. The elected political representatives were only bound by their conscience when making political decisions, but the need to secure democratic legitimacy and the competition for voters means that political leaders must engage with the voters; if not in regular party meetings, then at least during recurring election campaigns.

The political leader–people connection marks a huge difference from the ancient regime, where the king's power was based on a divine right to rule. In liberal democracy, the right to rule is established by free and fair elections that are assumed to manifest and communicate the will of the people. However, in the classical conception of representative democracy (Weber 2015 [1921]), elected politicians are portrayed as a sort of elected kings; they are still supposed to make authoritative decisions by themselves without involving the people. When the voters have spoken on Election Day, the elected politicians are free to make all the necessary decisions without further consultation and the government can command the bureaucracy to implement laws and secure compliance (Olsen 1978).

In reality, elected politicians and political leaders are obliged to engage with political party members and their local constituencies to secure re-election, and they are forced to work with social and economic stakeholders, community leaders, and social movements to gain political support and achieve their goals. As regards the latter, Heclo (1978) has famously demonstrated how political sub-committees in the US Congress involve a broad range of organized interests in policymaking. Similarly, in a small group of northern European countries, politicians have regularly orchestrated tripartite negotiations with peak labor-market organizations to generate support for legislation (Schmitter & Lembruch 1979). Politicians may also engage in dialogue with social movements. Hence, Heifetz (1994) has shown how, during the 1960s, US President Lyndon B. Johnson had to involve and negotiate the protest movements led by Martin Luther King to deal with the highly contentious civil rights issue. In the same way, the South African government negotiated the abolition of apartheid with the anti-apartheid movement led by Nelson Mandela (Spence & Welsh 2010).

However, interaction with organized interests seldom gives rise to the formal and permanent changes in the institutions of government that remain largely untouched in the face of the more or less informal and sporadic negotiations with interest organizations and social movements. Moreover, relevant and affected citizens are rarely involved in discussions with their elected representative in relation to concrete efforts to solve pressing societal problems. Indeed, elected politicians and political leaders are relatively insulated from the citizens they are representing and spend most of their time raising money for their respective re-election campaigns, processing legislative proposals in specialized political committees, and engaging in political communication via traditional mass media and new social media. In sum, despite the critical relationship between political leaders and the voting population, there is hardly any direct participation in policy deliberation, as politicians seem to operate in a political sphere that is seldom penetrated by citizens, who tend to remain passive spectators to the mediatized process through which government and the opposition present and debate alternative policy solutions (Edelman 1988; Manin 1997; De Beus 2011).

The traditional and institutionalized absence of systematic two-way communication between political leaders and their followers has been legitimized by a less than favorable view of the competences of voters (Ingham 2016). Hence, Schumpeter (2010 [1942]: 253) maintains that for politicians to respect the will of the people, "it must be something more than an indeterminate bundle of vague impulses loosely playing about given slogans and mistaken impressions." According to Schumpeter (2010 [1942]: 261), the average voter does not know what he or she wants and has little knowledge of politics and the problems discussed in politics, since "he expends less disciplined effort on mastering a political problem than he expends on a game of bridge." Hence, there is little to gain from interacting with the voters during the election period, as "the typical citizen drops to a lower level of mental performance as soon as he enters the political field, he argues and analyses in a way which he would readily recognize as infantile within the sphere of his real interest" (Schumpeter 2010 [1942]: 261). This serves to explain why modern representative democracy developed into a system for elite competition in which political leaders rarely engage with their actual and potential followers, thus undermining the circular process of motivation and power exchange on which political leadership is founded and becomes truly transformative.

THE TENSION BETWEEN POLITICAL LEADERSHIP AND DEMOCRATIC EGALITARIANISM

Recent research argues that liberal democracy is founded on a fundamental tension between the collective self-determination of the sovereign people and the exercise of political leadership (Kane & Patapan 2012). Hence, liberal democracy builds on the idea that everybody belonging to a particular local or national demos should be able to influence the decisions that affect their lives. At the same time, it recognizes the need for political leaders who can skillfully unify the plural and divided people, provide solutions to pressing problems, and help to define and achieve collective goals and visions for societal development. As such, the decision-making competence in liberal democracy is simultaneously placed in the hands of the members of the local or national demos and in the hands of a particular group of political leaders with the power to make binding decisions for all of society. Let us take a closer look at each of the poles in this tension and the attempt to overcome and handle the tension in order to understand the contemporary challenge to political leadership in Western democracies.

Modern democracy builds on the idea of a sovereign people who determine their own affairs and are able to influence their own living conditions. The people are sovereign in the sense that nobody over or beside them can challenge their right to collective self-determination; there is no king, religious authority, or all-powerful technocrat capable of dictating political decisions made through collective decision-making based on some basic democratic rights and norms about freedom, fairness, and equity. The people are assumed to be homogenous in the sense that everyone possesses the same competence and possibilities for free and equal access to participate in the decision-making process. Elections and voting procedures build on the principle of "one person, one vote." All votes should be counted, and they count evenly; and in the deliberative processes preceding elections and voting procedures, all arguments should be heard and openly discussed. In sum, the right of the sovereign people to collective self-determination is essentially egalitarian, since all citizens are supposed to have an equal influence on the political governance of society and the economy.

The democratic idea of the sovereign people stands in sharp contrast to the idea of a sovereign political leadership that assumes that every society requires political leaders who can foster and nurture the process through which the people become a people and begin to speak coherently about and discover their collective interests and future aspirations (Kane & Patapan 2012). Political leaders are deemed necessary to identify and diagnose problems that call for collective action, defining and prioritizing societal goals, crafting viable solutions, and securing support for their implementation (Tucker 1995). As such, political leaders tend to concentrate (and even monopolize) the power to make authoritative governance decisions. They may receive advice from their administrative aids and be influenced by competing coalitions of private actors, but they ultimately have the responsibility to govern our increasingly complex and fragmented societies.

Political leaders are recruited and selected competitively by political parties that are organized with the purpose of winning and exercising government power. From joining a party to becoming part of the party leadership and representing the party in political negotiations about public governance solutions is a long journey. "Going all the way" requires particular personal traits, competences, and resources, including determination, insight and education, charisma, political astuteness, experience, argumentative and rhetorical skills, media coverage, good contacts, and so on. These traits, competences and resources are equally distributed across the population but tend to become concentrated in a particular political class, and even sometimes in particular families, clans, or dynasties, from where most of the top-level political leaders are drawn (Landemore 2020). In sum, political leaders tend to form an elite, which breaks with the egalitarian democratic norms.

The contrast between the egalitarian conception of the self-determining people and the somewhat elitist political leadership is further amplified by the fact that the appraisal of political leadership predates democratic theory (Grint 2010) and continues to play a crucial role in contemporary democracies. Plato praised the knowledge and expertise of political leaders, who he depicted as "philosopher kings," whereas Aristotle highlighted the prudence and rhetorical skills of political leaders, who must combine the appeal to logos, pathos, and ethos. Machiavelli discards the ideas about political leaders' reliance on wisdom, prudence, and skills of persuasion, claiming instead that they must be prepared to ruthlessly do whatever it takes to win, exercise, and hold on to political power. The conception of a sovereign political leadership is further developed and epitomized by Hobbes, who claims that the absolute power of the king is a condition for securing social order.

Locke and other liberal democratic thinkers had to find a way to combine the idea of a self-determining people with the need for political leadership. They aim to solve the problem and ease the tension between democratic egalitarianism and political elitism by arguing that, in a modern democracy, the political leaders come from the people, are elected by the people and rule for the people;

in other words, the political leaders somehow incarnate the will of the people, at least in the sense that they are appointed by and thus represent them.

There are several reasons why the model of democratic representation fails to eliminate the tension between democratic egalitarianism and the elitism associated with political leadership. First, the link between the voters and their political representatives is thin. The elected political leaders rarely know exactly why they were elected and what the voters expect of them. Moreover, the political parties that may help to connect the political representatives with their voters during the election period have very few members, and the activity level is low (Mair 2013). In the US, the political parties hardly exist outside of regular election campaigns. Voters may use traditional mass media and new social media to convey political messages to elected politicians and political leaders, but there is a profound lack of constructive two-way dialogue in these media. Some political leaders use focus groups to obtain input from their typical voters and to test new ideas and slogans, but this is a poor alternative to face-to-face dialogue between the people and the political leaders. Hence, it is difficult to ensure correspondence between the political representatives and the represented people; not because the people are short on articulated interests, opinions, or ideas, but because the mechanism for linking voters with their political representatives through elections and political parties is weak.

Second, there is no guarantee that elected political leaders see themselves as representatives of the people with a mission to promote general interests and create public value. Most political leaders are primarily interested in re-election and spend considerable time and energy on creating and maintaining coalitions that can provide public support and help finance their election campaign. In addition, many elected politicians seem to pursue their own interests and use their public office to benefit themselves, their family, their local constituency, and the socioeconomic actors that support them financially (Mause 2014; Bardhan & Mookherjee 2018). Political leaders may formulate a set of ambitious election pledges to win an election but then fail to honor them because of "changing circumstances," "economic necessities, " or "external pressures" from globalization. This kind of political cynicism tends to lead to a breakdown in the relation of representation from above.

Lastly but importantly, there seems to be a rise of growing "anti-politics" in the electorate, which further undermines the relation of representation (Stoker 2006; Hay 2007). Some voters are so dissatisfied with the current forms of politics and the apparent political impotence via-à-vis complex problems (e.g., the financial crisis, refugee crisis, climate crisis) that they refuse to participate in elections and forsake the political institutions of representative democracy, thus undermining the representative relation from below.

All of these points and arguments go to show how attempts to overcome the tension between democratic egalitarianism and the elitism associated with political leadership by insisting on the near-perfect representational leaders–led relation are failing to do the trick. Hence, the tension persists and calls for political and democratic innovation in order to avoid the development of a widening gulf between the people and their political leaders that may spur the rise of anti-democratic forms of authoritarian populism.

CHALLENGES TO SOVEREIGN POLITICAL LEADERSHIP

There are other challenges to political leadership than those arising from the tension from the demand for democratic egalitarianism and the resulting need to find better ways of connecting political elites with the people they are supposed to represent. Let us briefly catalogue some of these challenges to flesh out a fuller image of how recent developments and events have problematized political leadership in representative democracies.

Solving pressing societal problems is a key political leadership task but increasingly difficult, as the world is currently facing a large number of wicked problems that are complex, tangled and hard to understand, conflicting policy goals, no standard solutions, a need for specialized knowledge, a large number of stakeholders with different interests, and a high risk of conflict (Rittel & Webber 1973; Head 2008). Such problems cannot be solved singlehandedly by political leaders and their usual crowd of administrative aides and policy advisors; they require input from and negotiations with societal actors who can provide the knowledge, ideas and support needed to stimulate innovation and to secure the implementation of new and bold solutions (Head & Alford 2015). Politicians increasingly recognize the need for input from lay actors and appreciate its role in designing and implementing relevant policy solutions (Christiansen & Nørgaard 2003; Lees-Marshment 2015; Hendriks & Lees-Marshment 2019), but the interaction with relevant and affected policy actors remains informal and unsystematic, thereby preventing political leaders from reaping the full benefit from this type of policy crowdsourcing (Aitamurto & Chen 2017).

The challenge provided by the pervasive wicked problems and the need for input to make promising but provisional solutions is mirrored by the institutional insulation of political leaders from societal actors. Politicians are often buried in highly specialized political committee work and seldom come out to meet and interact with relevant stakeholders. Participation in new forms of networked governance tends to be monopolized by public managers who act as gatekeepers who regulate the contact between elected politicians and external actors. This institutional insulation risks creating an unfortunate tunnel vision that prevents policy innovation. Politicians also tend to have very little interaction with the downstream actors responsible for policy implementation. They are supposed to focus on "steering" and leave the "rowing" to administrative actors and private contractors (Osborne & Gaebler 1993). This division of labor prevents politicians from influencing the many small but crucial decisions made in the course of implementation, which limits the impact of their political leadership.

The popular image of what constitutes a good politician seems to have shifted considerably from the mid-twentieth century to the beginning of the twenty-first century (Clarke et al. 2018). Earlier, citizens expected politicians to be sincere, hardworking, strong, skillful, and moderate, and to possess and express a noble and elevated set of political competences that separated them from the general population. Today, citizens increasingly expect politicians to be all of the above—while at the same time appearing "normal," "approachable," and "in touch" with reality and ordinary people. This new and conflicting demand for politicians who are not merely supposed to be brilliant statespersons capable of exercising political leadership *for* the people but also expected to be genuine and authentic politicians *of* the people is supported by the mass media, which regularly poll which top-level political leader the voters would like to invite for a beer and barbecue and invite politicians to participate in entertainment programs where they cook, dance, and quiz. While there is certainly nothing wrong with the demand for elected politicians to appear "down to earth," the problem is that the attempts made by politicians to appear as strong and clever statespersons with a high degree of perseverance while at the same time presenting as a nice, relatable person you would like to invite over is pretty close to being a performative contradiction. Hence, the challenge for political leaders is to be distant enough to be trusted as a competent governor of the affairs of the state while having enough proximity to the voters to appear empathetic and a man/woman of the people.

Speaking of the people, the civic culture is transformed as citizens appear to be less allegiant and more assertive (Dalton & Welzel 2014). Their institutional confidence, philanthropic faith, and norm compliance is dwindling, while at the same time citizens increasingly praise their civil liberty to decide how they will live their lives, demand equal opportunities for everyone and believe that people should have a voice in collective decisions at various levels (Dalton & Welzel 2014: 291–2). Anti-authoritarian sentiments nurtured by half a century of educational expansion and cultural revolution tend to erode citizen faith in expert knowledge and political elites while boosting confidence in their ability to participate in and influence public governance decisions (Warren 2002). The increasingly assertive, competent, and critical citizenry wants to participate more actively and directly in public decision-making than the institutions of representative democracy tend to allow for—and that poses a major challenge to the usual way of exercising political leadership.

Political leadership is now mediatized 24/7. While both traditional media and new social media provide good opportunities for transformational political leadership aiming to sketch out possible and desirable futures that resonate with cherished norms and values, the current mediatization of politics has created a drama democracy that places a high premium on personal point scoring, political conflict and rivalry, and demonstration of the capacity for swift and determined action leading to short-term solutions (Klijn 2014). The Trump era has provided evidence of how challenging things can become when a president seemingly believes he can rule the world by social media, launching personal attacks and promising populist, quick-fix solutions, such as promises to stop immigration by building a wall on the US–Mexican border. The mediatized drama democracy suppresses fact-based political debate, trust-based political collaboration between opposing parties, a shared focus on salient policy issues, and the production of long-term solutions to wicked and unruly problems.

Finally, there are a number of factors that tend to disempower political leaders in Western democracies. The globalization of economic transactions, physical and digital communication, and the strategic horizons of public governance at various levels subject political leaders to pressures from pro-cesses and events they can neither control nor affect, because power is widely dispersed and the institutional mechanisms for transnational and multi-level governance are weak (Kennett 2008). Economic pressures from recurring periods of austerity combined with the hegemony of neoliberal economic discourse seem to dictate market-conform policy answers that are backed by the disempowering catchphrase: "There is no alternative" (McBride & Evans 2017). Digital informatization means that political decision-makers have unlimited access to multiple, redundant, parallel, and competing streams of information, which tends to create a paralyzing information overload; and at the same time a scarcity of relevant, validated and reliable knowledge upon which elected politicians can act (Workman et al. 2009). The rise of strategic managerialism as a part of New Public Management (NPM) means that the strategic decision-making power of public managers is strengthened at the expense of the political leaders, especially since public service organizations are given greater autonomy vis-à-vis central government through increased structural devolution (Christensen & Lægreid 2002). The off-loading of public tasks, such as service production, and the monitoring of public regulation to private actors who are notoriously difficult to influence and hold to account undermines the capacity of political leaders to deliver public goods and produce particular public value outcomes (Hay 2007).

INTERACTIVE POLITICAL LEADERSHIP

The summary analysis of the challenges to political leadership presented above attests to the need to empower the political leaders in liberal democracies while simultaneously enhancing their interaction with relevant and affected actors who can help to provide much-needed input that allows politicians to better understand the problems at hand, get new ideas for their solution and develop the joint ownership to the solutions that would enable their implementation. Indeed, enhanced interaction between political leaders and their increasingly assertive, critical, and competent followers will help the former to solve wicked problems by stimulating policy innovation; break the insulation of elected politicians so as to facilitate learning and adjustment in all phases of the policy process; further demonstrate the approachability and empathy of political leaders; and create a space for slow, collaborative, and well-informed policymaking as an antidote to the mediatized drama democracy. Enhanced interaction between political leaders and those who are bound by their decisions may also help to draw attention to the problems and needs of the electorate, provide a broader selection of solutions from which to choose, construct a relevant and solid foundation for joint decision-making, and refocus public governance on the co-creation of innovative public value outcomes.

Problem-focused deliberation between political decision-makers and citizens can produce better decisions, democratic legitimacy, and social justice if it stimulates learning, facilitates broad-based participation, and allows minority groups to be heard (Fung 2015). On the downside, the effort to involve citizens in policymaking systematically may undermine the primacy of politics by allowing unelected lay actors to participate in and influence political decision-making. However, enhanced interaction between political leaders and their followers does not mean that the political leaders surrender their political power and authority to citizens. The latter may provide valuable input to the decision-making process and try to influence the result, but the elected politicians tend to remain in charge of making the final decisions that may go against the preferences of citizens. Still, the deliberative interaction will enable politicians to justify their choices, which in turn will result in increased respect for politicians (Gutmann & Thompson 2004).

Over the years, we have seen many forms of citizen participation in public governance (Fung 2006). The range of participants and the method for recruitment differ, as do the forms of interaction and the influence of the deliberative interaction on final outcomes. The policy issues have also changed from planning problems via budgeting to a broader set of governance questions, including education reform, health care, social inclusion and employment, the accommodation of racial and ethnic diversity, and climate change. Finally, whereas for many years citizen participation in mini-publics was initiated by public administrators aiming to improve the effectiveness and legitimacy of public governance, the last two decades have seen a growing number of examples of elected politicians initiating interaction with citizens (Fung 2015). The purpose of the politically initiated venues for policy interaction has varied from attempts to co-design constitutional governance reforms (Grant 2013; Landemore 2014) and to handle thorny issues such as abortion (Field 2018) or make budget cuts (Siebers & Torfing 2018) to attempts to solve wicked policy problems at the national, regional, and/or local levels (Koppenjan et al. 2009; Ercan 2014; Sørensen & Torfing 2019a; Agger 2021). Interviews with a large sample of political leaders in five Anglophone countries reveal how politicians value formal and informal interaction with citizens, because such interaction provides useful inputs to their decisions, connects them to everyday people and enables the testing of advice from other sources (Hendriks & Lees-Marshment 2019).

The political initiation of policy deliberation with citizens—whether individuals, groups, or interest organizations—bears witness to the development of an interactive political leadership defined as a systematic attempt of elected politicians to engage a broad range of relevant and affected actors, including citizens, communities, and civil society associations, in collaborative interaction processes through which problems are framed and defined and solutions are designed, endorsed and carried out (Ansell & Torfing 2017; Sørensen & Torfing 2019a; Sørensen 2020). Interactive political leadership is an antidote to the heroic political leadership aimed at solving great societal challenges by developing and executing smart and enlightened solutions that are hardly discussed with anybody and therefore enjoy little popular support. It builds on the basic idea that elected politicians' performance of the basic political leadership function will be greatly improved by interaction with relevant and affected actors who can help to clarify and add nuance to the policy problem, qualify and enrich the ideas for policy solutions, and develop democratic ownership to solutions that facilitate implementation. To illustrate, French President Emmanuel Macron learned the limitations of his heroic political leadership the hard way: in an attempt to solve the climate crisis, he launched new legislation raising the prices of gasoline and diesel, but the lack of consultation, collaboration and public justification led to the nationwide "yellow vest" protest movement that criticized the unequal economic impact of the rising prices, which were bound to deepen social inequality, especially in rural areas. A more interactive political leadership involving relevant and affected actors could potentially have found ways to compensate those hit by the massive price spikes, thereby avoiding the massive climate policy backlash in France.

Fortunately, there are many examples of interactive political leadership (Piattoni 2011; Heiden & Krummenacher 2011; Hertting & Kugelberg 2017;

Table 3.1   Interactive political leadership—drivers and barriers

Drivers	Barriers
Many countries are marked by an alarming decline in citizen trust in politicians, which prevents the latter from launching necessary structural reforms	The classic role perception is that political leaders should go it alone rather than involving ignorant, self-interested amateurs in policymaking
Many politicians are dissatisfied with being sidelined and marginalized policy experts and executive civil servants. They must create alliances with external actors (e.g., citizens)	Many politicians (especially at the national level) are driven by ideology, thus making it difficult for them to engage in pragmatic problem-solving with citizens
Many politicians are frustrated with how NPM has reduced their role to merely defining the overall goals and budget frames and are looking for a new, more active policymaking role	Representative democracy is built on competition for voters, media attention and political control, all of which are diluted if politicians become one among many actors engaged in interactive policymaking
Political leaders feel the pressure from urgent policy problems but are caught in a political stalemate due to the lack of inspiring input	Many politicians are unwilling to accept the risk associated with collaborative policymaking that may force them to adopt solutions they dislike
Many politicians are tired of having to defend political decisions against criticism from citizens and organized stakeholders and are searching for ways to construct common ownership	The scarcity of time and resources that politicians have at their disposal often make them think they cannot afford to invest in lengthy participatory and deliberative processes

Sørensen et al. 2020). A recent study of Dutch mayors has revealed how most tend to see themselves as "bridging-and-bonding mayors" rather than "get-it-done mayors" (Karsten & Hendriks 2017). Hence, their principal aim is not to push through their own policy ideas but rather to bring different groups of people together and unite them through a democratic process of policy deliberation. Problem-focused policy deliberation with citizens is much easier to orchestrate at the local level because of the physical proximity, although digital tools may help national-level politicians to engage in regular discussions with their local constituency (Neblo et al. 2018).

A further enhancement of interactive political leadership holds the promise of improving political leadership in turbulent times while reconnecting political leaders with their competent, critical, and assertive followers, who are increasingly fragmented and divided over a broad range of political, economic, and cultural issues. Despite the current embryonic forms of interactive political leadership, its promotion is more noble ambition than fact. To envisage the prospect for advancing interactive political leadership, Table 3.1 draws on Ansell and Torfing (2017) in charting some of the main drivers of and barriers to thinking about and practicing political leadership in Western democracies. Although it is possible to identify strong drivers of political leaders to engage in deliberative interaction with different groups of followers, the barriers are considerable, and researchers and practitioners must work hard to find ways of overcoming them by developing and cultivating new role perceptions for elected politicians and experimenting with new institutional designs that facilitate problem-focused interaction without adding to an already strained time budget.

BUILDING PLATFORMS AND ARENAS FOR INTERACTIVE POLITICAL LEADERSHIP

Advancing interactive political leadership requires the creation of institutional platforms and arenas that can support the interface between politicians and citizens and facilitate sustained interaction. The construction of platforms and arenas is the focal point of the new research on "generativity" (Zittrain 2006; Post 2009; Foerderer et al. 2014) and "generative governance" (Ansell & Gash 2008; Ansell & Miura 2020). Generativity refers to a capacity to leverage unprompted action without determining its content. To illustrate, the internet allows users to easily discover and exploit widely distributed resources and data to construct their own websites or communication structure. Generativity has been explored in many different sub-fields. New research on public governance talks about generative governance, defined as governance that facilitates and enables the emergence of productive interaction among distributed actors (Ansell & Torfing 2021). There are many examples of generative governance. Reflexive law mandates distributed actors to come together to carry out important public tasks, and it provides a legal framework for their interaction. The construction of quasi-markets creates legal procedures for public and private service providers to compete for contracts and customers. Finally, devolution authorizes lower-level jurisdictions to undertake different tasks, whether alone or together.

The generative governance concept offers a new perspective on public governance that breaks with the bureaucratic idea that all public tasks must be carried out by an agency with a particular position in the public hierarchy and division of labor and in accordance with explicit rules and budget frames. Instead, the idea is that the public sector provides resources, opportunities, storylines and frameworks that mobilize and guide different public and/or private actors who may come together to co-create public value outcomes. Generative governance may combine generative tools (e.g., open-access data, digital simulation of urban planning) with generative processes (e.g., design thinking, design experiments) and generative institutions (e.g., platforms, arenas) (Ansell & Torfing 2021). The latter are particularly relevant for promoting and supporting interactive political leadership.

Platforms are relatively permanent opportunity structures that facilitate the formation, adjustment, and proliferation of different arenas that bring together distributed actors such as politicians and relevant and affected groups of individual and/or organized citizens in sustained and value-producing interaction. For example, Gouillart and Hallett (2015) describe the functioning of local engagement platforms in London that allow a dispersed Somali community to engage in issue-specific interaction with public decision-makers, and Aragón et al. (2017) describe an online platform created by Barcelona City Council to stimulate discussion about its strategic plan for the city with local citizens. Platforms can accomplish multiple tasks to support interactive political leadership: they may advertise their existence to the public and thus draw attention to the possibility for participation and interaction in relation to a specific set of governance issues. They also provide visible contact points for those wanting to participate in policy interaction. Sometimes they will impose a specific set of access rules determining who can participate in policy interaction, how they participate and to what end. Platforms tend to provide rules, resources, and communication systems that help to lower the transaction costs of sustained interaction and deliberation. They also provide procedures, routines, and templates, making it easy to initiate policy interaction, exploit the results, and create spin-off processes. Finally, they may provide advice, assistance, and feedback to those in charge of leading and managing interactive policy arenas.

To illustrate, in 2015, Gentofte Municipality in Denmark created a new type of Task Committee that has provided a platform for the creation of more than thirty-five problem-focused arenas for interactive political leadership, each committee typically bringing together ten citizens and five local councilors (Sørensen & Torfing 2019a). The new platform is described in the local steering documents, and the municipality has established a clear set of procedures about the initiation, modus operandi, and leadership of these Task Committees and how they report back to the City Council that issues their mandate. The platform has also created an internal network of administrative facilitators that facilitates ongoing discussions about how best to support the interaction between the local councilors and the diverse group of citizens. We shall return to discuss some of the key design features of this platform below.

Whereas the platforms are few, relatively permanent, and have the creation of arenas as their key purpose, the arenas they engender are many, temporary, and focused on the facilitation of collaborative interaction and production of outputs and outcomes. Arenas are institutional frameworks for interactions that provide specific mandates, self-regulated agendas and timelines, physical and digital opportunities for meeting and discussing problems and solutions, ground rules governing interaction, mechanisms for conflict mediation, and a facilitative leadership that helps to ensure progress. Arenas may create spin-off agendas, tasks and activities that new arenas may help to initiate and organize. The membership of the new arenas may be the same, different, or overlapping with old ones.

Platforms are typically constructed by governments aiming to enhance interaction between public decision-makers and relevant and affected citizens. Think tanks, civil society organizations and ideational associations aiming to strengthen democratic governance may also provide platforms for interactive policy deliberation with participation of elected politicians and interested citizens. However, governments tend to be the key provider of platforms for interactive political leadership, as they not only have the capacity and resources to do so but can also forge a close link between the interactive policymaking process and the political leaders responsible for using the citizen input and drawing on co-created policy proposals when making authoritative decisions.

The typical way that governments may use platforms and arenas to connect elected politicians and citizens and foster interactive political leadership is illustrated in Figure 3.1.

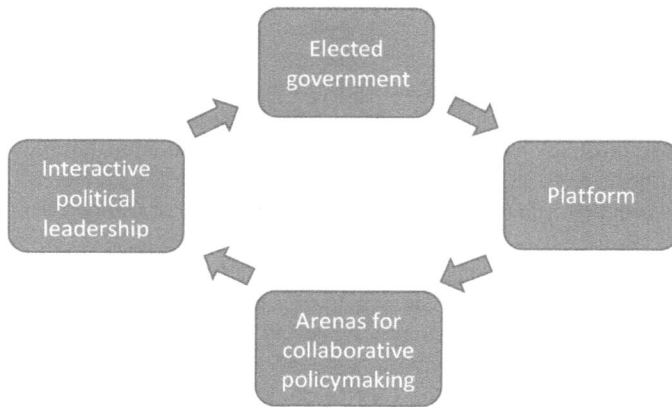

Figure 3.1   *How platforms and arenas foster interactive political leadership*

The construction of platforms and arenas for interactive political leadership is a new and exciting task for governments. For researchers, it calls for further research investigating the impact of institutional design on political participation and collaborative governance (Alexander 2005; Fung 2003, 2006; Krogh 2022). For government officials, it involves a series of important design choices. Let us briefly consider three crucial design choices and their likely impacts.

The first choice concerns the membership of interactive policy arenas. One option is to let citizens deliberate on their own and without any politicians to divert attention, and perhaps try to put pressure on citizens to adopt a particular solution. Another option is to have a mixed membership that forces elected politicians and citizens to deliberate with each other and try to reach agreement on a joint set of recommendations. The trend in mini-publics, such as the much-used citizen juries, is to let citizens deliberate on their own while having access to policy-relevant knowledge and expertise presented to them by scientists or policy experts. While this may help to prevent systemic logics based on political power and economics to distort the deliberative process, policy uptake may end up being low, since elected politicians will tend to feel little ownership of the citizen-crafted solutions.

This problem might be solved by a mixed-membership design that may enhance policy uptake by developing joint ownership of new and bold policy solutions. A comparison of case studies of interactive political leadership arenas in the Netherlands (Michels & de Graaf 2010) and New South Wales in Australia (Hendriks & Lees-Marshment 2016), where elected politicians were presented with policy proposals developed by citizens alone, with case studies of Task Committees in Gentofte in Denmark shows that mixed membership tends to produce much higher policy uptake. While conclusive evidence will require further studies, there is good reason to expect the result from the comparative analysis to hold up. Direct politician–citizen interaction helps to create realistic expectations regarding joint policy solutions while at the same time recruiting strong supporters among elected politicians who will help to convince other politicians to follow the recommendations.

The second choice concerns the method for recruiting the citizens who are to participate in interactive policy arenas. The common method is to issue an open invitation and let citizens self-select based on "first come, first served." This method is easy to use and merely requires broadcasting the call, but the downside is that the open invitation method tends to create a large participatory self-selection bias, as those who end up participating are often the white, retired middle class, who have both the time and resources to participate. Another method is random selection, as often used in citizen juries. While this may create a representative sample of citizens with whom politicians can interact, the selected citizens may not be interested in participating. A third method is to elect the citizen participants. However, organizing an election of citizen representatives is both time-consuming and carries the risk of (very) low voter turnout, meaning that the elected representatives might not be representative of the affected demos.

Finally, the citizens may be appointed by the elected politicians and the administrative aides with a view to securing participation from a broad range of different but relevant citizen voices. This method requires a broad knowledge of the relevant participants with different backgrounds, experiences, and ideas, which is not always available. However, the platform for the creation of the Gentofte Task Committees in Denmark has found a new and promising way of solving this problem: when drafting a written mandate for a new interactive policy arena, the local councilors outline ten different competence profiles for the citizens they want to include. Citizens who think they match one or more of these profiles can sign up on a municipal webpage, and the City Council then makes the final selection by comparing the competence profiles with the citizens who signed up. Citizens who are not selected are offered participation in working groups, seminars, and hearings (Sørensen & Torfing 2019a).

The final choice concerns who is exercising leadership within interactive policy arenas. Since citizens are seldom sufficiently competent and experienced leaders of policy processes, the question becomes whether politicians or administrators lead the interactive processes between events and meetings or perhaps whether a professional third-party facilitator should be asked to lead and manage the process. The choice of leadership model is by no means an easy one. Politicians and administrators both know the policy area well, but the politicians may want to participate actively in the interaction process rather than functioning as facilitators, and the administrators may be good at preparing and organizing meetings and taking minutes, but they often have no professional skills when it comes to facilitating collaborative processes and spurring innovation. Alternatively, one might hire professional third-party facilitators who will have the skills to engage the participants in fruitful discussions and drive the process to a conclusion. However, external facilitators tend to have little knowledge of the policy area in question and may fail to understand and take into account the often-sensitive political ramifications of the process. The institutional design of the Gentofte Task Committees aimed to balance several of these concerns (Sørensen & Torfing 2019a). Two of the participating politicians were appointed as formal chairs of the Task Committees, and they welcomed and concluded all of the meetings, but specially trained administrators prepared and managed the interactive processes in the meetings using techniques drawn from design thinking. In effect, the politicians felt strong ownership over the collaborative endeavor but were free to participate in the discussions, which were professionally facilitated by knowledgeable facilitators who fully understood the logic of appropriate action in a politically charged environment.

TOWARD A NEW FORM OF HYBRID OR COMPOUND DEMOCRACY?

In many cases, interactive political leadership may merely serve to provide input on the basis of which governments make better-informed and perhaps even more innovative solutions, thus limiting the direct democratic influence of citizens to the idea-generating phase. As Michels and de Graaf (2010) show, however, the positive effects on democracy of interactive political leadership are not limited to direct citizen influence on policy solutions; based on case studies of local participatory policymaking in two Dutch cities, they find that participation in interactive policymaking may enhance and widen democratic engagement, create responsibility for public matters, encourage people to listen to different opinions and strengthen democratic legitimacy. As such, interactive political leadership tends to supplement the traditional forms of representative democracy with new forms of democratic participation in deliberative processes that compensate for the decline of the representative function of political parties and elections (Cain et al. 2006).

Institutional forms of representative democracy and institutional forms of participatory and deliberative democracy may co-exist and support each other within new forms of hybrid or compound democracy deliberately aimed at combining different forms of democracy to achieve the positive impacts of each of them (Sørensen & Torfing 2019b). Representative democracy gains its democratic legitimacy from free and fair elections based on universal suffrage, and it may support participatory and deliberative forms of democracy by creating platforms and arenas for interactive political leadership and discussing, amending, and endorsing proposals from interactive policymaking arenas and ensuring their implementation. Participatory and deliberative democracy that brings together politicians and citizens in interactive policymaking processes gains its democratic legitimacy from the inclusion of relevant and affected actors, and may support representative democracy by providing a space for politicians to discuss politics with each other and with interested, competent, and committed citizens who may provide important and useful input that help to stimulate policy learning while building joint ownership of new, bold policy solutions.

Combining new participatory and deliberative forms of democracy with established forms of representative democracy helps us to transcend the traditional either/or thinking that has dominated democratic theory, where one camp has cheered for the expansion of participatory forms of democracy based on deliberation in self-governing communities while another has warned against going down this road, insisting on the preservation of the existing forms of representative democracy, perhaps with a few adaptations. The challenge, however, is to avoid a bifurcation of democracy that creates competing centers of legitimate political power. Hence, we must find ways of linking the two forms of democracy. One option is to let representative democratic institutions decide when and how to initiate participatory and deliberative processes, let the mandated interactive decision-making arenas be relatively self-governed and then allow representative government to make the final decision about whether to endorse the new proposals and how to fund and implement them. This might function particularly well if there is a mixed membership of the interactive policy arena that helps align the two different democratic mechanisms and foster joint ownership of solutions.

In sum, interactive political leadership may improve the role, quality, and impact of political leadership and help to democratize public governance. New experiments with platforms and arenas for interactive political leadership are promising and seem to be relatively robust, although they may fare better in countries with consensus rather than majoritarian democracy, relatively high trust in elected politicians, strong and well-organized civil societies, and a public bureaucracy capable of supporting reforms and new forms of interactive policymaking. This caveat identifies a genuine paradox: the countries that need the new forms of interactive policymaking and democracy the most may also experience the greatest difficulties launching successful reforms.

REFERENCES

Agger, A. (2021). Democratic Innovations in Municipal Planning: Potentials and Challenges of Place-Based Platforms for Deliberation between Politicians and Citizens. *Cities, 117*, 103317.

Aitamurto, T. & Chen, K. (2017). The Value of Crowdsourcing in Public Policymaking: Epistemic, Democratic and Economic Value. *The Theory and Practice of Legislation, 5*(1), 55–72.

Alexander, E. R. (2005). Institutional Transformation and Planning: From Institutionalization Theory to Institutional Design. *Planning Theory, 4*(3), 209–23.

Ansell, C. & Gash, A. (2008). Collaborative Governance in Theory and Practice. *Journal of Public Administration Research and Theory, 18*(4), 543–71.

Ansell, C. & Miura, S. (2020). Can the Power of Platforms Be Harnessed for Governance? *Public Administration, 98*(1), 261–76.

Ansell, C. & Torfing, J. (2017). Strengthening Political Leadership and Policy Innovation through the Expansion of Collaborative Forms of Governance. *Public Management Review, 19*(1), 37–54.

Ansell, C. & Torfing, J. (2021). *Public Governance as Co-Creation: A Strategy for Revitalizing the Public Sector and Rejuvenating Democracy*. Cambridge: Cambridge University Press.

Aragón, P., Kaltenbrunner, A., Calleja-López, A., Pereira, A., Monterde, A., Barandiaran, X. E. & Gómez, V. (2017). Deliberative Platform Design: The Case Study of the Online Discussions in Decidim Barcelona. In Ciampaglia, G., Mashhadi, A. & Yasseri, T. (Eds.), *Social Informatics 2017, Lecture Notes in Computer Science, 10540*. Cham: Springer.

Bardhan, P., & Mookherjee, D. (2018). *A Theory of Clientelistic Politics versus Programmatic Politics* (No. dp-317). Boston University, Department of Economics.

Blondel, J. (1987). *Political Leadership*. London: Sage.

Burns, J. M. (1978). *Leadership*. New York: Harper & Row.

Cain, B. E., Dalton, R. J. & Scarrow, S. E. (Eds.) (2006). *Democracy Transformed? Expanding Political Opportunities in Advanced Industrial Democracies*. Oxford: Oxford University Press.

Christensen, T. & Lægreid, P. (2002). New Public Management: Puzzles of Democracy and the Influence of Citizens. *Journal of Political Philosophy, 10*(3), 267–95.

Christiansen, P. M. & Nørgaard, A. S. (2003). *Faste forhold, flygtige forbindelser: Stat og interesseorganisationer i Danmark i det 20. Århundrede.* Aarhus: Aarhus University Press.
Clarke, N., Jennings, W., Moss, J. & Stoker, G. (2018). *The Good Politician: Folk Theories, Political Interaction, and the Rise of Anti-Politics.* Cambridge: Cambridge University Press.
Dalton, R. J. & Welzel, C. (Eds.) (2014). *The Civic Culture Transformed: From Allegiant to Assertive Citizens.* New York: Cambridge University Press.
De Beus, J. (2011). Audience Democracy: An Emerging Pattern in Postmodern Political Communication. In Brants, K. & Voltmer, K. (Eds.), *Political Communication in Postmodern Democracy* (19–38). London: Palgrave Macmillan.
Edelman, M. (1988). *Constructing the Political Spectacle.* Chicago, IL: University of Chicago Press.
Ercan, S. A. (2014). Same Problem, Different Solutions: The Case of "Honour Killing" in Germany and Britain. In Gill, A. K., Strange, C. & Roberts, K. (Eds.), *"Honour" Killing and Violence* (199–216). London: Palgrave Macmillan.
Field, L. (2018). The Abortion Referendum of 2018 and a Timeline of Abortion Politics in Ireland to Date. *Irish Political Studies, 33*(4), 608–28.
Foerderer, J., Kude, T., Schütz, S. & Heinzl, A. (2014). Control Versus Generativity: A Complex Adaptive Systems Perspective on Platforms. *35th International Conference on Information Systems.*
Fraser, C. (2020). Donald J. Trump and the Politics of Democratic Dysfunction. *Fast Capitalism, 17*(1), 165–82.
Fung, A. (2003). Recipes for Public Spheres: Eight Institutional Design Choices and Their Consequences. *Journal of Political Philosophy, 11*(3), 338–67.
Fung, A. (2006). Varieties of Participation in Complex Governance. *Public Administration Review, 66*(1), 66–75.
Fung, A. (2015). Putting the Public Back into Governance: The Challenges of Citizen Participation and Its Future. *Public Administration Review, 75*(41), 513–22.
Gouillart, F. & Hallett, T. (2015). Co-Creation in Government. *Stanford Social Innovation Review, 13*(2), 40–7.
Grant, J. A. (2013). Consensus Dynamics and Global Governance Frameworks: Insights from the Kimberley Process on Conflict Diamonds. *Canadian Foreign Policy Journal, 19*(3), 323–39.
Grint, K. (2010). *Leadership: A Very Short Introduction.* Oxford: Oxford University Press.
Gutmann, A. & Thompson, D. F. (2004). *Why Deliberative Democracy?* Princeton, NJ: Princeton University Press.
Hartley, J. & Benington, J. (2010). *Leadership for Healthcare.* Bristol: Policy Press.
Hay, C. (2007). *Why We Hate Politics.* Cambridge: Polity Press.
Head, B. W. (2008). Wicked Problems in Public Policy. *Public Policy, 3*(2), 101–18.
Head, B. W. & Alford, J. (2015). Wicked Problems: Implications for Public Policy and Management. *Administration & Society, 47*(6), 711–39.
Heclo, H. (1978). Issue Networks and the Executive Establishment. *Public Administration Concepts Cases, 413*(413), 46–57.
Heiden, N. & Krummenacher, P. (2011). The Role of Citizen Forums in Local Development Planning in Switzerland. In Torfing, J. & Triantafillou, P. (Eds.), *Interactive Policymaking: Metagovernance and Democracy* (227–42). Colchester: European Consortium for Political Research Press.

Heifetz, R. A. (1994). *Leadership without Easy Answers* (vol. 465). Cambridge, MA: Harvard University Press.

Helms, L. (Ed.) (2012). *Poor Leadership and Bad Governance: Reassessing Presidents and Prime Ministers in North America, Europe and Japan*. Cheltenham: Edward Elgar Publishing.

Hendriks, C. M. & Lees-Marshment, J. (2016). Personalised Deliberation: How Political Leaders Connect with their Publics. In *Australian Political Science Association Conference, University of New South Wales, Sydney*, 26–8.

Hendriks, C. M. & Lees-Marshment, J. (2019). Political Leaders and Public Engagement: The Hidden World of Informal Elite–Citizen Interaction. *Political Studies*, *67*(3), 597–617.

Hertting, N. & Kugelberg, C. (2017). Representative Democracy and the Problem of Institutionalizing Local Participatory Governance. In Hertting, N. & Kugelberg, C. (Eds.), *Local Participatory Governance and Representative Democracy* (1–17). New York: Routledge.

Ingham, S. (2016). Popular Rule in Schumpeter's Democracy. *Political Studies*, *64*(4), 1071–87.

Kane, J. & Patapan, H. (2012). *The Democratic Leader: How Democracy Defines, Empowers, and Limits Its Leaders*. Oxford: Oxford University Press.

Karsten, N. & Hendriks, F. (2017). Don't Call Me a Leader, but I Am One: The Dutch Mayor and the Tradition of Bridging-and-Bonding Leadership in Consensus Democracies. *Leadership*, *13*(2), 154–72.

Kennett, P. (Ed.) (2008). *Governance, Globalization and Public Policy*. Cheltenham: Edward Elgar Publishing.

Klijn, E. H. (2014). Political Leadership in Networks. In Rhodes, R. A. W. & Hart, P. T. (Eds.), *The Oxford Handbook of Political Leadership* (403–17). Oxford: Oxford University Press.

Koppenjan, J., Kars, M. & Voort, H. V. D. (2009). Vertical Politics in Horizontal Policy Networks: Framework Setting as Coupling Arrangement. *Policy Studies Journal*, *37*(4), 769–92.

Krogh, A. H. (2022). Facilitating Collaboration in Publicly Mandated Governance Networks. *Public Management Review*, *22*(4), 631–53.

Landemore, H. (2014). Democracy as Heuristic: The Ecological Rationality of Political Equality. *The Good Society*, *23*(2), 160–78.

Landemore, H. (2020). *Open Democracy: Reinventing Popular Rule for the Twenty-First Century*. Princeton, NJ: Princeton University Press.

Lees-Marshment, J. (2015). *The Ministry of Public Input: Integrating Citizen Views into Political Leadership*. London: Palgrave Macmillan.

Mair, P. (2013). *Ruling the World: The Hollowing of Western Democracy*. London: Verso.

Manin, B. (1997). *The Principles of Representative Government*. Cambridge: Cambridge University Press.

Masciulli, J., Molchanov, M. A. & Knight, W. A. (2016). Political Leadership in Context. In Molchanov, M. A. & Masciulli, J. (Eds.), *The Ashgate Research Companion to Political Leadership* (23–48). London: Routledge.

Mause, K. (2014). Self-Serving Legislators? An Analysis of the Salary-Setting Institutions of 27 EU Parliaments. *Constitutional Political Economy*, *25*(2), 154–76.

McBride, S. & Evans, B. M. (Eds.) (2017). *The Austerity State*. Toronto: University of Toronto Press.

Michels, A. & De Graaf, L. (2010). Examining Citizen Participation: Local Participatory Policy Making and Democracy. *Local Government Studies*, *36*(4), 477–91.

Neblo, M. A., Esterling, K. M. & Lazer, D. M. J. (2018). *Politics with the People: Building a Directly Representative Democracy.* New York: Cambridge University Press.

Olsen, J. P. (Ed.) (1978). *Politisk organisering: organisasjonsteoretiske synspunkt på folkestyre og politisk ulikhet.* Oslo: Universitetsforlaget.

Osborne, D. & Gaebler, T. (1993). *Reinventing Government: How the Entrepreneurial Spirit Is Transforming the Public Sector.* Reading, MA: Addison-Wesley.

Piattoni, S. (2011). Reconnecting Representative and Participatory/Deliberative Democracy in Italy: The Case of Tuscany and Trentino. In Torfing, J. & Triantafillou, P. (Eds.), *Interactive Policy Making, Metagovernance and Democracy* (187–204). Colchester: European Consortium for Political Research Press.

Post, D. G. (2009). The Theory of Generativity. *Fordham Law Review*, *78*(6), 2755–66.

Rittel, H. W. & Webber, M. M. (1973). Dilemmas in a General Theory of Planning. *Policy Sciences*, *4*(2), 155–69.

Sartori, G. (1987). *The Theory of Democracy Revisited.* Chatham, NJ: Chatham House Publishers.

Schmitter, P. C. & Lembruch, G. (Eds.) (1979). *Trends towards Corporatist Intermediation.* London: Sage.

Schumpeter, J. A. (2010 [1942]). *Capitalism, Socialism and Democracy.* London: Routledge.

Siebers, V. & Torfing, J. (2018). Co-Creation as a New Form of Citizen Engagement: Comparing Danish and Dutch Experiences at the Local Government Level. *International Public Management Review*, *18*(2), 187–208.

Sørensen, E. (2020). *Interactive Political Leadership: The Role of Politicians in the Age of Governance.* Oxford: Oxford University Press.

Sørensen, E. & Torfing, J. (2019a). Designing Institutional Platforms and Arenas for Interactive Political Leadership. *Public Management Review*, *21*(10), 1443–63.

Sørensen, E. & Torfing, J. (2019b). Towards Robust Hybrid Democracy in Scandinavian Municipalities? *Scandinavian Political Studies*, *42*(1), 25–49.

Sørensen, E., Hendriks, C. M., Hertting, N. & Edelenbos, J. (2020). Political Boundary Spanning: Politicians at the Interface between Collaborative Governance and Representative Democracy. *Policy and Society*, *39*(4), 530–69.

Spence, J. & Welsh, D. (2010). *Ending Apartheid.* London: Routledge.

Stoker, G. (2006). Public Value Management: A New Narrative for Networked Governance? *The American Review of Public Administration*, *36*(1), 41–57.

Tucker, R. C. (1995). *Politics as Leadership.* Columbia, MO: University of Missouri Press.

Van Wart, M. (2013). Lessons from Leadership Theory and the Contemporary Challenges of Leaders. *Public Administration Review*, *73*(4), 553–65.

Warren, M. E. (2002). What Can Democratic Participation Mean Today? *Political Theory*, *30*(5), 677–701.

Weber, M. (2015 [1921]). Bureaucracy. In Waters, T. & Waters, D. (Eds.), *Weber's Rationalism and Modern Society: New Translations on Politics, Bureaucracy, and Social Stratification* (73–127). New York: Palgrave Macmillan.

Workman, S., Jones, B. D. & Jochim, A. E. (2009). Information Processing and Policy Dynamics. *Policy Studies Journal*, *37*(1), 75–92.

Zittrain, J. L. (2006). The Generative Internet. *Harvard Law Review*, *119*(7), 1975–2040.

4. From policy program implementation to public value creation

The perceived essence of governing has long been to produce public policies that define problems, goals, and solutions together with particular courses of action and inaction. Policies are articulated in legislation and regulation and implemented through a series of specific programs that make targeted, short-term interventions in society and the economy in order to create temporary improvements of various sorts. The focus on public policies and programs tends to produce an *inward gaze* within the public sector on the political negotiations through which problems and goals are defined, the role of experts and policy advisors in creating feasible policy solutions, and program designs and the role of downstream administrative agencies, public managers, and street-level bureaucrats in effectively implementing new policy programs. The key question tends to be how elected politicians and their administrative aides can produce bold, effective, and feasible policy programs that are dutifully implemented by frontline staff. The increasing mediatization and presidentialization of politics seems to have enhanced the pace of public policymaking, with political leaders aiming to demonstrate their political resolve by launching a spate of symbolic policy reforms backed by expert reports, but often with little concern for the possible future effects and how they are evaluated, thus triggering implementation scandals that come back to haunt them. Hence, the fast-paced executive policy machine tends to become increasingly insulated from its social and economic environment (Nielsen 2021).

Since the insulation of the mediatized executive policy circuit from the rest of society risks feeding the growing distrust in elected government, it is quite fortunate that we are now witnessing a growing appreciation of the public sector contribution to the production of public value outcomes. Based on the seminal work of Moore (1995), we see an increasing focus on how the public sector can produce solutions that have value for citizens and society at large. The new and emerging focus on public value production might be most pronounced in countries such as Australia, Denmark, the Netherlands, and in North America, where Moore's theory of public value management has been effectively translated to public managers through public leadership training programs. As we shall see, the focus on public value outcomes creates a new *outward gaze* in the public sector that increasingly asks how public managers and employees can produce public value and how external societal stake-holders can contribute to this value production (Bryson et al. 2014). The new emphasis on public value production through the collaborative involvement of external stakeholders may help to enhance the legitimacy of public governance and restore trust in elected government as it becomes clear that the public sector serves the public and seeks to engage the public in collaborative forms of governance that tend to promote a sense of common ownership over policy solutions.

This chapter aims to study the implications of and conditions for the shift from the inward-looking focus on the design and implementation of policy programs to a more outward-looking focus on public value outcomes. It first scrutinizes the bureaucratic preoccupation with the formation of policy programs and the attempt of New Public Management (NPM) to broaden the original focus on bureaucratic rule-following to include concerns for the production of measurable results. The next section presents a critical analysis of the growing fragmentation of the public sector into a plethora of insulated public agencies that results from the efforts of NPM to reduce complexity through the creation of special-purpose agencies and secure efficient service delivery through performance management. Following this analysis, the public value concept is introduced as part of a wider theory of public value management. Public value is argued to be a game-changer that opens up the public sector for the involvement of an array of public and private actors in producing governance solutions. The chapter is rounded off with a discussion of the barriers to the collaborative efforts to produce public value outcomes and the proactive strategies for achieving such outcomes.

PUBLIC GOVERNANCE AS POLICYMAKING

In representative democracy, elections are relatively short-lived episodes. Hence, what stands out as the essence of governing modern societies is the production of public policy that frames and guides the implementation of more targeted programs, which in turn provides regulation, services, and transfer payments to citizens and private businesses. Once voters and political parties have provided their input in terms of support and demands to the political system, what is then left for government is to govern particular policy sectors through the production of laws and regulations. The importance of policy-making is reflected at the research level by the emergence of policy science as a major sub-field of political science (Lasswell 1970; Heclo 1972). Encouraged by the belief that ideology was dead, the new policy science started off with a rather rationalistic view of policymaking as social engineering (Tribe 1972). Soon after, however, the belief in rational decision-making leading to com-prehensive reforms was problematized by: (1) the insistence that policy actors have a bounded rationality (Simon 1990); (2) the recognition of the contingent coupling of problems and solutions (Kingdon 1984); and (3) the observation that the policy process is often incremental and only takes small steps forward depending on the positive evaluation of the last one (Lindblom 1979).

Today, the public policy agenda is set through mediatized political debates in which mass media provide a wide selection of agenda items, and the incumbent government and the opposition pick and choose the items that resonate with their current political goals and aspirations (Green-Pedersen & Stubager 2010). The formulation of comprehensive policy solutions, however, is often left to experts and bureaucrats, with interest organizations and lobbyists participating in formal and informal hearings and consultations and elected politicians entering late in the process to close the political deal through negotiations within the government and with oppositional parties. When new policy programs are finally politically endorsed, they are implemented top-down, and responsibility for program delivery is allocated to a specific department or agency. As such, the policy process tends to be governed by the chain of government into which a selected group of media people and lobbyists is integrated. This is at least the image of the policy process that is sketched out in much of the policy literature. Hence, according to Sabatier (1991), political scientists have tended to focus on either a specific type of institution (e.g., media, legislatures, political parties, government officials, interest groups, administrative agencies, local governments) or on specific types of behavior outside those institutions (public opinion, negotiation, voting, political socialization).

This all goes to show how policymaking has been largely internal to government and focused on questions such as what the problem is, how to find a feasible solution, how to secure political support, and how to ensure that solutions are carried out effectively. The latter question about implementation has especially drawn considerable attention. The risk of implementation failure has been explained either by obstacles arising at different levels in the overly long implementation chains stretching from national government to local frontline agencies (Pressman & Wildavsky 1973) or by the coping strategies of discretionary street-level bureaucrats, who are caught in a crossfire between legal requirements, budget constraints, citizen demands, and their own professional aspirations (Lipsky 1980). Still, both of these explanations remain focused on factors internal to the political-administrative system of government.

The attempt to govern society and the economy through public policymaking has focused the attention of both policymakers and public administration scholars on the internal working of government. Even when the effect of policy programs is assessed, the interest is often on how downstream actors perceive the utility of new policies (Patzelt & Shepherd 2009) and whether they are decoupling their local practices from new policies (Meyer & Rowan 1977;

Briscoe & Murphy 2012). Of course, there have been frequent attempts to measure results and assess policy program outcomes, but such policy evaluations seldom lead politicians and executive civil servants to make major policy revisions. Elected governments seem to be more interested in solving new and emerging problems than spending time reading lengthy evaluation reports and mending past failures.

The bottom line is that the design and implementation of policy is seen as a fundamental way of governing modern societies and largely perceived as internal government activities. With the social and economic sub-systems becoming increasingly self-regulated and difficult to influence from the outside and citizens and societal stakeholders becoming more competent, critical, and assertive, an internal-looking, government-driven policymaking process focusing on political goals, coalition-building, and effective implementation becomes a liability. In our complex and fragmented societies, policymaking is likely to fail; and when it does, the blame will solely be on the government, as external societal actors have at best played a limited role as bystanders in policy design and implementation. And the government losing the blame game may fuel the growing distrust in elected government that is observed in many Western countries (Foster & Frieden 2017).

THE CRITIQUE OF THE PREDOMINANCE OF BUREAUCRATIC RULE-FOLLOWING AND THE NEW FOCUS ON RESULTS

The public policymaking machine was first and foremost bureaucratic, meaning that both the policy process and the implementation of new policy programs should follow clearly specified formal rules and procedures. Transparent rule-following is important as it reduces the element of formal and informal discretion that would potentially make room for subjective concerns, private interests, and outright corruption, which undermines the legality and objectivity of public administration. As such, public employees are expected to obediently observe written rules when making decisions about how to administer and implement policy decisions. This point is well taken by public employees, who save considerable amounts of time by relying on clearly defined rules instead of making administrative decisions from scratch. As the number of bureaucratic rules grows, however, they begin to act as a straitjacket for the making of sound decisions (Downs 1967), and the efforts to match a particular situation with a relevant set of rules become increasingly demanding (March & Olsen 1989).

But while public employees could build an entire career on obediently following explicit rules and minimizing the number of mistakes and blunders, as the critics of public bureaucracy rightly point out, it is not enough to excel in rule-following if the result is poor or even absent (Osborne & Gaebler 1993). Following bureaucratic rules to the letter may actually prevent effective problem-solving, which often calls for professional discretion and a flexible interpretation and application of particular rules. Following this argument, advocates of NPM went on to recommend a greater focus on the actual results. After all, it is not so important that doctors and nurses are following detailed administrative protocols as long as they manage to treat a large number of patients and perform the operations required. The focus on results rather than rules brings the policymaking machine closer to the citizens and private businesses on the receiving end. The new focus on customer satisfaction is important and a welcome alternative to the traditional focus on inflexible rule compliance.

It is by no means easy to ensure the efficient production of results (defined as output per input) in the public sector. NPM relies on public choice theory that is highly skeptical about the ability of the public sector to deliver results. Public bureaucracies are large and ossified (Downs 1967), public employees are self-interested and self-serving (Lane 2006), public agencies are not exposed to competition (Walsh 1995), and there is little effort to measure and report results and to sanction underperformance (Jackson 1988). The cure to these problems suggested by NPM was, first, to subject public service delivery agencies to competition for both contracts and customers through a combination of privatization, outsourcing, and commercialization and, second, to introduce an elaborate system of performance management combined with a strengthening of the role of public leaders so as to facilitate the conditional sanctioning of performance results (Hood 1991).

Performance management has been high on the public sector agenda for the last three decades, where citizen demands for high-quality services have been rising and public resources scarce (Van Dooren et al. 2015). The idea is to create a formal system for providing precise, relevant, and transparent performance information and systematically to analyze and benchmark the performance of administrative units in order to provide critical management feedback, including negative sanctions on low-performers and repeated instructions about how to improve performance (Barber 2007).

Despite the many problems associated with performance management, such as sub-optimizing, goals displacement, gaming, increasing transaction costs, and the crowding out of the intrinsic task motivation and public service motivation of public employees (Bohte & Meier 2000; Hood & Peters 2004; Jacobsen & Andersen 2015; Musso & Weare 2020), its introduction helped to shake up the public sector and refocus the attention of public managers and employees on the citizens and service users now perceived as "customers." Hence, the new success criterion for public employees was that they should be service-minded and deliver what customers want and need. This meant that the public sector finally discovered that there was a world outside and scores of citizens to be served. Still, the principal instrument to secure efficient service delivery was performance management focused on the internal government mechanics, thus aiming to solve both the problem with long implementation chains by measuring performance all the way down to frontline agencies and the problem with "rogue," street-level bureaucrats by strengthening public management based on transactional and transformational leadership (Ansell et al. 2017).

In sum, NPM merely reasserted the demand for the efficient implementation of policy programs. The focus on results rather than rules prompts the public sector to gauge the demands of service users and wider society, but the ultimate ambition of NPM is to provide a clear line of sight from the apex of government all the way down to the service-delivering agencies to ensure efficient service production based on measurement, reporting, and sanctions (Barber 2007). Questions regarding public regulation and service outcomes are seldom raised, and reflections about the societal value that the public sector produces are prevented by the neoliberal and public choice discourse of which NPM is a part. Here, the public sector is broadly perceived as a parasite, squandering the value produced in the private sector; it should be cut back, exposed to fierce competition, and heavily disciplined to reduce its lavishness.

INSULATION, FRAGMENTATION AND JOINED-UP GOVERNMENT

The introduction of performance management in the public sector further strengthened the inward gaze of public delivery agencies. Public managers were told to focus on how to deliver better results by motivating and monitoring their employees, trimming their organizations and making the most of their budgets, which were subjected to annual cuts reflecting anticipated productivity gains. The inward-looking gaze was further strengthened by the agentification of the public sector. In an effort to reduce the complexity of the daily operations of public agencies and enhance local autonomy and flexibility in pursuit of centrally defined targets, NPM created increasing amounts of special- or single-purpose agencies that were responsible for specific policy programs and governed based on an arm's-length principle (Bouckaert et al. 2010; Verhoest 2018). Each of the special-purpose agencies received a budget frame, a number of employees, a particular mission, and a clear set of targets to achieve, and it was up to the local leaders and managers to use the resources to produce results.

The combined effect of the introduction of performance management and the construction of special-purpose agencies was the growing insulation of public agencies and increasing public sector fragmentation (Torfing &

Triantafillou 2013). The latter was further augmented by the outsourcing of public services to private companies in the newly created quasi-markets, where the public and providers competed for service contracts and to attract customers. While we should be careful not to wish ourselves back to the old unicentric and hierarchical governance system proffered by Weberian-style bureaucracy, the enhanced insulation and fragmentation is undoubtedly problematic in a world where most policy problems cut across singular agencies and clearly demarcated policy areas. After many years, NPM began recognizing the problems associated with increasingly "differentiated policy" (Rhodes 1997), and the cure was "joined-up government."

The idea of joined-up government was promoted to enhance coordination and provide more holistic problem-solving and service delivery. Separate central policy departments and local delivery agencies were urged to concentrate on delivering joint outcomes regardless of organizational boundaries (Kavanagh & Richards 2001; Ling 2002; Bogdanor 2005). The focus is no longer merely on producing a measurable output in terms of large numbers of services of a certain quality, but on outcomes in terms of solutions to cross-cutting wicked problems. However, joined-up government tends to adopt an intra-governmental perspective focused on cross-departmental and inter-agency collaboration. Hence, there is no escape from the traditional, inward-looking public policy perspective, although the outcome focus undermines this perspective by shifting the attention to providing solutions to societal problems and drawing attention to the manifold actors who, in a holistic perspective, can contribute to public value production.

As part of the overall assessment of NPM, one might argue that viewed as an effort to counteract the growing fragmentation that greatly enhanced the ungovernability of the public sector, the call for joined-up government was too little, too late. Moreover, if different government departments and agencies each have their own mission, budget frame and performance targets and are subjected to regular performance assessments, the prospects for inter-organizational collaboration are dim. Finally, the idea of joined-up government was dwarfed by competing ideas of how to produce public value in networks and partnerships involving a plethora of public and private actors.

THE DISCOVERY OF PUBLIC VALUE AND THE NEW FOCUS ON OUTCOMES

Given the problems associated with the narrow public governance focus on policy programs, it is difficult to overestimate the positive impact of the discovery of public value and the development of the public value management perspective. First, instead of perceiving the public sector as a parasitic drain on the value production in the private sector, the public sector is described as a unique type of organization with a distinct revenue source (taxation) and a distinct form of value (public value) (Moore 1995, 2000). The public sector does not produce private value (profit) for a small group of shareholders but rather politically mandated public value (social purpose). Public value is defined as what is valuable to the public and what the public values. There is no pre-given or uniform understanding of what public value is but rather an ongoing debate and struggle to define its precise content. There is also a built-in tension between what is valuable to a particular group and what is valuable for society at large. Hence, it may appear to be valuable for students to all get the same high grades, but this is not particularly good for society, which will have problems matching students with jobs on a meritocratic basis. Such trade-offs are likely to emerge in public value production because there is no common utility function—only ongoing attempts at reaching agreement on what constitutes public value. As such, public value is inextricably linked to democratic deliberation and political decision-making.

Second, the public value perspective goes against the grain of classical bureaucracy and NPM, rejecting the stereotypical conception of public managers as unimaginative bureaucrats and wasteful squanderers of value extracted from the private sector. Instead, it portrays public managers as curious explorers and change agents aiming to discover and define what would be valuable for the public sector to do in order to meet social needs and solve societal problems. Like their private sector counterparts, public managers are inventive, well intentioned, and mission-driven. As such, the public value perspective helps public managers to restore their self-worth as public managers after years of bureaucracy-bashing and to regain their status in society, which is a prerequisite for performing their tasks well (Rhodes & Wanna 2007: 407).

Finally, the public value produced by public service organizations is not supposed to be validated merely by individual consumers operating in the new service markets based on free choice of service providers but supposedly subject to democratic political debate between public managers, elected politicians and relevant stakeholders (Moore 1995). Public managers constantly attempt to develop new public value propositions, and they must seek the authorization of these propositions to go ahead. Hence, they must garner support from elected politicians and stakeholders in their authorizing environment before trimming their organization and building the operational capacities needed to produce and deliver public value to users, citizens, private businesses, and other target groups. Together, the relations between public value, the authorizing environment and the operational capacities make up the "strategic triangle," which helps public managers to understand the strategic challenges at stake when governing and to reflect on the complex choices they face (Moore 1995).

The public value perspective maintains that a public organization is not merely founded on a broad set of public values, such as democracy, transparency, fairness, equity, and the common good (Bozeman & Jørgensen 2007). It also produces public value, such as law and order, health care, social assistance, education, environmental protection, public security, cultural diversity, sustainable transport, and so on, catering to the needs of different social and economic groups and/or society at large (Moore 1995; Bryson & Crosby 2005).

Moore (1995) discovered the public value perspective in conversations with public managers participating in training programs at the Harvard Kennedy School of Government. Public managers were found to be engaged in exploring how to expand the production of public value, and they sought to generate political support for the social purpose they wanted to pursue and to build public organizations fit for the task. The discovery and development of the public value perspective fueled and systematized the efforts of public managers to enhance the production of public value. This is especially true in countries where public leadership programs have played a major role in disseminating the public value perspective.

In Australia, the public value perspective has been used as a key reference point in the Aboriginal community and Western Australia arts sectors, and the Labor-led south Australian government uses it extensively, as well documented by Ballintyne and Mintrom (2018). The Australia and New Zealand School of Government Program provides an interesting example of the application of the public value framework by two public leaders meeting in a training program for executive leaders (Padula 2018). Rod Chenhall was the Director of Correction Services in New South Wales and struggling to find enough community service options for offenders, while Graham Bradshaw headed the New South Wales transport services and thought that he had plenty of public spaces surrounding railroad stations requiring attention. By joining forces and getting support from their respective organizations, they could help to advance public value production by letting offenders work off their community service by tidying train station carparks, walkways, gardens, and concourses that were open and accessible after hours and on weekends, when the offenders had time off from their normal jobs.

In the Netherlands, the public value perspective has framed the strategic management efforts of the Social Insurance Bank, the Public Health Department in Utrecht, and the Literacy Foundation of the Netherlands— just to mention a few examples. The former pays out social benefits to different target groups and is dedicated to delivering high-quality services and value to its users by focusing on the intention of individual welfare schemes rather than the letter of the law. The organization is highly adaptive, and its leaders and managers are committed to exploring innovative solutions. To bolster value-driven service improvement, the Netherlands has seen the formation of an Institute for Public Value, which uses action research to stimulate the use of the public value triangle in public service production. A flagship project focuses on how to measure the public value of new social welfare initiatives.

In the US, the leadership training programs offered by the Harvard Kennedy School of Government have boosted the use of the public value perspective among executive public managers. Indeed, there are examples of public value management throughout the US. In King County in Washington State, for instance, the public value framework has been applied in strategic planning, programmatic investments, and the attempt to enhance lean management focused on user needs. The adoption of the countywide strategic plan has strengthened the focus on major goals identified by county leadership and artic-ulated public interests via active community group involvement. Programmatic investments based on deep public engagement include a reduced transit fare pass for low-income residents, an equity-based parks and open space invest-ment plan, and a long-term plan to move toward zero youth detention. Finally, a new "LEAN" management framework asks every department and program to identify relevant user groups, reflect on what is important to them and then find process improvements and operational efficiencies to better meet public needs and increase public value. The executive branch tends to create a vision for enhancing public value production, and the legislative branch acts on and revises major policy proposals. The engagement of external stakeholders is critical to final adoption at the county level and in many cases supported by a popular vote. Overall, the public value framework has helped King County to consider how to develop and implement public value propositions and to do a better job engaging the most affected and under-resourced communities.

Finally, in Denmark, where the public management perspective has received considerable attention, the performance management system in the regional health-care systems, which seemed to enhance productivity but neither quality nor effectiveness, has been thoroughly reformed with inspiration from Moore (1995) and Porter (2010). The new, reformed system is a value-based system aimed at assessing the outcomes of the public care systems by measuring improved patient health.

Use of the public value perspective in Brazil (Pereira et al. 2017), Iran (Mahjoob et al. 2021) and Sri Lanka (Karunasena & Deng 2012) attests to how it would appear to have penetrated public sectors around the globe. In a less explicit way, it can also be seen as undergirding the new focus on mission-driven innovation in the public sector (Eggers & Macmillan 2013; Kattel & Mazzucato 2018). Public sector innovation is not driven by profit but rather by problems requiring attention that call for new and better solu-tions. Public managers and employees encounter numerous problems in their day-to-day attempts to deliver high-quality services and effective governance, and they sometimes respond to these problems by designing and implementing new and bold solutions that fix pressing problems (Torfing 2016). On a much bigger scale, however, the public sector also attempts to tackle major societal challenges by articulating new grand missions—whether traveling to Mars, solving the climate crisis, or putting an end to poverty—that call for radical innovation. The UN Sustainable Development Goals (SDGs) are examples of mission statements that seem to trigger public innovation aimed at creating public value for particular target groups as well as society at large. The UN SDGs are setting the agenda in an increasing number of countries around the world, thereby forcing governments and societal actors to reconsider how they can contribute to public value production (Ansell et al. 2022).

The discovery of the public value perspective and its explicit or implicit use in different countries and policy sectors shifts the focus from how to ensure successful program implementation to how to generate value for different target groups, as well as society more broadly. Aspiring to produce valuable outcomes for users, citizens, communities, and society at large tends to question existing policy programs and trigger innovation based on an empathetic dialogue with affected citizens and a critical reframing of the problem or challenge that must be tackled. As we shall see, the new value-based focus on outcome also raises questions about how different public and private actors can help to enhance public value production.

PUBLIC VALUE MANAGEMENT AS A GAME-CHANGER

While the public value perspective rejects the neoliberal bureaucracy-bashing associated with NPM, it seems to be a direct continuation of NPM in one particular respect: it readily assumes that public leadership should be strengthened by letting (and making) public managers manage (Normann 2001). Public managers must find and connect with their inner entrepreneurial spirit and take upon them the responsibility for developing new and inspiring public value propositions. True, they must muster support for their ideas from key political and societal actors in their authorizing environment, and public employees and users further down the value chain should be involved in co-producing public value solutions (Benington & Moore 2011), but the whole process of enhancing public value production is driven by public managers. As Moore (2021: 219) himself explains in a recent publication aimed at defining the essence of the public value perspective, "The core idea is a simple one: public managers should be focused on 'creating public value' from the assets entrusted to them by the public." Actors other than public managers do not really enter into the equation.

The managerialism inherent to Moore's formulation of the public value perspective must be challenged. As soon as the public sector begins to focus broadly on the production of public value outcomes rather than more narrowly on the administration of particular policy programs, it becomes clear how a wide range of public and private actors, including service users, citizens, and civil society actors, may contribute to defining and producing public value (Stoker 2006; Alford 2010; Page et al. 2015; Bryson et al. 2017; Crosby et al. 2017). Hence, the public value perspective encourages the public sector to embrace a collaborative governance approach that assumes that resources, competences, and ideas are distributed and shared by manifold actors who must collaborate to do together what neither of them can achieve on their own.

In short, public value is a game-changer, since focusing on public value production immediately brings into view a broad range of public and private organizations and lay actors who can contribute to public value creation. Public managers may have a privileged vantage point because they have abundant time, expertise, power, and authority, but their professionally trained employees have firsthand knowledge of the conditions on the ground, the users have direct experience with problems that need fixing, interest organizations have insights into the needs of different user groups and ideas for how to meet them, private businesses have access to new technologies and investment capital, and local communities have resources that can be mobilized in the implementation phase. Moreover, we must never forget that the public sector is politically led and that elected politicians play a key role in defining the public value aspirations of the public sector and launching bold reforms in response to new public sector missions. Bringing together all of these actors in cross-boundary collaboration may be helpful in generating new public value outcomes (Crosby et al. 2017).

The intrinsic link between the new public value focus and collaborative governance has three important implications: first, public value creation is not an exclusive task for public managers, as it transcends and cuts across organizational and sectoral boundaries and frequently mobilizes citizens, social entrepreneurs, and so on who are attracted by the prospect of contributing to the production of value for society at large. Second, the new emphasis on collaborative public value creation places a premium on networks and partnerships, turning public leaders into conveners of relevant and affected actors and facilitators of collaboration in settings where power is distributed and shared, which renders both the formulation of public value propositions and the organizational strategies for implementation a joint effort. Third, public managers must take up the task of linking their elected principals with the societal actors participating in public value creation and involving them in the metagovernance of the networks and partnerships through which public value is produced.

STIMULATING THE COLLABORATIVE PRODUCTION OF PUBLIC VALUE OUTCOMES

The public value perspective tends to open up the public sector in two important ways. First, it supplements the internal focus on program performance with a broader focus on the societal impact of the public sector and how this impact is valued by different target groups and society in general. Second, it paves the way for the involvement of a plethora of public and private actors in the production of public value outcomes. This dual impact of the public value perspective may contribute to enhancing the legitimacy of public governance by facilitating the provision of valuable inputs to the decision-making process and producing outcomes that have real value to external actors.

It goes without saying that the opening of the public sector to its external environment must neither undermine its internal commitment to fairness, transparency, and legality nor jeopardize the effective and efficient delivery of public policy programs. Core public values must also be upheld when the public sector engages external actors in formulating and achieving public value outcomes. That is not always easy, however, as power asymmetries, opaque decision-making processes, and the need for the flexible adaptation of rules and laws may threaten traditional bureaucratic values. In much the same way, efficient and effective policy implementation may be problematized by coordination problems arising in collaborative processes, where many different actors must contribute to goal attainment. While public managers must pay attention to and should seek to mitigate these problems through proactive leadership, they can also appreciate how the collaborative production of public value outcomes may strengthen core public values, such as the right of intensely affected actors to be involved in public decision-making and improve implementation by mobilizing resources and creating a sense of common ownership over innovative public value outcomes.

The prospect of reaping the fruits of the collaborative involvement of external actors in the production of public value outcomes, as well as the ability to mitigate associated problems, begs the question of how the public sector can stimulate the collaborative creation of public value outcomes (Ansell & Torfing 2021). Let us briefly consider five conducive factors.

Strategic management. The attempt to create a public sector with a strong focus on collaborative public value production may rely on strategic management, defined as the long-term attempt of situated actors to transform the modus operandi of their organization by formulating and implementing major goals, strategies, and plans based on a prospective analysis of the internal and external environment (Nag et al. 2007). The contemporary field of strategic management contains numerous schools of thought (Ferlie & Ongaro 2015) that may provide different recommendations. However, a synthetic view of how strategic management can help to stimulate the collaborative production of public value outcomes may point to the need of executive public managers to clarify the overall mission and goals of the organization together with the need for stakeholder involvement; to facilitate and manage strategic learning to allow new strategies to emerge and flourish, creating space for middle managers to use their entrepreneurial competences and inputs from external actors to discover new ways of enhancing public value production; and to praise and readily embrace the micro-level efforts of frontline personnel to uncover the needs behind the demands of users, citizens, and organized stakeholders and to work together with them to develop and test prototypes of new public value solutions (Torfing et al. 2021).

Public value scorecards. In order to advance the production of public value, it must be measured to facilitate assessment and development. Building on Kaplan and Norton (1996), Moore (2012) has suggested that the public sector may use a public value scorecard to properly determine whether public value has, in fact, been created by a particular government organization. Such a scorecard may endeavor to measure financial costs and mission achievement, unintended positive and negative consequences, user satisfaction, and broader social outcomes. Further along these lines, Meynhardt et al. (2014) have developed a concrete measurement tool aiming to determine whether a particular public initiative is useful, decent, politically acceptable, a good experience, and perhaps even profitable. The tool can be used by both public and private organizations and may thus support discussions of whether and how public organizations produce solutions of value to society.

Platforms for collaborative governance. Collaborative governance platforms aim to facilitate the creation, adaptation, and multiplication of more temporary arenas for collaborative governance (Ansell & Gash 2018). Platforms are relatively permanent institutions that help to attract relevant and affected actors, provide a communication system facilitating interaction, offer organizational templates that make it easy to initiate collaboration, and give access to relevant knowledge and practical advice. In short, platforms aim to reduce the transaction costs of collaborating. The construction of collaborative governance platforms is part of a new type of generative governance that facilitates and enables the emergence of productive interaction among distributed actors who come together to explore the possibilities for creating public value outcomes (Ansell & Torfing 2021).

New role perceptions and mindsets for public managers and frontline staff. Promoting the collaborative production of public value outcomes hinges on the development of new role perceptions and mindsets for public managers and the employees in frontline agencies. As long as public managers perceive their role as "rule-enforcers" (bureaucracy) or "efficiency drivers" (NPM) and public employees perceive their role as "rule-followers" (bureaucracy) or "service-minded delivery agents" (NPM), the public sector will remain trapped in its traditional, inward-looking focus on administering its policy program portfolio. To stimulate the shift toward a more outward-looking focus on the production of social purpose together with societal actors, public managers must begin to see themselves as "value-driven team captains" and public employees must see themselves as "public value co-creators." A new mindset focusing on how to identify and realize potentials for public value creation and how to do so together with relevant and affected actors is also essential.

Social accountability. Involving external actors such as citizens, private firms, and civil society organizations in producing public value solutions challenges the traditional forms of accountability in the chain of government whereby shifting principals delegate decision-making competence to agents and hold them to account for their actions and inactions. Collaborative networks and partnerships are notoriously difficult to hold to account because there are many different actors involved in joint decision-making based on deliberation, consensus seeking, and tacit dissent. In addition, it is difficult to measure the public value produced by new initiatives as the target group may be diffuse. Finally, it is difficult to see who supported particular outputs and outcomes and therefore also difficult to hold the responsible actors to account. One way of solving the inherent accountability problem is to ask collaborative governance arenas to produce non-technical public accounts of how they perceived their mission and how they contributed to public value production. Such accounts will allow local target groups and beneficiaries to critically scrutinize new collaborative endeavors, pose clarifying questions to the collaborative governance arenas, and eventually pass judgment. This kind of bottom-up accountability has been referred to as "social accountability" (Fox 2015) and it may work well in relation to collaborative public value production, especially if central public authorities prompt local collaborations to respond to critical questions and negative assessments.

While these and other factors may prove to be conducive to stimulating public value creation based on collaborative governance, ultimately there is no quick fix—only hard work, bold moves and learning from experience. The stakes are high, however, since there is much to gain in terms of enhanced public legitimacy at both the system and program levels.

REFERENCES

Alford, J. (2010). Public Value from Co-Production with Clients. In Moore, M. H. & Benington, J. (Eds.), *Public Value: Theory and Practice* (144–57). Basingstoke: Palgrave Macmillan.

Ansell, C. & Gash, A. (2018). Collaborative Platforms as a Governance Strategy. *Journal of Public Administration Research and Theory*, *28*(1), 16–32.

Ansell, C. & Torfing, J. (2021). *Public Governance as Co-Creation: A Strategy for Revitalizing the Public Sector and Rejuvenating Democracy*. Cambridge: Cambridge University Press.

Ansell, C., Sørensen, E. & Torfing, J. (2017). Improving Policy Implementation through Collaborative Policymaking. *Policy and Politics*, *45*(3), 467–86.

Ansell, C., Sørensen, E. & Torfing, J. (2022). *Co-Creation for Sustainability: The UN's SDGs and the Power of Local Partnerships*. Bingley: Emerald.

Ballintyne, K. & Mintrom, M. (2018). Towards Whole-of-Government Enhancement of Public Value: An Australian Case. *Policy Design and Practice*, *1*(3), 183–93.

Barber, M. (2007). *Instruction to Deliver*. London: Politico Publishing.

Benington, J. & Moore, M. H. (Eds.) (2011). *Public Value: Theory and Practice*. Basingstoke: Palgrave Macmillan.

Bogdanor, V. (Ed.) (2005). *Joined-Up Government*. Oxford: Oxford University Press.

Bohte, J. & Meier, K. J. (2000). Goal Displacement: Assessing the Motivation for Organizational Cheating. *Public Administration Review*, *60*(2), 173–82.

Bouckaert, G., Peters, B. G. & Verhoest, K. (2010). *The Coordination of Public Sector Organizations: Shifting Patterns of Public Management*. London: Springer.

Bozeman, B. & Jørgensen, T. B. (2007). Public Values: An Inventory. *Administration & Society*, *39*(3), 354–81.

Briscoe, F. & Murphy, C. (2012). Sleight of Hand? Practice Opacity, Third-Party Responses, and the Interorganizational Diffusion of Controversial Practices. *Administrative Science Quarterly*, *57*(4), 553–84.

Bryson, J. M. & Crosby, B. C. (2005). *Leadership for the Common Good: Tackling Public Problems in a Shared-Power World*. San Francisco, CA: Jossey-Bass.

Bryson, J. M., Crosby, B. C. & Bloomberg, L. (2014). Public Value Governance: Moving beyond Traditional Public Administration and the New Public Management. *Public Administration Review*, *74*(4), 445–56.

Bryson, J., Sancino, A., Benington, J. & Sørensen, E. (2017). Towards a Multi-Actor Theory of Public Value Co-Creation. *Public Management Review*, *19*(5), 640–54.

Crosby, B. C., Hart, P. & Torfing, J. (2017). Public Value Creation through Collaborative Innovation. *Public Management Review*, *19*(5), 655–69.

Downs, A. (1967). *Inside Bureaucracy*. Boston, MA: Little, Brown and Company.

Eggers, W. D. & Macmillan, P. (2013). *The Solution Revolution: How Business, Government, and Social Enterprises Are Teaming Up to Solve Society's Toughest Problems*. Boston, MA: Harvard Business Press.

Ferlie, E. & Ongaro, E. (2015). *Strategic Management in Public Services Organizations: Concepts, Schools and Contemporary Issues*. Abingdon: Routledge.

Foster, C. & Frieden, J. (2017). Crisis of Trust: Socio-Economic Determinants of Europeans' Confidence in Government. *European Union Politics*, *18*(4), 511–35.

Fox, J. A. (2015). Social Accountability: What Does the Evidence Really Say? *World Development*, *72*(C), 346–61.

Green-Pedersen, C. & Stubager, R. (2010). The Political Conditionality of Mass Media Influence: When Do Parties Follow Mass Media Attention? *British Journal of Political Science*, *40*(3), 663–77.

Heclo, H. (1972). Policy Analysis. *British Journal of Political Science*, *2*(1), 83–108.

Hood, C. (1991). A Public Management for All Seasons? *Public Administration*, *69*(1), 3–19.

Hood, C. & Peters, G. (2004). The Middle Aging of New Public Management: Into the Age of Paradox? *Journal of Public Administration Research and Theory*, *14*(3), 267–82.

Jackson, P. (1988). The Management of Performance in the Public Sector. *Public Money & Management*, *8*(4), 11–16.

Jacobsen, C. B. & Andersen, L. B. (2015). Is Leadership in the Eye of the Beholder? A Study of Intended and Perceived Leadership Practices and Organizational Performance. *Public Administration Review*, *75*(6), 829–41.

Kaplan, R. S. & Norton, D. P. (1996). *The Balanced Scorecard: Translating Strategy into Action*. Boston, MA: Harvard Business School Press.

Karunasena, K. & Deng, H. (2012). Critical Factors for Evaluating the Public Value of E-Government in Sri Lanka. *Government Information Quarterly*, *29*(1), 76–84.

Kattel, R. & Mazzucato, M. (2018). Mission-Oriented Innovation Policy and Dynamic Capabilities in the Public Sector. *Industrial and Corporate Change*, *27*(5), 787–801.

Kavanagh, D. & Richards, D. (2001). Departmentalism and Joined-Up Government. *Parliamentary Affairs*, *54*(1), 1–18.

Kingdon, J. W. (1984). *Agendas, Alternatives, and Public Policies*. Boston, MA: Little, Brown & Co.

Lane, J. E. (2006). *Public Administration and Public Management: The Principal–Agent Perspective*. London: Routledge.

Lasswell, H. D. (1970). The Emerging Conception of the Policy Sciences. *Policy Sciences*, *1*(1), 3–14.

Lindblom, C. E. (1979). Still Muddling, Not Yet Through. *Public Administration Review*, *39*(6), 517–26.

Ling, T. (2002). Delivering Joined-Up Government in the UK: Dimensions, Issues and Problems. *Public Administration*, *80*(4), 615–42.

Lipsky, M. (1980). *Street-Level Bureaucracy: Dilemmas of the Individual in Public Services*. New York: Russell Sage Foundation.

Mahjoob, S. R., Daneshfard, K. & Mirsepassi, N. (2021). Designing a Model for the Role of Government in Promoting Social Capital via a Public Value Creation Approach in the Governmental Organizations of Iran. *Social Capital Management*, *8*(2), 209–33.

March, J. G. and Olsen, J. P. (1989). *Rediscovering Institutions*. New York: The Free Press.

Meyer, J. W. & Rowan, B. (1977). Institutionalized Organizations: Formal Structure as Myth and Ceremony. *American Journal of Sociology*, *83*(2), 340–63.

Meynhardt, T., Gomez, P. & Schweizer, M. (2014). The Public Value Scorecard: What Makes an Organization Valuable to Society? *Performance*, *6*(1), 1–8.

Moore, M. H. (1995). *Creating Public Value: Strategic Management in Government*. Cambridge, MA: Harvard University Press.

Moore, M. H. (2000). Managing for Value: Organizational Strategy in For-Profit, Nonprofit, and Governmental Organizations. *Nonprofit and Voluntary Sector Quarterly*, *29*(S1), 183–204.

Moore, M. H. (2012). *Recognizing Public Value*. Cambridge, MA: Harvard University Press.

Moore, M. H. (2021). Creating Public Value: The Core Idea of Strategic Management in Government. *International Journal of Professional Business Review*, *6*(1), e219.

Musso, J. A. & Weare, C. (2020). Performance Management Goldilocks Style: A Transaction Cost Analysis of Incentive Intensity in Performance Regimes. *Public Performance & Management Review*, *43*(1), 1–27.

Nag, R., Hambrick, D. C. & Chen, M. (2007). What Is Strategic Management, Really? Inductive Derivation of a Consensus Definition of the Field. *Strategic Management Journal, 28*(9), 935–55.

Nielsen, S. W. (2021). *Entreprenørstaten*. Copenhagen: GAD.

Normann, R. (2001). *Service Management*. Chichester: Wiley.

Osborne, D. & Gaebler, T. (1993). *Reinventing Government: How the Entrepreneurial Spirit Is Transforming the Public Sector*. Reading, MA: Addison-Wesley.

Padula, M. (2018). *ANZSOG Case Program Changing Outlooks: Thinking Small for Big Change*, available at: file:///C:/Users/Jtor/Downloads/2018-204.1_Changing-Outlooks-collaborating-for-change-CC%20(1).pdf.

Page, S. B., Stone, M. M., Bryson, J. M. & Crosby, B. C. (2015). Public Value Creation by Cross-Sector Collaborations: A Framework and Challenges of Assessment. *Public Administration, 93*(3), 715–32.

Patzelt, H. & Shepherd, D. A. (2009). Strategic Entrepreneurship at Universities: Academic Entrepreneurs' Assessment of Policy Programs. *Entrepreneurship Theory and Practice, 33*(1), 319–40.

Pereira, G. V., Macadar, M. A., Luciano, E. M. & Testa, M. G. (2017). Delivering Public Value through Open Government Data Initiatives in a Smart City Context. *Information Systems Frontiers, 19*(2), 213–29.

Porter, M. E. (2010). What Is Value in Health Care? *New England Journal of Medicine, 363*(26), 2477–81.

Pressman, J. L. & Wildavsky, A. (1973). *Implementation*. San Francisco, CA: University of California Press.

Rhodes, R. A. W. (1997). *Understanding Governance: Policy Networks, Governance, Reflexivity and Accountability*. Buckingham: Open University Press.

Rhodes, R. A. W. & Wanna, J. (2007). The Limits to Public Value, or Rescuing Responsible Government from the Platonic Guardians. *Australian Journal of Public Administration, 66*(4), 406–21.

Sabatier, P. A. (1991). Toward Better Theories of the Policy Process. *Political Science & Politics, 24*(2), 147–56.

Simon, H. A. (1990). Bounded Rationality. In Eatwell, J., Milgate, M. & Newman, P. (Eds.), *Utility and Probability* (15–18). London: Palgrave Macmillan.

Stoker, G. (2006). Public Value Management: A New Narrative for Networked Governance? *The American Review of Public Administration, 36*(1), 41–57.

Torfing, J. (2016). *Collaborative Innovation in the Public Sector*. Washington, DC: Georgetown University Press.

Torfing, J. & Triantafillou, P. (2013). What's in a Name? Grasping New Public Governance as a Political-Administrative System. *International Review of Public Administration, 18*(2), 9–25.

Torfing, J., Ferlie, E., Jukić, T. & Ongaro, E. (2021). A Theoretical Framework for Studying the Co-Creation of Innovative Solutions and Public Value. *Policy & Politics, 49*(2), 189–209.

Tribe, L. H. (1972). Policy Science: Analysis or Ideology? *Philosophy & Public Affairs, 2*(1), 66–110.

Van Dooren, W., Bouckaert, G. & Halligan, J. (2015). *Performance Management in the Public Sector*. London: Routledge.

Verhoest, K. (2018). Agencification in Europe. In Ongaro, E. & Thiel, S. V. (Eds.), *The Palgrave Handbook of Public Administration and Management in Europe* (327–46). London: Palgrave Macmillan.

Walsh, K. (1995). *Public Services and Market Mechanisms: Competition, Contracting and the New Public Management.* London: Macmillan International Higher Education.

5. From control- to trust-based governance and management

Public governance involves the formulation and achievement of common goals, and it is inextricably linked to control, since someone must have the power to make and enforce authoritative decisions to ensure goal attainment. As mentioned in Chapter 2, the chain of government connecting voters, government officials, and public employees combines delegation with control: voters control the elected politicians, who in turn control the administrators and street-level bureaucrats. In multi-level governance systems such as the European Union, the supranational level controls the national (and sub-national regional) level, which in turn control the local level when it comes to compliance with laws, rules, and regulations. Control aims to prevent drift and chaos and to attain a particular set of goals by ensuring that actors do what they are supposed to do. It regulates action through the use of more or less binding norms and rules, creates incentives for actors to comply with the normative and regulatory prescriptions, monitors their actual behaviors and results, and uses conditional rewards to sanction their performance. In sum, control is important for ensuring both democratic and effective governance. Ultimately, voters want to control how public money collected through general taxation is spent, and elected politicians want to ensure that democratic, political decisions are carried out according to plan and that they generate the desired results without costing too much. As such, control is essential for performance as well as accountability.

Liberal societies aim to control the formulation, implementation, and impact of public decisions with the least possible amount of force; for example, by facilitating dialogue about means and ends and seeking to create a sense of broad-based ownership of authoritative decisions in the hope that actors will internalize the goals and voluntarily commit to using the most effective tools to achieve them. However, the attempt to minimize the use of force in public control systems cannot hide the fact that, in classical forms of bureaucracy, control is exercised top-down, it tends to constrain the behavior of frontline staff and it therefore tends to come into conflict with human demands for autonomy, self-realization, and justice (Argyris 2017). While some people might be prepared to argue that subordinate public employees at the bottom of the hierarchy must dutifully accept constraining control mechanisms, such as the obligation to follow rules and to have their work monitored closely, these forms of control may undermine public employee motivation to use their professional norms and competences to do a good job, and they may limit the scope for frontline collaboration and innovation. Indeed, control can be a buzz-kill, and too much of it risks creating an atmosphere of mistrust that hampers communication and leads to low work-life satisfaction—and correspondingly to a high staff turnover rate. Finally, control is expensive as well as intrusive: the costs of controlling thousands of staff members are high and may lead to organizational ossification (Downs 1967).

Defined as the acceptance of the risk of vulnerability to the actions of others, trust is often praised as the antidote to control; if we trust people's competences and intentions, control is less necessary. Trust not only allows us to scale down our efforts to control behaviors and results but also has a value in itself; it motivates people to improve performance (Harris et al. 2013), speeds up communication (Covey 2006), and creates an autonomous space for the collaborative exploration and exploitation of new ideas (Nooteboom 2013). For these and other reasons, there is growing interest in trust-based forms of governance and management. Hence, whereas the public governance ortho-doxy used rule-following and performance management to enhance control, today there is renewed effort in the public sector to unleash the potential of trust to enhance innovation, efficiency, and effectiveness. Trust is sometimes even extended beyond the public sector to citizens and stakeholders, who are entrusted to hold important resources and ideas that are worth taking into account and to focus on common interests and public value enough to prevent the predominance of private interests.

This chapter aims to explore the current turn to trust-based governance and management. It begins with a review of the schism inherent to the public governance orthodoxy and its attempt to combine centralized control with pro-fessional autonomy. It then considers how New Public Management (NPM) added a new layer of control to the rule-based bureaucratic compliance mech-anisms by introducing an elaborate system of performance management and managerial control intended to prevent opportunistic behavior on the part of public employees. Against this control-fixated governance legacy, the idea and potential of trust-based governance and management is revisited and linked to new theoretical developments that reject the principal–agent model, which seems to undergird much of the recent efforts to secure frontline compliance. This account prompts a discussion of the positive potential of trust-based gov-ernance and management and the scope conditions for realizing this potential. The chapter concludes with discussion of how to balance control and trust, perhaps superseding the dichotomy altogether.

BETWEEN CENTRALIZED CONTROL AND PROFESSIONAL AUTONOMY

From its very inception, public bureaucracy emphasized the need for hierarchical control and downstream compliance with administrative rules and regulations. Weber assumed that public employees were well trained, competent, and motivated by noble intentions, such as serving democratically elected politicians, respecting core bureaucratic values, and advancing public interests. Still, public organizations were supposed to be most effective when governed top-down based on centralized command and control and when public employees were following written rules that prevented unreasonable considerations from shaping outcomes. Indeed, bureaucratic control is important for several reasons. First, it enables elected politicians to delegate the implementation of political decisions to public managers and employees who will use their skills and competences to carry out political decisions by means of creating and complying with explicit rules that lead to expected outcomes. Second, control secures legality and budget discipline and prevents the abuse of office. Finally, the development of a control culture helps to create stability in public organizations and their outputs and outcomes. Citizens tend to place a premium on predictability when it comes to public regulation and service provision.

The advantage of bureaucratic control over control via market-based price mechanisms or clan-based norms and traditions comes from the fact that it is based on the hiring, training, and monitoring of personnel following impersonal rules anchored in a legitimate political authority (Ouchi 1979). Bureaucratic rules can be trusted to be authoritative. Rules are rules, and they are neither subverted by powerful market actors nor constantly reinterpreted by whimsical guardians of obscure traditions or religious dogmas. They are supposedly legitimate and rational—and for the most part written down for all to see and follow, thereby allowing non-compliance to be identified and punished. Rules are imposed through top-down hierarchical authority, and those not following them are met with legal and rational sanctions (Jørgensen & Larsen 1987).

Bureaucracy relies on public employees following the rules and doing their jobs in return for public respect and a decent wage. With the development of the modern welfare state, however, the well-trained public professions (e.g., doctors, schoolteachers, social workers) were not only expected to be allegiant but also to invest their knowledge, skills, and competence in delivering high-quality welfare based on professional discretion and intuition. This required the expansion of the local autonomy of the professionally trained public employees, which should be given a certain space of self-regulation based on professional standards and norms controlled by the peer group. This recognition paved the way for the introduction of "professional rule" based on a tacit agreement that the welfare professions would obtain a high degree of self-regulated autonomy in their working lives in return for their unwavering commitment to use their skills and competences to deliver high-quality welfare (Byrkeflot 2011; Ackroyd 2016).

Professional rule entrusts the welfare professions to govern themselves because they are well trained, competent, and dedicated to their work and because the professional community seeks to uphold and enforce a set of professional norms and values (Noordegraaf 2016; Six 2018). Moreover, it goes without saying that the local professional autonomy in the hospital, school, or job center is circumscribed and constrained by centrally defined laws, rules, and regulations, and further constrained by centralized budget decisions. The co-existence of local, trust-based autonomy and centralized, rule-based, control creates a schism in the modern welfare state. Hence, the co-habitation of bureaucracy and professional rule requires continuous effort to balance local trust and centralized control. When the balance tips toward greater professional autonomy, the welfare professions are often accused of being too powerful and failing to listen to their political principals. In contrast, when the balance tips toward centralized control, the welfare professionals tend to accuse government of undermining service quality by building control systems that straitjacket frontline personnel. Finding the right balance requires constant dialogue between central government and the representatives of the welfare professions, frequently leading to some sort of welfare corporatism focusing on negotiations with professional organizations (Byrkeflot 2011).

In sum, professional rule partially breaks with the unchallenged rule of hierarchical control in public bureaucracy by enhancing the local autonomy of particular welfare professions that are trusted because of their professional qualifications and professional self-discipline, which includes both strict rules regarding entry into the profession and the collective effort to uphold professional norms, values, and ethics. The local, trust-based autonomy is confined by bureaucratic rules and regulations that determine the scope for local autonomy and merge with professional norms and standards to shape local self-regulation.

PRINCIPAL–AGENT THEORY AND THE QUEST FOR CONTROL THROUGH PERFORMANCE MANAGEMENT

Although the bureaucratic control model is still going strong (Walton 2005), its heyday was in the 1960s and 1970s, when it was combined with varying degrees of professional rule. Already in the late 1960s, however, public choice theorists and neoliberal politicians and commentators started criticizing public bureaucracy for being inflexible (Downs 1967), costly (Niskanen 1971) and more concerned with ensuring rule compliance than producing actual results and satisfying service users (Osborne & Gaebler 1993). Civil servants may build an entire career on slavishly following bureaucratic rules and regulations without really delivering high-quality outputs or producing desirable outcomes. Moreover, as the number of rules increases, they may actually become a barrier to dealing flexibly with the needs of citizens or private enterprises. This problem is aggravated by the fact that different administrative agencies have different rules that may be in conflict with each other, thus preventing holistic service production. Finally, bureaucratic rules may be administered by strict and paternalistic welfare professionals who think they know more about what the social clients need than the clients themselves (Calder 1995).

In an attempt to address these problems, NPM recommends that the public sector pay more attention to the effective production of results than to compliance with bureaucratic rules (Osborne & Gaebler 1993). This shift in attention creates a new focus on the behavior of the public employees responsible for delivering results, and the criticism of these employees is exceedingly harsh, as it tends to imply that welfare professionals are self-interested knaves rather than benevolent knights (Le Grand 1997). Drawing on principal–agent theory (Lane 2005), the increasingly autonomous and powerful professions are accused of exploiting the information asymmetries inherent to principal–agent relations in order to pursue opportunistic behavior that tends to make public services poor and costly. Principals hire agents to perform particular tasks in the public sector, but they lack precise and reliable information about the actual competences and performance of the agents and the actual costs of solving the tasks in question. Assuming that the hired agents are rational, utility-maximizing *homo economicus*, public employees are depicted as cheats who strive to minimize their effort while maximizing their own personal remuneration.

The NPM solution is to pressure public organizations by letting them compete with private service providers for contracts and customers. To deal with the pressure from this market-based competition, public organizations must import management techniques from the private sector (Hood 1991). Hence, they must introduce a strict performance management regime with clear goals and budget frames, strong demands for the documentation of meticulously measured results, and conditional rewards and punishments (Dooren et al. 2015). Barber's *Instruct to Deliver* (2007) is emblematic of the performance measurement movement and became the bible for leading politicians and executive public managers in several Western countries. As mentioned in the previous chapter, it describes how a line of sight is created by clearly communicating policy and service goals, planning their implementation, requesting regular performance reports from all levels of government, and continuing to follow up on performance problems. Further down the organization at the program delivery level, public managers should exercise transactional leadership, combining sticks and carrots to motivate frontline staff to give their best and to pursue efficient and effective implementation.

Although performance management backed by transactional leadership may have contributed to improving public budgets and secure policy implementation, the detrimental impact on the motivation of public employees is considerable. The excessive use of control-fixated performance management and transactional leadership risks creating a workforce of cynics who only work to receive financial rewards and not because they enjoy what they are doing and think it has value for others (Moynihan 2010).

The research on employee motivation assumes that public employees cannot be reduced to *homo economicus* and that they are driven by a mixed bag of motivations: (1) *extrinsic motivation*, which is based on self-interest and drives action based on the desire to receive performance-related rewards and to avoid punishment (Sansone & Harackiewicz 2000); (2) *intrinsic motivation*, which is hedonistic and refers to the empowering feeling enjoyed by employees who use their knowledge and skills to competently and efficiently accomplish a task they deem meaningful (Franco et al. 2002); and (3) *public service motivation*, defined as "an individual's orientation to delivering service to people with the purpose of doing good for others and society" (Hondeghem & Perry 2009: 6). There is good reason to assume that it is more important to enhance the intrinsic motivation and public service motivation than the extrinsic motivation of public employees, which is promoted by performance management and transactional leadership (Bentzen & Torfing 2020). While extrinsic, incentive-driven motivation fails to produce the expected positive effects on the performance of public service organizations (Perry et al. 2009), intrinsic motivation and public service motivation tend to enhance work engagement, job satisfaction and organizational commitment (Pandey & Stazyk 2008), together with public performance and the production of desirable outcomes (Naff & Crum 1999; Andersen et al. 2014).

If the crowding out effect of performance management was the only negative impact, it would be sufficient to counterbalance transactional leadership with a transformative leadership aiming to "crowd in" the intrinsic motivation and pro-social public service by seeking "to develop, share, and sustain a vision intended to encourage employees to transcend their own self-interest and achieve organizational goals" (Jacobsen & Andersen 2015: 832). However, it is well established in the literature that attempts at solving the principal–agency problem by means of performance management also lead to goal displacement and sub-optimization (Bohte & Meier 2000), enhance standardization of services and hamper public innovation (Moynihan 2013), spur gaming and window dressing that seek to produce apparent rather than real results (Hood 2006), and increase transaction costs and internal administrative burdens, thereby taking away resources from service delivery (Herd & Moynihan 2019; Musso & Weare 2020). Considering the many unintended negative effects of performance management, of which the crowding out of hedonistic and pro-social forms of motivation is the main concern, it is easy to understand why the public sector has been looking for alternatives (Bentzen & Torfing 2020).

STEWARDSHIP THEORY AND THE DISCOVERY OF TRUST-BASED GOVERNANCE AND MANAGEMENT

The growing criticism of control-fixated performance management has triggered the search for more trust-based forms of governance and management (Sardiello & Alexius 2019; Niedlich et al. 2021). Researchers and practitioners alike have recommended the introduction of new, trust-based governance models anchored in stewardship theory as an alternative to principal–agent theory.

Stewardship theory emerged in corporate governance research in the early 1990s (Donaldson & Davis 1991; Davis et al. 1997; Muth & Donaldson 1998) and appeared in public sector research a decade later (Dicke 2002; Schillemans 2008; Van Slyke 2007). In their seminal article, Donaldson and Davis (1991) first describe how corporate governance has been influenced by principal–agent theory, which claims that shareholder interests will only be safeguarded in firms where the chief executive officer (CEO) is *not* also the board chair and where the board has created proper incentives and control mechanisms that curb the CEO's ability to act opportunistically in ways that make shareholders incur a loss, as compared to a situation in which the CEO has direct control over the corporation. Rejecting the underlying *homo economicus* model, Donaldson and Davis (1991) then proceed to argue that far from being a self-interested slacker, the CEO will typically want to be a good steward of the corporate assets, obtain intrinsic satisfaction from doing the job well, and carry out unrewarding tasks out of some sense of duty and pro-social respect for the shareholders. It follows that the corporate performance of CEOs does not depend on incentive and control schemes but rather on the creation of empowering structures that include having the CEO chair the board of directors, thus concentrating power and authority in one person (see also Bentzen & Torfing 2020).

There have been several attempts at empirically validating either principal–agent or stewardship theory as the allegedly "best way" to conduct governance in private or public organizations. Although recent results do produce partial support for the positive impact of the stewardship model, the findings do not provide unequivocal answers to the question about the relative superiority of principal–agent or stewardship theory (Donaldson & Davis 1991; Davis et al. 1997; Schillemans 2013). Hence, most research tends to stress the contingency of the performance of models derived from principal–agent and stewardship models on different cultural, contextual, and situational factors. In empirical reality, the two models also seem to be combined depending on traditions, political preferences, and asset specificity. Hence, stewardship theory does seem to offer a complete substitute for agency-based governance, but as an alternative model based on different motivational assumptions that may modify, balance, or transform existing agency-based governance practices (Caers et al. 2006).

In line with this, Schillemans (2008) observes how stewardship theory helps us to move beyond the clash of interests between equally self-interested principals and agents in the public sector and to chase away the fear that contract-bound agents—be they public employees, public agencies, or private service deliverers—may exploit the principals' limited information, time, resources, and knowledge to shirk and do less to provide public solutions and services than they are contractually obliged to do. Assuming, with stewardship theory, that subordinate agents in the public sector are not "individualistic, opportunistic and self-serving" but rather "collectivistic, pro-organizational and trustworthy" (Davis et al. 1997: 20) may help us to avoid wasting public money on costly systems of control-based performance management (McCubbins et al. 1987) and avoid alienating and demotivating public employees who become subject to close and frequent monitoring that reeks of punishment (Meier & Krause 2003; Jacobsen et al. 2014).

Stewardship theory criticizes both the critical diagnosis of slacking and shirking advanced by principal–agent theory and the control-focused cure offered by performance management, and it simultaneously provides the foundation for a new trust-based governance model that nurtures the hedonistic and pro-social goals of public employees. The argument is not that subordinate agents are exclusively motivated by professional aspirations and pro-social goals but rather that a governance model that supports hedonistic and pro-social motivation and empowers the agents also enables the principals to tap into the otherwise hidden resources, ideas, and energies of their agents. Hence, despite the structurally defined power asymmetries, principals and agents may actually share the same goals and motivations, thereby creating benefits for public leaders, employees, users, and society in general (Schillemans 2008). As such, it is reasonable to expect nurses to be motivated by improving public health, elderly care assistants to be driven by the ambition to provide a dignified life for the elderly and social workers to strive to enhance the employability of unemployed persons and to help them find employment. Stewardship theory suggests that we draw on the consequences of this insight for public governance (see Bentzen & Torfing 2020).

Table 5.1   Comparison of agency and stewardship theory

	Principal–agent theory	Stewardship theory
Motivation of agents/ stewards	Extrinsic motivation based on self-interest	Intrinsic motivation based on professional self-realization and pro-social orientation
Goals of public leaders and employees	Conflicting: principals and agents have diverging interests	Shared: there is considerable goal congruence
Role of public leaders	Reduce the risk of shirking by enhancing control through strict performance management based on objectives, performance indicators, regular evaluation, and corrective measures	Absorb risk of shirking by enhancing trust through the promotion of dialogue, coaching, empowerment, and joint learning
Type of public leadership	Transactional, top-down	Transformative, distributive, horizontal
The role and organization of power in governance	High "power distance" allows powerful, formal leaders to regulate and discipline less powerful employees	Low "power distance" facilitates knowledge-sharing between empowered peers, coordination based on shared outcome responsibility and self-governance within mutually agreed boundaries

Source: Adapted from Bentzen & Torfing (2020); Schillemans (2008); Hernandez (2012).

The best way to capture the novelty, basic features, and consequences for public governance of the new stewardship theory is to compare it with the old principal–agent theory. Table 5.1 provides such a comparison.

Two relatively coherent governance stories seem to emerge from the comparison. Principal–agent theory assumes that agents are motivated by individual utility maximization and envisages a conflict between principals and agents in which the former is bound to lose unless they develop an elaborate system of performance management and transactional leadership based on discipline and control. In contrast, stewardship theory assumes that public employees are motivated by carrying out meaningful tasks that create value for others and that the goals of public leaders and the employees who are stewarding them are basically the same or will tend to be congruent, thus paving the way for public managers to engage in a trust-based, learning-focused dialogue with their employees about visions, goals, and tools. Such a dialogue calls for a combination of servant leadership aiming to promote the self-development of the employees (Reinke 2004), transformational leadership aiming to give direction to their efforts (Bass & Riggio 2006), and horizontal and distributed leadership facilitating team-based self-regulation (Gronn 2002; Pearce et al. 2008; Bolden 2011).

Empirically, the contrasted stories and practices of public governance can be combined in different ways. A recent study of Dutch quasi-autonomous agencies conducted a survey experiment, finding that the perception of the actual use of elements from stewardship theory is lower than what the respondents would regard as optimal (Schillemans & Bjurstrøm 2020). This deficit might be explained by the continued predominance of the NPM paradigm among public administrators, and it begs the question of what can be gained by shifting the balance more in the direction of trust-based governance supported by stewardship theory.

Trust-based governance encourages leaders and managers to share power, information, and resources with employees. Peters (1996: 51) explained long ago that we should expect that "more empowered workers should be willing to work harder, share more ideas with management, and treat their clients more humanely since they are themselves being treated better." This expectation resonates well with empirical studies of staff empowerment in private service firms (see Fernandez & Moldogaziev 2011), which show how trust-based power sharing improves effectiveness and productivity (Kirkman & Rosen 1999), promotes innovativeness (Spreitzer 1995) and increases employee job satisfaction (Kirkman & Rosen 1999), organizational commitment (Lawler et al. 1992, 1995; Kirkman & Rosen 1999; Guthrie 2001), and job involvement (Coye & Belohlav 1995). There is a dearth of studies on the impact of employee empowerment in the public sector and relatively few positive examples of what a gravitational shift from control-fixated governance toward trust-based governance may accomplish. A notable exception, however, is the independent Dutch homecare provider Buurtzorg, which is based on self-governing nursing teams and has managed to produce high employee and user satisfaction while cutting costs (Drennan et al. 2018; Gray et al. 2015).

Stewardship theory provides a radical, trust-based alternative to control-based principal–agency theory, but there are also other theories about "sociocracy" (Eckstein 2016; Cumps 2019) and the "evolutionary-teal organization" (Laloux 2014) that subscribe to the idea of wide-ranging trust in the competences and intentions of public employees.

Sociocracy is a guide for the creation of agile and resilient public organizations based on conscious and effective collaboration (Eckstein 2016; Cumps 2019). Hence, organizational governance is a result of decisions influenced by everyone who is affected by them. Agreement rests on consent aimed at identifying and resolving objections to particular courses of action based on empirical evidence and transparent access to all available knowledge and information. The responsibility for initiating and implementing decisions is shared across all levels of the organization, and assuming such responsibility involves doing what is necessary to achieve common objectives and to remove barriers, thus ultimately producing the continuous improvement of organizational outputs and outcomes (Cumps 2019). The whole process is supported by an organizational structure that establishes self-regulating circles of relevant actors at all levels and links these circles in ways that combine top-down directional leadership with bottom-up influence (Eckstein 2016). The crux of the argument, however, is that the trust-based dual-linkage of self-regulating circles at the top and bottom of the organization facilitates proactive innovation and the flexible adaptation of strategies, structures, and services that tend to produce a dynamic resilience in the face of turbulence.

The "evolutionary-teal organization" portrayed by Laloux (2014) is set out in contrast to "conformist-amber organizations" aiming to enhance compliance through formal roles and top-down control within hierarchical bureaucracies; "achievement-orange organizations" seeking to outperform competing organizations through management by objective, internal accountability, and innovation; and "pluralistic-green organizations" aspiring to enhance quality by means of value-based leadership, empowerment, and stakeholder involvement. New and emerging teal organizations are based on three breakthrough principles: self-management, wholeness, and evolutionary purpose. They successfully establish self-management structures based on the formation of self-management teams with fluid roles and distributed leadership. The self-managing teams may co-exist with varying amounts of hierarchical leadership, but everybody in the organization—whether executive leaders or team members—is empowered to make decisions based on transparent real-time information and advice from relevant and affected actors. Ad hoc meetings aiming to foster agreement rather than consent are called when needs arise. As in stewardship theory, employees are perceived as "reasonable people that can be trusted to do the right thing" (Laloux 2014: 80). The need for control is limited because high-level performance is ensured through a combination of intrinsic motivation, peer emulation, and external demands. In the daily operations of the organizations, people are invited to use all aspects of their individual personality, including their emotional, intuitive, and spiritual sides that are normally suppressed by bureaucratic achiever organizations. The evolutionary-teal organization develops when leaders open themselves to the complex wholeness of the world and the discovery of new, emerging solutions that seem right and are based on wisdom beyond rationality. Last but not least, the primary purpose of the organization is not organizational self-preservation based on an unchallenged mission statement and organizational format laid down by an executive leadership group but rather the pursuit of new and evolving formats and goals based on the collective intelligence of managers, employees, and external stakeholders who flexibly adjust organizational strategies and structures to new and changing circumstances and new, collectively formulated meanings.

THE JOB ACTIVITIES CENTER EXAMPLE

While stewardship theory supports the idea of trust-based relations between managers and employees, the new theories of sociocracy and the evolutionary-teal organization go on to recommend the formation of self-regulated teams of public employees. This additional recommendation links trust along the vertical axis of manager–employee relations with trust along the horizontal axis of peer-to-peer relations. Many successful public and private organizations are based on this formula. Buurtzorg (public sector), FAVI (private industry) and Morningstar Farms (vegetarian and vegan food) are well-known examples (see Getz 2009; Kirkpatrick 2010; Gray et al. 2015; Laloux 2014). Another fresh example is found in a recent study of the Job Activities Center (JAC) in Gentofte, a Danish municipality (Bentzen & Torfing 2020). JAC provides empowering activities, education, and job training for adults with disabilities. The target group consists of citizens who struggle to gain a foothold in the labor market because of physical, psychological, and/or social challenges. JAC serves about 400 adults from Gentofte and other municipalities in the Copenhagen Capital Region, providing outreach and outplacement to private firms. It has about one hundred employees, including a group of seven leaders. When the new executive leader of JAC took office in 2012, the organization seemed to be based on hierarchical and compartmentalized steering. Allegedly, it had a "gossipy" culture and a "bossy" leadership style, and a challenging financial situation necessitated layoffs. The new leader exploited this crisis to set a new, positive agenda that encouraged the remaining personnel to stand together, to "give more than they take," and to become actively involved in developing and governing JAC. This was assumed to help to enhance the service quality and to recruit more paying municipal customers in the long run, thus improving the financial situation.

In the gradual shift to a new, trust-based governance model focused on staff empowerment, three things proved important: the careful selection of a new, visionary, and unified leadership team; supportive involvement of the trade union and shop stewards; and clear communication with all staff members about the kind of commitment and involvement expected of them as JAC employees. Nevertheless, the first two years were somewhat conflict-ridden, until the new governance model finally received general acceptance.

Today, the daily operations at JAC are carried out by self-regulated teams that are responsible for distributing tasks, determining whether specific users fit their program, selecting and developing professional methods, and taking financial decisions within their allocated budget. The teams are also responsible for recruiting new employees. While a member of the leadership team participates in the selection process, it is otherwise driven by the team members who will end up working together with the new employee. This procedure tends to make the new employees feel "chosen" by their new workmates. The teams are also responsible for allocating wage bonuses, and the process has proven to run surprisingly smoothly, with an exceedingly high level of satisfaction with the outcome. The Best Place to Work survey found that 77% of the employees are satisfied with the wages they receive for the work they are doing. Finally, if a team encounters problems or disputes that it is unable to solve on its own, it can request assistance from an external team leader, who offers to coach and advise the team.

While the delegation of leadership responsibilities to self-governing teams in which leadership is exercised in a horizontal and distributed way is relatively common, the massive involvement of all employees in the strategic leadership decisions, as found in JAC, remains relatively rare. Strategic task forces comprising leaders and selected employees were responsible for developing the overall organizational strategy for JAC in two consecutive rounds over the first five years, and a new, third round is underway. A new assessment and documentation tool was also developed by a joint task force. In addition, the entire staff body was involved in a process leading to financial cuts and layoffs. The executive leadership openly informed the staff at a plenary meeting about the poor financial situation, and the leadership received many ideas and suggestions that helped turn the budget around with a limited number of layoffs. The employees felt that they had real influence on the budget process. They were listened to and taken seriously. Finally, at a later stage, the organizational structure was changed through a joint process whereby the employees ended up designing two alternative organizational diagrams that were put to a vote.

The result of JAC's adoption of a trust-based governance model is irrefutably impressive. In 2018 and 2019, JAC received the "best public workplace" award in Denmark, and it was awarded the title "best public workplace in Europe" in 2019, 2020, 2021 and 2022 by the European organization Best Place to Work. This result was achieved based on three important outcomes: first, employee motivation and well-being receive top scores. All of the responding employees in the Best Place to Work survey say that they experience more well-being and work engagement, and 100% of them answer that JAC is a "fun place to work." In the last two years, less than 2% of the JAC employees have left.

Second, the perceived user satisfaction, user empowerment, and overall quality of the work delivered by the JAC employees have all increased. Hence, the external assessment of the quality of work conducted by the national Social Auditing Agency gives JAC a score of 4.8 out of 5 and concludes that all citizens served by JAC appear trusting and satisfied and feel that they receive high-quality services that help them to develop their full potential as human beings (Socialtilsyn Hovedstaden 2019).

Third, the overall organizational performance, including cost efficiency, has improved. Employee input helped JAC to deliver the same or better service for less, and in the period 2013–18, illness absenteeism fell by 30%, which saves JAC and the municipality a considerable amount of money.

Despite these positive outcomes, the trust-based governance and management model that JAC practices also has a dark side. First, the transaction costs of employee participation in local team meetings and plenary staff meetings are relatively high: trust-based collaboration along the horizontal and vertical axes simply takes time, although we should remember that time is also saved when decisions are implemented based on joint ownership. Second, the mismatch between the new trust-based governance model and a large group of staff members who were uninterested in taking more responsibility and participating in self-regulated goal attainment resulted in the laying off of 20% of the original employees. As reported above, however, the employee turnover has been extremely low since then. Finally, the new model does leave much space for disagreement and conflict between the employees and organizational leadership. The executive leader claims that instead of "us" and "them," the reforms at JAC have created a "we." While this may enhance productivity, there is a risk of totalitarianism if protests and grievances are seen as a threat to this all-inclusive "we." Despite these problems, the JAC experience bears witness to the achievements made possible by a turn from control- to trust-based governance.

ADVANCING TRUST-BASED GOVERNANCE AND MANAGEMENT

While the JAC example shows what trust-based governance and management may look like in practice, much more work is required to flesh out the basic skeleton, as there are many unanswered questions pertaining to organization, process, and leadership—and not least to how organizations can make the shift from control- to trust-based governance. An inventory of measures that can help set public organizations on the course to trust-based governance involves: scaling down the number of bureaucratic rules to a bare minimum (e.g., by giving employees the right to challenge obsolete or burdensome rules, which are then eliminated if the executive management group cannot come up with a clear defense); reducing the number of performance targets to no more than a handful, which is usually what public employees and managers can have in their head when going about their daily duties; and ensuring that performance targets are meaningful, possible to impact and in accordance with key professional norms in the area. To these defensive measures, which merely endeavor to limit the negative effects of control-based governance, we must add some more offensive measures, such as the introduction of new forms of performance evaluation aimed at spurring mutual learning and lesson-drawing; the creation of platforms and arenas for vertical organizational dialogue about organizational goals and strategies; experimentation with self-regulating teams; and the combination of team-based performance evaluation with assessments of public leaders and managers.

Examining this tentative inventory, emerging problems and dilemmas come to mind. Central authorities may insist on tight performance management, which helps to ensure compliance, whereas local-level service organizations may want to reduce performance control to spur innovation. A trust-based work environment with few controls may be more productive and effective, but performance measurement provides data enabling the identification of best practices and administrative failures, thus enabling systematic efforts to improve productivity and effectiveness. Managers may trust their employees' competences and intentions and therefore lift their foot from the control pedal, but their employees may not trust them to accept the mistakes and errors that eventually follow from the employees' exploitation of the space created by trust-based management (Bentzen 2019). These and other similar dilemmas call for reflection and cautious progress toward trust-based governance and management.

The shift from control- to trust-based governance appears highly context-dependent. Countries and sectors dominated by the public governance orthodoxy may see little change, whereas countries characterized by strong traditions for professional rule, low power distance between managers and employees, and a low degree of work structuration may excel in trust-based governance. Differences between policy and service areas may also call for varying degrees of control with the actual public employee performance. The police may require body cameras to control the behavior of police officers and prevent police brutality, but they are unwarranted in public schools, daycare facilities, and health clinics, where the personnel are expected to provide care for their clients. Likewise, external control with the ability of security workers to follow protocol when inspecting nuclear power plants must be tighter than control with parks and recreation employees, where failure to follow rules and regulations is unlikely to be hazardous. Moreover, some employees may be uncomfortable with working in a trust-based environment in which they are expected to assume greater responsibility for their own initiatives and results and to interact closely with their colleagues. Education and training may determine the preferences of public employees and their reactions to trust-based management. Finally, based on prior observations of employee behavior and assessments of the quality of their relationship to the managers, some groups of employees will appear more trustworthy than others. Differences in context mean that the shift from control-based to trust-based governance will be rather uneven across countries, sectors, and employee groups.

A contingency approach to control and trust that reflects on dilemmas and context variation is implicit to the notion of smart trust (Covey et al. 2012). Whereas "blind trust" believes that trust is always called for and should be applied universally, "smart trust" analyzes the situation and context and aims to cope with emerging problems. When taking a cautious and reflective approach to trust-based management, the chances are good that trust-based management will enhance collaboration, innovation, effectiveness, and quality in public service production. This conclusion begs the question of how to advance trust-based governance. In Denmark, co-creation has been advanced as a strategy for de-bureaucratization and the enhancement of trust-based governance (Krogh 2018, 2019; Bentzen 2022). Hence, instead of making top-down reforms aiming to reduce bureaucratic rules and performance targets and building a trust-based working environment, public managers and employees work closely together to identify problems and ways forward. They frequently develop and test prototypes of new forms of governance and revise them until the desired outcomes are achieved. A key tool involves managers and employees in governance labs, where they discuss administrative rules and performance targets to eliminate them, change them, reconstruct their meaning, or simply keep them as they are. Thus far, the experience with co-created governance reforms is that they create a sense of joint ownership of robust transformations, which improves performance while fostering a thriving working environment and growing user satisfaction.

BALANCING TRUST AND CONTROL

New theories and empirical studies recommend that public organizations cut back their elaborate control systems to prevent them from spinning out of control and adopt a more trust-based governance and management style. As seen above, studies show that the impact of trust-based governance and management reforms is no less than astonishing, as they tend to produce a triple win for managers (enhance efficiency), employees (self-realization and improve working environment), and citizens (better service quality). Nevertheless, legitimate public pressures for enhanced transparency, accountability, and control tend to be growing, which makes it increasingly difficult to navigate between the Scylla of excessive control and the Charybdis of unbounded trus.

As such, the challenge for elected politicians and their administrative aides is to find ways of balancing control and trust in public governance and management. Some measure of control with public sector performance and results is needed for elected politicians to steer resource allocation and make well-informed political priorities, for public managers to secure proper implementation of policy programs, for professionally trained employees to see how they are doing and make needed adjustments, and for citizens to maintain trust in government. At the same time, enhanced governance and management based on wide-ranging trust in the competences and intentions are needed to cut the costs of control, speed up communication, improve efficiency and quality, and make room for local collaboration, innovation, and user involvement. Finding the right balance is difficult and will tend to require some trial and error and learning from experience.

In the beginning, the challenge will often be how to move public organizations in the direction of more trust-based governance and management. If mutual trust between public leaders and employees is low, positive upward-going trust spirals must be initiated through dialogue and carefully controlled and evaluated experimentation. To stimulate reforms, public leaders may take a leap of faith and involve employees in eliminating unnecessary and burdensome rules and performance targets. Likewise, public employees may want to develop and broadcast a new professional identity stressing the public service motivation of the profession and its willingness to upgrade its skills, use best practices, engage in dialogue with political leaders and administrative managers, and enforce laudable professional norms and values through inter-collegial supervision. Virtuous circles of mutual trust-building are often sparked by unilateral invitations to trust or be trusted. When the positive upward-going trust spirals are in place, the next challenge is to prepare for perceived breaches of trust that may be a result of misunderstandings, unintended externalities, or the pursuit of self-interest. While building trust takes a long time, it can be ruined in a flash. Hence, having procedures for conflict mediation in situations with breaches of trust is crucial for the preservation of trust.

The balancing act is often perceived as a zero-sum game in which more trust must necessarily lead to a loss of control and vice versa. Interestingly, however, some forms of control may support trust-based governance and management. If public leaders are capable of controlling a few basic parameters, they may actually be better able to trust their employees to have considerable freedom as to what they think best produces efficient, high-quality solutions. This mechanism is clearly visible in the Culture and Leisure Department in the City of Copenhagen, where the head of department gave the employees considerable freedom from bureaucratic rules and performance indicators provided that the different administrative units respected their budget limits, maintained low illness absenteeism, and secured high user-satisfaction levels. Only if one or more of these control parameters was compromised would there be cause to tighten performance control to diagnose and solve the problems. Conversely, as long as the control parameters were intact, the employees would enjoy considerable autonomy, which would in turn help them to accept the basic forms of control.

In sum, the control–trust balance depends on context and may vary over time. Moreover, it can be shifted toward trust-based governance and management based on dialogue, learning, and concrete trust-building efforts made by committed public leaders and employees. Finally, it can be maintained by exploiting mutually reinforcing synergies between control and trust.

REFERENCES

Ackroyd, S. (2016). Sociological and Organizational Theories of Professions and Professionalism. In Dent, M., Bourgeault, I. L., Denis, J. & Kuhlmann, E. (Eds.), *The Routledge Companion to the Professions and Professionalism* (33–48). London: Routledge.

Andersen, L. B., Heinesen, E. & Pedersen, L. H. (2014). How Does Public Service Motivation among Teachers Affect Student Performance in Schools? *Journal of Public Administration Research and Theory, 24*(3), 651–71.

Argyris, C. (2017). *Integrating the Individual and the Organization*. New York: Routledge.

Barber, M. (2007). *Instruction to Deliver*. London: Politico.

Bass, B. M. & Riggio, R. E. (2006). *Transformational Leadership*. Mahwah, NJ: Lawrence Erlbaum Associates.

Bentzen, T. Ø. (2019). The Birdcage Is Open, but Will the Bird Fly? How Interactional and Institutional Trust Interplay in Public Organizations. *Journal of Trust Research, 9*(2), 185–202.

Bentzen, T. Ø. (2022). Co-Creation: A New Pathway for Solving Dysfunctionalities in Governance Systems? *Administration & Society, 54*(6), 1148–77.

Bentzen, T. Ø. & Torfing, J. (2020). Does Stewardship Theory Provide a Viable Alternative to Control-Fixated Performance Management? *Administrative Sciences, 10*(4), 1–19.

Bohte, J. & Meier, K. J. (2000). Goal Displacement: Assessing the Motivation for Organizational Cheating. *Public Administration Review, 60*(2), 173–82.

Bolden, R. (2011). Distributed Leadership in Organizations: A Review of Theory and Research. *International Journal of Management Reviews, 13*(3), 251–69.

Byrkeflot, H. (2011). Healthcare States and Medical Professions: The Challenges from NPM. In Christensen, T. & Lægreid, P. (Eds.), *The Ashgate Research Companion to New Public Management* (147–60). Farnham: Ashgate.

Caers, R., Bois, C. D., Jegers, M., Gieter, S. D., Schepers, C. & Pepermans, R. (2006). Principal–Agent Relationships on the Stewardship–Agency Axis. *Nonprofit Management and Leadership, 17*(1), 25–47.

Calder, M. C. (1995). Child Protection: Balancing Paternalism and Partnership. *The British Journal of Social Work, 25*(6), 749–66.

Covey, S. M. (2006). *The Speed of Trust: The One Thing That Changes Everything*. New York: Free Press.

Covey, S. M., Link, G. & Merrill, R. R. (2012). *Smart Trust: Creating Prosperity, Energy, and Joy in a Low-Trust World*. New York: Simon & Schuster.

Coye, R. W. & Belohlav, J. A. (1995). An Exploratory Analysis of Employee Participation. *Group & Organization Management, 20*(1), 4–17.

Cumps, B. (2019). *From Competition to Collaboration: Case Studies in Financial Services*. London: Henry Stewart Talks.

Davis, J. H., Schoorman, F. D. & Donaldson, L. (1997). Davis, Schoorman, and Donaldson Reply: The Distinctiveness of Agency Theory and Stewardship Theory. *The Academy of Management Review*, *22*(3), 611–13.

Dicke, L. A. (2002). Ensuring Accountability in Human Services Contracting: Can Stewardship Theory Fill the Bill? *The American Review of Public Administration*, *32*(4), 455–70.

Donaldson, L. & Davis, J. H. (1991). Stewardship Theory or Agency Theory: CEO Governance and Shareholder Returns. *Australian Journal of Management*, *16*(1), 49–64.

Dooren, W. V., Bouckaert, G. & Halligan, J. (2015). *Performance Management in the Public Sector*. London: Routledge.

Downs, A. (1967). *Inside Bureaucracy*. Boston, MA: Little, Brown & Co.

Drennan, V. M., Calestani, M., Ross, F., Saunders, M. & West, P. (2018). Tackling the Workforce Crisis in District Nursing: Can the Dutch Buurtzorg Model Offer a Solution and a Better Patient Experience? A Mixed Methods Case Study. *BMJ Open*, *8*(6), e021931.

Eckstein, J. (2016). Sociocracy: An Organization Model for Large-Scale Agile Development. In *Proceedings of the Scientific Workshop Proceedings of XP2016* (1–5). New York: Association for Computing Machinery.

Fernandez, S. & Moldogaziev, T. (2011). Empowering Public Sector Employees to Improve Performance: Does It Work? *The American Review of Public Administration*, *41*(1), 23–47.

Franco, L. M., Bennett, S. & Kanfer, R. (2002). Health Sector Reform and Public Sector Health Worker Motivation: A Conceptual Framework. *Social Science & Medicine*, *54*(8), 1255–66.

Getz, D. (2009). Policy for Sustainable and Responsible Festivals and Events: Institutionalization of a New Paradigm. *Journal of Policy Research in Tourism, Leisure and Events*, *1*(1), 61–78.

Gray, B. H., Sarnak, D. O. & Burgers, J. S. (2015). *Home Care by Self-Governing Nursing Teams: The Netherlands' Buurtzorg Model*. New York: Commonwealth Fund.

Gronn, P. (2002). Distributed Leadership as a Unit of Analysis. *The Leadership Quarterly*, *13*(4), 423–51.

Guthrie, J. P. (2001). High-Involvement Work Practices, Turnover, and Productivity: Evidence from New Zealand. *Academy of Management Journal*, *44*(1), 180–90.

Harris, J., Caldwell, B. J. & Longmuir, F. (2013). *A Culture of Trust Enhances Performance*. Melbourne: Australian Institute for Teaching and School Leadership.

Herd, P. & Moynihan, D. P. (2019). *Administrative Burden: Policymaking by Other Means*. New York: Russell Sage Foundation.

Hernandez, M. (2012). Toward an Understanding of the Psychology of Stewardship. *Academy of Management Review*, *37*(2), 172–93.

Hondeghem, A. & Perry, J. L. (2009). EGPA Symposium on Public Service Motivation and Performance: Introduction. *International Review of Administrative Sciences*, *75*(1), 5–9.

Hood, C. (1991). A Public Management for All Seasons? *Public Administration*, *69*(1), 3–19.

Hood, C. (2006). Gaming in Targetworld: The Targets Approach to Managing British Public Services. *Public Administration Review*, *66*(4), 515–21.

Jacobsen, C. B. & Andersen, L. B. (2015). Is Leadership in the Eye of the Beholder? A Study of Intended and Perceived Leadership Practices and Organizational Performance. *Public Administration Review*, *75*(6), 829–41.

Jacobsen, C. B., Hvitved, J. & Andersen, L. B. (2014). Command and Motivation: How the Perception of External Interventions Relates to Intrinsic Motivation and Public Service Motivation. *Public Administration*, *92*(4), 790–806.

Jørgensen, B. & Larsen, B. (1987). Control: An Attempt at Forming a Theory. *Scandinavian Political Studies*, *10*(4), 279–99.

Kirkman, B. L. & Rosen, B. (1999). Beyond Self-Management: Antecedents and Consequences of Team Empowerment. *Academy of Management Journal*, *42*(1), 58–74.

Kirkpatrick, D. (2010). *What Is Self-Management?* Sacramento, CA: Morning Star Self-Management Institute.

Krogh, A. H. (2018). *Evalueringsrapport: Projekt "Kerneopgaven i centrum" i Høje-Taastrup Kommune*. Roskilde: Institut for Samfundsvidenskab og Erhverv.

Krogh, A. H. (2019). *Evalueringsnotat: Projekt Nybureaukratisering i Odder Kommune*. Roskilde: Institut for Samfundsvidenskab og Erhverv.

Laloux, F. (2014) *Reinventing Organizations*. Brussels: Nelson Parker.

Lane, J. E. (2005). *State Oversight of Higher Education: A Theoretical Review of Agency Problems with Complex Principals*. Philadelphia, PA: Annual Conference of the Association for the Study of Higher Education.

Lawler, E., Mohrman, S. A. & Ledford, G. E. (1992). The Fortune 1000 and Total Quality. *Quality and Participation*, *15*, 6–10.

Lawler, E., Mohrman, S. A. & Ledford, G. E. (1995). *Creating High Performance Organizations: Impact of Employee Involvement and Total Quality Management*. San Francisco, CA: Jossey-Bass.

Le Grand, J. (1997). Knights, Knaves or Pawns? Human Behaviour and Social Policy. *Journal of Social Policy*, *26*(2), 149–69.

McCubbins, M. D., Noll, R. G. & Weingast, B. R. (1987). Administrative Procedures as Instruments of Political Control. *Journal of Law, Economics & Organization*, *3*(2), 243–77.

Meier, K. J. & Krause, G. A. (2003). The Scientific Study of Bureaucracy: An Overview. In Krause, G. A. & Meier, K. J. (Eds.), *Politics, Policy, and Organizations: Frontiers in the Scientific Study of Bureaucracy* (1–19). Ann Arbor, MI: University of Michigan Press.

Moynihan, D. P. (2010). From Performance Management to Democratic Performance Governance. In O'Leary, R., Van Slyke, D. M. & Kim, S. (Eds.), *The Future of Public Administration around the World: The Minnowbrook Perspective* (21–31). Washington, DC: Georgetown University Press.

Moynihan, D. P. (2013). Advancing the Empirical Study of Performance Management: What We Learned from the Program Assessment Rating Tool. *The American Review of Public Administration*, *43*(5), 499–517.

Musso, J. A. & Weare, C. (2020). Performance Management Goldilocks Style: A Transaction Cost Analysis of Incentive Intensity in Performance Regimes. *Public Performance & Management Review*, *43*(1), 1–27.

Muth, M. & Donaldson, L. (1998). Stewardship Theory and Board Structure: A Contingency Approach. *Corporate Governance: An International Review*, *6*(1), 5–28.

Naff, K. C. & Crum, J. (1999). Working for America: Does Public Service Motivation Make a Difference? *Review of Public Personnel Administration*, *19*(4), 5–16.

Niedlich, S., Kallfaß, A., Pohle, S. & Bormann, I. (2021). A Comprehensive View of Trust in Education: Conclusions from a Systematic Literature Review. *Review of Education, 9*(1), 124–58.

Niskanen, W. A. (1971). *Bureaucracy and Representative Government*. Chicago, IL: Aldine Atherton.

Noordegraaf, M. (2016). Reconfiguring Professional Work: Changing Forms of Professionalism in Public Services. *Administration & Society, 48*(7), 783–810.

Nooteboom, B. (2013). Trust and Innovation. In Bachmann, R. & Zaheer, A. (Eds.), *Handbook of Advances in Trust Research* (1006–124). Cheltenham: Edward Elgar Publishing.

Osborne, D. & Gaebler, T. (1993). *Reinventing Government: How the Entrepreneurial Spirit Is Transforming the Public Sector*. Reading, MA: Addison-Wesley.

Ouchi, W. G. (1979). A Conceptual Framework for the Design of Organizational Control Mechanisms. *Management Science, 25*(9), 833–48.

Pandey, S. K. & Stazyk, E. C. (2008). Antecedents and Correlates of Public Service Motivation. In Perry, J. L. & Hondeghem A. (Eds.), *Motivation in Public Management: The Call of Public Service* (101–17). Oxford: Oxford University Press.

Pearce, C. L., Conger, J. A. & Locke, E. A. (2008). Shared Leadership Theory. *The Leadership Quarterly, 19*(5), 622–8.

Perry, J. L., Engbers, T. A. & Yun, S. (2009). Back to the Future? Performance-Related Pay, Empirical Research, and the Perils of Persistence. *Public Administration Review, 69*(1), 39–51.

Peters, B. G. (1996). *The Future of Governing: Four Emerging Models*. Lawrence, KS: University Press of Kansas.

Reinke, S. J. (2004). Service before Self: Towards a Theory of Servant-Leadership. *Global Virtue Ethics Review, 5*(3), 30–57.

Sansone, C. & Harackiewicz, J. M. (Eds.) (2000). *Intrinsic and Extrinsic Motivation: The Search for Optimal Motivation and Performance*. Amsterdam: Elsevier.

Sardiello, T. & Alexius, S. (2019). Time for Trust? Post-New Public Management Reforms in the Swedish Social Services. In *EGOS Conference, Edinburgh, United Kingdom*, July 4–6.

Schillemans, T. (2008). Accountability in the Shadow of Hierarchy: The Horizontal Accountability of Agencies. *Public Organization Review, 8*(2), 175–94.

Schillemans, T. (2013). Moving beyond the Clash of Interests: On a Stewardship Theory and the Relationships between Central Government Departments and Public Agencies. *Public Management Review, 15*(4), 541–62.

Schillemans, T. & Bjurstrøm, K. H. (2020). Trust and Verification: Balancing Agency and Stewardship Theory in the Governance of Agencies. *International Public Management Journal, 23*(5), 650–76.

Six, F. (2018). Trust in Public Professionals and Their Professions. In Searle, R., Nienaber, A. M. & Sitkin, S. (Eds.), *Routledge Compendium to Trust* (Routledge Companions in Business, Management and Accounting, 361–75). Abingdon: Routledge.

Socialtilsyn Hovedstaden (2019). Tilsynsrapport. Available online: https://jacinfo.gentofte.dk/-/media/Websites/   SOJOBAKT/Dokumenter/Til koebsydelse-Tilsynsrapport-Gentofte-kommune-JAC-Gentofte-2019.pdf?la=da&hash=D0E9522D109C173ECC3CCB0D98266E7420874D28.

Spreitzer, G. M. (1995). Psychological Empowerment in the Workplace: Dimensions, Measurement, and Validation. *Academy of Management Journal, 38*(5), 1442–65.

Van Slyke, D. M. (2007). Agents or Stewards: Using Theory to Understand the Government–Nonprofit Social Service Contracting Relationship. *Journal of Public Administration Research and Theory*, *17*(2), 157–87.

Walton, E. J. (2005). The Persistence of Bureaucracy: A Meta-Analysis of Weber's Model of Bureaucratic Control. *Organization Studies*, *26*(4), 569–600.

6. From the efficient use of existing resources to the mobilization of new ones

The restless expansion of public governance and administration in modern societies requires enormous amounts of public resources gathered through a combination of direct and indirect taxes, tariffs, user fees, land sales, and so on. Public revenues are collected by bodies of local, regional, and national government and allocated for various purposes through political budget deals. In the labor-intensive public sector, revenue is largely spent on hiring public employees, managers, and experts who work hard to carry out routine functions, but who also contribute to developing new ways of governing society and the economy (Mazzucato 2013). Transfer payments to disadvantaged citizens and businesses also figure prominently on public budgets. The operational costs of public institutions (e.g., schools, universities, hospitals, nursing homes) are high, and the construction of vital infrastructures (e.g., roads, bridges, harbors, airports) requires large public investments. Finally, in many countries, the costs of maintaining national security and expanding military capacities are exorbitant.

For many years, the conventional wisdom was that the public sector alone should pay for the growing costs of public service delivery, social assistance, public regulation, and the physical infrastructure for the increasingly demanding population and business sector. From the 1970s onward, however, a series of economic crises put severe pressure on public finances. Public debt increased drastically, and neoliberal and neoconservative political parties demanded that government be reduced in both size and scope. The public governance orthodoxy combining bureaucratic and market-confirming governance tools aimed to make ends meet through a combination of budget cuts, increased efficiency, and outsourcing. This was no easy task, as cutbacks often met with fierce opposition, efficiency increases only produced limited, short-term cost savings and the gains from outsourcing waned over time. Moreover, in the increasingly globalized economy marked by strong competition between nation-states, the pursuit of the different austerity measures led to a "race to the bottom" (Rudra 2008), which left many Western countries with a run-down public sector that failed to meet the high expectations of elected politicians, professionally trained employees and the increasingly affluent middle classes. In some countries, enhancing taxation (or making it more progressive) offers a viable strategy for escaping the financial pinch. In others, the same fiscal improvement might be achieved by improving employment levels, thus raising the aggregate tax revenues. However, many countries have severe political and economic constraints on enhancing taxation and the employment rate.

In this unfortunate situation, it is important to remember that there are always more resources outside the public sector than inside it and new ways in which the public sector can tap into these resources. One way forward would be the more systematic use of co-production and co-creation to mobilize the societal resources required to alleviate poverty and enhance sustainable growth and human well-being. Hence, leveraging resources through the co-production of public services and co-creation of service systems, urban planning and public governance solutions provide a welcome supplement to the endless attempts to use existing resources more efficiently and an attractive alternative to continued austerity policies and rising taxes, especially because co-production and co-creation not only mobilize valuable resources, such as the time, energy, and labor of scores of users, volunteers, and citizens, but they also provide fresh ideas and public support for new and bold solutions.

This chapter explores the shift from the orthodox public governance focus on the efficient exploitation of the existing resources to a new focus on the mobilization of additional resources through co-production and co-creation. It begins with the story of how the public sector expanded in the postwar era, was hit by a growing number of fiscal problems that undermined its legitimacy and subsequently aimed to escape the fiscal squeeze between growing expectations to service production and the limited public resources by focusing on the three Es: economy, efficiency, and effectiveness. It then introduces and defines the co-production and co-creation concepts and shows how these new collaborative forms of governance may help to mobilize resources and make ends meet in the public sector. Co-production and co-creation are parts of a new form of generative governance aimed at turning the public sector into a platform for bringing together relevant and affected actors in collaborative processes that aim to foster innovative public value outcomes. The conclusion discusses the conditions for transforming the public sector into a platform for co-creation and for enhancing the use of co-production and co-creation.

THE GROWTH OF THE TAX-FINANCED PUBLIC SECTOR

In the late nineteenth century, European governments spent less than 10% of GDP on the public sector. In the period from 1915 to 1945, public spending was generally volatile, particularly for the countries that were more involved in the First and Second World Wars. In the postwar period, public expenditure grew rapidly, especially from 1960 to 1980, and then slowed down during the economic crisis in the 1990s that was caused by a combination of a new oil shock and restrictive monetary policies. Nevertheless, in the twenty-first century, public expenditure exceeds 50% of GDP in many European countries. The increase in absolute terms during the last century is much larger than the increase in relative terms, since the level of GDP per capita increased substantially.

The dramatic growth in public spending reflects how the public sector has assumed a growing responsibility for solving public problems and tasks and meeting citizen needs. Early in the previous century, the low levels of public spending were just enough for governments to maintain public order and protect property rights. With the growth of industrialism, however, the pressure for social welfare reform spurred the rise of social expenditure, although there were notable differences between countries that developed universalistic or corporatist welfare systems versus those that maintained a liberal welfare state relying on individual responsibility for personal welfare and one's family (Esping-Andersen 1990). The massive increase in social spending in the second half of the twentieth century was largely driven by the expansion of public education and health care and enabled by increased public taxation. In the period from 1920 to 1980, taxation as a share of GDP increased drastically, more than doubling across all Western countries, albeit with notable differences between countries with different welfare state regimes.

The rise of tax-financed public expenditure reflects the basic idea informing the public governance orthodoxy that the public sector should merely rely on its own budgets, organization, and employees to meet societal and individual demands. In some majority-Roman-Catholic countries, the subsidiarity principle demands that the family and local communities and charity organizations shall first do what they can to help disadvantaged people before passing responsibility on to the public welfare system. In other countries, private social insurance systems based on actuarial principles have aimed to take some of the burden from the state by rejecting the socialization of personal risks. Nevertheless, the public sector has ended up with a huge responsibility for the provision of social welfare, public regulation, and infrastructural investments, and it must find ways to shoulder the burden through enhanced taxation, user fees, and the sale of public assets (e.g., land for private development).

The expansion of a tax-financed public sector was flying in the face of Lockean liberalism, which otherwise recommended a minimalist night-watchman state. Conservatives such as Hayek and North American libertarians such as Friedman and Nozick have since criticized the public welfare system for seizing private property through taxation and reducing the incentive to work. Some countries saw the occasional rise of anti-tax movements, but they never amounted to much, and most people were ready to demand and consume the help offered by public welfare programs, even if some were unwilling to pay for it (Citrin 1979). Today, the largest anti-tax movement possibly consists of people trying to cheat tax authorities by not declaring their income correctly or hiding money in offshore banks and companies.

FROM FISCAL CRISIS TO CUTBACKS, OUTSOURCING, AND EFFICIENCY CAMPAIGNS

The oil crises in 1973, 1979 and 1990 and, more recently, the financial crisis in 2007–8 triggered economic recessions that emphasized the necessity of social welfare programs while simultaneously lowering tax revenues. This pinch made it difficult for the tax-financed public sector to make ends meet and forced it to exploit its resources—in terms of its public finances, organization, and personnel—more efficiently. Consequently, expenditure-cutting outsourcing, lean-based rationalization, and across-the-board budget cuts became permanent fixtures in public organizations.

The practice of outsourcing public services to private actors is as old as the public sector itself, and it is found in sectors as diverse as military defense, digital solutions, public utilities, and specialized social services such as health (Kelman 2002). In the wake of the fiscal crises since the 1970s, however, neoliberal politicians, commentators and public choice theorists joined forces in criticizing the inefficiency of the public sector, which allegedly lacked the disciplining force of the market mechanism to drive costs down and to improve quality. In response, a suggestion was made that publicly financed services would be both better and less costly if they were more often produced and delivered by private companies competing for contracts and customers (Amirkhanyan et al. 2007; Bel & Fageda 2007). New Public Management (NPM) reforms paved the way for the outsourcing of public services through the creation of quasi-markets in which both public and private service providers could bid on the production of public services, contracts were negotiated and signed, and the results were monitored and assessed on a regular basis (Gaebler & Osborne 1993). The strong belief in market efficiency made outsourcing a popular political ploy. The hope was that outsourcing would cut costs and shrink the public sector. There were several reports of significant economic gains from outsourcing (Domberger & Jensen 1997), but the early enthusiasm for outsourcing soon began to dwindle because of the frequent absence of the conditions for successful outsourcing (few bidders, high transaction costs, and lack of transparency), the discovery of a series of unintended consequences of service contracting (lower quality, high cost of monitoring results, and delivery insecurity), and the progressive decline in the average net gains from 2000 to 2015 (Boardman & Hewitt 2004; Davies 2008; Petersen et al. 2015). In addition, there was growing evidence of systematic trade-offs between economic efficiency and quality (Lowery 1998; Sclar 2000) as well as between economic efficiency and other relevant public goals, such as equity, accountability, and responsiveness (Brown et al. 2006). Finally, the increased use of outsourcing did not seem to reduce the size of the public sector, creating instead a new regulatory bureaucracy (Alonso et al. 2015). In sum, the reality of outsourcing did not seem to meet the massive expectations of its political and academic advocates.

If outsourcing did not solve the fiscal crisis, then perhaps the efficiency of the public sector could be enhanced by changes and reforms engineered by public managers using performance data to rationalize service production by reducing slack and removing red tape. Enhancing productivity is notoriously difficult in the low-tech, labor-intensive public service sector. This is problematic because salaries in the public sector tend to rise in response to rising salaries in the private sector, which generally experiences high productivity and therefore can afford to pay higher wages. Hence, Baumol's so-called "cost disease" thesis explains the rising unit costs in the public sector by the fact that a surgeon in a public hospital may not be able to perform a by-pass operation faster but will still want a higher salary to match the salary development of comparably educated professionals in other sectors. NPM refused to accept defeat, instead launching a spate of public productivity campaigns aimed at organizing public service production more efficiently while curbing wage increases. Two of the well-known tools have been Total Quality Management (TQM) and LEAN production methods.

TQM has been a key tool for enhancing public sector efficiency. It uses performance data to detect and eliminate errors, streamline service production, and improve user satisfaction by rewarding employees for exceptionally good performance and ensuring that other employees are brought up to speed with how to improve the efficient delivery of high-quality services. TQM was very popular in the 1980s and 1990s (Ahire et al. 1995) but this waned when it became clear how difficult it was to measure quality in public service production and that transactional leadership based on pecuniary rewards often backfired because it created so much envy among staff members and strengthened the extrinsic employee motivation at the expense of more important forms of motivation, such as intrinsic task motivation and public service motivation.

In this light, the parallel use of LEAN production methods in public administration appeared to present a suitable alternative to TQM (Womack & Jones 1996). The goal of LEAN is easier to operationalize, as it aims to improve efficiency while maintaining productivity and quality. Efficiency is improved by reconfiguring the operational process to cut slack (e.g., unnecessary waiting, superfluous motion, transport) over production and rework. Public service production is reconfigured through a simple process: first, the

change agents responsible for creating a leaner production process aim to
determine what is "value" and "waste," as seen from the customer's perspective. Second, they look for ways to reduce waste and enhance those activities
that add value without increasing the cost of the service or product. Finally,
they monitor results and appreciate how the new, lean production of services
or products frees up organizational resources that can be harvested and used
for other purposes (Radnor et al. 2012). Lean workshops focusing on rapid
improvement and deploying different tools are frequently used to cut slack and
boost efficiency. Recent research indicates that there are potential gains from
introducing LEAN into public service organizations and that the end-users
may benefit from it. However, the research also shows that LEAN typically
struggles to produce further gains after the initial correction of design faults.
Hence, LEAN is merely seeking to optimize the production of a given service
as opposed to trying to rethink that service and how it is produced, including
how the different operational processes interact to produce value and how the
end-user can contribute to value production (Radnor & Osborne 2013).

When both outsourcing and efficiency campaigns fail to produce sufficient budget improvements, public organizations must retreat to either
across-the-board cuts or more targeted budget cuts. Across-the-board budget
cuts are relentlessly egalitarian in the sense that all of the administrative enti-
ties at a certain level of governance must make the same proportional cuts to
their budgets. While such cuts are easy to communicate and administer, they
are blind to the actual needs and saving potential of different parts of the organization. However, the lack of precise information and political unwillingness
to prioritize between different public services areas, knowing that the victim
of cuts will inevitably think it unfair, means that across-the-board budget
cuts often win out. Neoliberal and neoconservative governments in the late
1970s and early 1980s had little success reducing public expenditure based
on across-the-board cuts despite the fierce ideological rhetoric about wanting
to dismantle the postwar welfare state consensus and political preferences
for "less state and more market" (Pierson 1994). Public social expenditure
continued to grow under both UK Prime Minister Margaret Thatcher and US
President Ronald Reagan, partly because of the economic recession and partly
because of the strong popular opposition to welfare cuts.

The welfare state seemed to have created its own supportive constituency
of people who benefited from the provision of public welfare, were employed
by the welfare state, or sympathized with its normative foundation in social
justice and solidarity. The resistance to welfare cuts served as a political
constraint on governments, both when introducing big, across-the-board
budget cuts and when targeting a particular area. Hence, when trying to cut
the budgets of schools, hospitals or particular groups, benefit claimants tended
to create a strong coalition of people and organizations against the cutbacks

that would visibly harm a particular target group—whereas the taxpayers who might benefit from budget reductions translated into small tax cuts hardly noticed what was going on (Kristensen 1980; Wilson 2021). To make matters worse, governments aiming to dismantle the welfare state sometimes began by reducing income taxes and giving tax relief to private businesses but never succeeded in making the corresponding welfare cuts. The result was a deepening of the public debt crisis, which in the 1980s was self-accelerating because of exceedingly high interest rates. Expanding military expenditure added further to the US debt crisis.

In sum, the attempt to make ends meet by making large cuts to social welfare programs has proven very difficult for governments that are blamed for the consequences of budget cuts and not infrequently punished by the voters. The point, however, is not that there have been no cutbacks at all, but rather that they were often smaller than leading politicians hoped for and only possible when accompanied by justification strategies arguing that the cuts would help to prevent the abuse of public means by tightening access, enhancing social equality by preventing affluent groups from receiving particular benefits or services, or increasing the incentives to work and sustain one's own living (Levy 1999; Green-Pedersen 2002).

RESOURCE MOBILIZATION BASED ON CO-PRODUCTION AND CO-CREATION

To make ends meet in the low-growth era following the heyday of public welfare expansion in the 1960s and 1970s, NPM pushed the agenda of outsourcing, efficiency campaigns and social expenditure cuts. These were very necessary—but also difficult—strategies for reducing public expenditure. The easiest and most effective strategy was often to use stealth tactics instead of going for big, publicly announced government initiatives. Hence, strengthening budget discipline through new and stricter budget laws prompting decentralized public agencies to make their own cuts in response to increasing costs, stopping the indexation of welfare benefits to price rises, and tightening the eligibility criteria of expensive welfare programs have been important tools for trimming public budgets in recent decades.

However, after more than forty years of attempts at cutting slack in the public sector, the opportunities to do so would appear to be close to exhausted. The most inefficient public service programs have been outsourced, waste has been eliminated by TQM and LEAN and public budget cuts have pushed the pace of work among public employees to the limit, leading to increasing incidences of stress, burnout, and breakdowns. Going much further down this road may not only prove difficult but also disastrous, since we risk losing support for the tax-financed public sector from two critical groups: the public employees and the citizens they are serving. So instead of going full steam ahead, we may want to throttle down and find alternative ways of mobilizing additional resources instead of merely trying to use the existing resources more efficiently. This is exactly what the growing appreciation of co-production and co-creation in the public sector aims to achieve.

The contribution of co-production to the provision of more and better public services was discovered by Nobel Prize laureate Elinor Ostrom in the 1970s and 1980s. Ostrom and her colleagues at Indiana University in Bloomington showed how local policing in the US could be improved by relying on active citizen participation in community policing (Ostrom et al. 1977; Ostrom 1978) and how public administrators encouraged citizens to contribute to the provision of urban infrastructure, such as sanitation (Ostrom 1996). These seminal studies set a new agenda for public administration research but did not receive the full and deserved attention from public administrators because they emerged during the hegemony of the public sector orthodoxy, which viewed citizens as either clients acted upon by public employees or as customers choosing between alternative welfare providers in a quasi-market. The public sector orthodoxy effectively prevented us from crossing the great divide between the public and private sectors and recasting citizens as co-producers (or indeed co-creators) of public services, public planning, and public solutions more broadly (Osborne & Strokosch 2013).

Today, there is growing interest in co-production and co-creation in most countries and policy sectors (Needham 2008; Alford & Yates 2016; Ansell & Torfing 2021). Individual citizens, local communities and civil society organizations are increasingly seen as important resources for producing and improving public services (Brandsen & Pestoff 2006; Alford 2009; Loeffler & Bovaird 2016). Likewise, multi-actor collaboration involving lay actors is lauded for its ability to create innovative public value outcomes while simultaneously fostering a sense of common ownership of their implementation (Bryson et al. 2017; Brandsen et al. 2018). There would thus appear to be an ongoing shift from perceiving the public sector as an almighty authority in Old Public Administration or an efficient service provider in NPM to viewing it as an initiator and orchestrator of co-production and co-creation, as the advocates of New Public Governance tend to do (Torfing et al. 2019).

While much of the literature uses the notions of co-production and co-creation interchangeably, we gain conceptual clarity by drawing a distinction between the two terms. As such, co-production can be defined as the productive exchange of experiences, knowledge, and resources between the service producers and service users involved in the production of a particular service (Brandsen & Honingh 2016). Similarly, co-creation can be defined as the collaborative process through which relevant and affected actors are defining common problems and challenges, and designing and implementing new and better solutions (Ansell & Torfing 2021). This definition reveals an important distinction between co-production and co-creation: whereas co-production is essentially a dyadic relation between a service user and service provider—mobilizing their competences and resources in producing a pre-defined service—co-creation involves a broader set of actors in the process of creating something new and innovative in the hope that the new solution will outperform the existing solution.

There are many good examples of co-production and co-creation. Beginning with co-production, there are numerous mundane examples, such as schoolchildren doing their homework to spur learning in public schools; citizens adding the ZIP code to envelopes and packages to ease the work of the postal services; taxpayers dutifully submitting their tax returns to the authorities; job seekers providing information about their skills, competences, and work experiences on the online Job Center portal to create a clear and attractive job profile; or patients dutifully going about their strength-training rehab exercises at home after a knee operation. There are also examples of volunteers co-producing public services for others. In Roskilde Municipality in Denmark, twenty local citizens were recruited as mentors for at-risk youth to keep them away from crime. The volunteer mentors thought it was an extremely meaningful task, and the young people they mentored were eager to keep out of trouble to avoid disappointing their mentor, who was helping them out of the goodness of their heart as opposed to being paid and/or wanting to control them. Moreover, their help freed up time for the public employees in the crime prevention agency, who could then help the at-risk youth to pursue an education and/or find work. Another example with a global reach is "Cycling without Age," which is present and active in many cities and countries worldwide. Here, volunteers drive elderly people from nursing homes round on rickshaw bicycles in return for their life story in order to enhance their social mobility and life quality. Nursing home staff report on how the residents are happier and less demanding when they go on such trips, even including examples of elderly residents with dementia having improved their communicative abilities because of the social contacts they develop with the volunteers.

Turning to co-creation, patients are frequently involved in developing new and better health-care service systems. In 2013, the New South Wales Clinical Excellence Commission in Australia implemented a system-wide change to promote patient-centered care designed in collaboration with a patient advisory committee. Each of the thirteen local health districts had tailored partnerships with patients, families, and caregivers that discussed the health-service priorities of their local community. The lay actors were involved in the design of the processes and new facilities as well as in the evaluation of the outcomes of the new organizational designs (Janamian et al. 2016).

Co-creation can also be used to solve the climate crisis by developing joint regulatory standards. Hence, the City of Oslo Business for Climate Network involves almost 150 private businesses in the achievement of Oslo's ambitious climate goals through the formation of a platform for joint problem-solving and enhanced implementation capacity. The platform involves private businesses at two different levels of commitment: a basic level, where the participating companies fulfill a set of minimum criteria and the chief executive officer simply expresses a willingness to adjust their business model and operations to joint climate goals; and a more ambitious level, where the local businesses are willing to actually cut their own emissions and work to make other firms do the same. This example from Oslo illustrates how the co-creation of regulations may stimulate mutual learning, joint action, and opportunities for more innovative, sustainable self-governance.

From the above, one might get the impression that co-creation is for Western societies only. This is far from the case. Inspired by government-launched programs and campaigns, the Youth Foundation of Bangladesh (YFB) has initiated an awareness and participatory action program to reduce the catastrophic impact that single-use plastic coming from local water transport systems has on rivers and local marine life. YFB works closely with the local municipality, the City Corporation, water transport leaseholders, and business organizations to raise awareness among passengers through information, signposting, and videos to provide additional waste bins, to keep launch areas and boats clean and tidy, to train transport personnel, and to monitor behavior and results (United Nations SDG Partnership Platform 2021).

These empirical examples all serve to demonstrate the value added by actively involving citizens and other lay actors in service production, urban planning, and creative problem-solving. New societal resources are mobilized to enhance service quality and spur the development of innovative solutions to reduce long-terms costs. While further emphasis on co-production and co-creation offers a promising strategy for the cash-strapped public sector (Ansell & Torfing 2021), we should not forget that neither co-production nor co-creation are entirely new phenomena. Osborne et al. (2018) have shown how co-production is not an add-on to public administration, but intrinsic to public services that are intangible, consumed at the point of their production and that have the user as the ultimate pivotal point in the service production process. Similarly, Røiseland and Lo (2019) have pointed to the fact that the joint creation of more or less innovative public solutions has been a common way of dealing with problems at the local governance level. Nevertheless, viewed in the light of the current predicament, co-production and co-creation seem to offer a new and welcome strategy for constructively combining public and private resources in the production of services and creation of novel solutions. A strategic effort to expand co-production and co-creation and reap the fruits thereof may not only provide the resources needed for the public sector to meet the high expectations to public services and the problem-solving capacity of the public sector but also provide fresh ideas that can help to improve public regulation and policymaking. Finally, it will foster a new way of connecting lay actors with the public sector and the governing elites, thereby enhancing the legitimacy of public governance and re-building trust relations.

Five crucial conditions may support the expansion of co-production and co-creation as a means to mobilize societal resources. First, the promotion of co-creation requires continuous effort to cultivate an active citizenship that recasts citizens from being clients or customers to being partners who actively influence public governance and administration and who share the responsibility for joint solutions (Heimburg et al. 2021). Involving citizens in workshops, living labs and other interactive processes based on two-way communication and using public websites to hail citizens as active contributors to public service production tends to empower citizens in ways that are conducive to co-production and co-creation.

Second, it is crucial that political leaders and public managers see citizens as valuable resources and assets (Mathie & Cunningham 2003), which can help to improve the public sector, rather than as obstacles to elite, technocratic decisions made by public officials who are convinced that they know better than the citizens themselves what they need and what is good for society. Realizing that lay-actor input can help expand the capacity of the public sector and provide fresh ideas to spur much-needed innovation helps public officials to invest in the orchestration of challenging and demanding co-creation processes.

Third, co-production and co-creation call for the development of new forms of public leadership and management that are more horizontal, distributive, relational, and integrative (Hofstad et al. 2021). Hence, co-creation processes cannot be led top-down through the use of sticks and carrots and based on pre-defined standards. The public and private partners must collaborate on an equal footing, meaning that leaders and managers must learn to lead through facilitation, delegation, intensive communication, and efforts to align a diverse set of actors.

Fourth, co-production and co-creation both require the expansion of decentralized, trust-based spaces for the continuous improvement of services and the innovation of entire service systems, urban planning, and public governance solutions. In short, there must be a "license to innovation" together with a new approach to risk management that perceives errors and mistakes as intrinsic to experiential learning processes and weighs risks against potential gains (Osborne & Brown 2011).

Fifth, co-production and co-creation will benefit from a shift from formative and summative evaluation to developmental evaluation, which asks critical questions about whether problems and tasks are properly understood, whether proposed solutions are adequate and will work in practice and the impact of different actions and efforts (Patton 2010).

Highlighting the conditions for expanding the role of co-production and co-creation in the public sector should not lead us to forget how there are also crucial barriers to such an expansion. First, many professionally trained public employees tend to think that they are perfectly capable of helping disadvantaged citizens and solving complex societal problems based on their own professional knowledge and without disturbing input from amateurs. Second, most public organizations have little or no experience with involving citizens and live a quiet life in relative isolation from the surrounding society. Their websites tell the citizens about rules and regulations by which they must abide and sometimes inform them about the choices they can make between different service providers, but seldom invite them to contribute to producing public value outcomes or influencing public governance decisions. Third, the uptake of recommendations and solutions developed in arenas for citizen participation and co-creation is often low, since elected politicians and public managers have little ownership of them if they have not participated in the creative problem-solving process. Finally, even when co-creation succeeds in mobilizing local ideas and resources and in developing new, bold, and feasible solutions that are endorsed by public authorities, making ends meet may not always help the public sector. Co-creation sometimes leads to new add-on solutions that the public sectors will have to finance, which exacerbates the fiscal problems and the need for economic prioritization.

The exercise of proactive leadership and strategic management may help to overcome the barriers to co-production and co-creation, thus allowing the public sector to reap the fruits of co-production and co-creation. Although this is an attractive scenario, we should bear in mind that co-production and co-creation also have a rarely mentioned dark side (Brandsen et al. 2019), which includes the risk of co-creation leading to the co-destruction of public value due to the participating lay actors' negligence, incompetence, and/or abuse of power. Hence, the co-creation of neighborhood security may foster a militant vigilantism that may end up hurting innocent people or creating a popular feeling of intimidation. Another dark but unintended consequence of co-creation is the risk of arena capture, which allows the resourceful, white middle class that typically participates and sets the tone in co-creation processes to bend joint decisions in their own direction and thus gain further advantages at the expense of other participants or those not participating.

A third risk is that the less resourceful citizens will come under heavy pressure to invest more in the co-production of their own services and the co-creation of local welfare solutions. Indeed, they may end up being stigmatized if they do not co-produce and co-create public value, thereby failing to live up to the new image of the active and contributing citizen who not only receives benefits but also helps to produce them. Finally, although co-creation may stimulate democratic debate with relevant and affected actors, there is a risk that public authorities will tend to suppress the disagreements arising in the discussions of problems and potential solutions because they want to produce small, quick wins that can help demonstrate the value of co-creation and secure support from the elected politicians, who are sometimes more skeptical about co-production and co-creation than the public administrators.

While we want to walk on the bright side of co-creation, it also has a dark side of which we should be aware to mitigate and counteract the negative risks that co-creation may sometimes entail. And we can only succeed in taming or conquering the beast by staring it straight in the eye. Denial of the dark side is not an option.

GENERATIVE GOVERNANCE

Recent decades have seen growing interest in co-production and co-creation as a way of mobilizing important resources that may enable the public sector to do more for less; or perhaps the same amount of public resources either by simply adding in-kind resources or by contributing to the development of innovative solutions based on the actual needs of different citizen groups. As discussed in Chapter 3, co-production and co-creation may be stimulated by a stronger focus on "generativity." Generativity means "tending to generate," which in turn refers to attempts to facilitate the emergence of something useful. Giddens (1994), for example, talked about generative welfare as a new type of welfare policy aiming to empower, train, and educate people to improve their ability to master the risky situations in their lives and to secure their own welfare through gainful employment. Another example is from the field of linguistics, which uses the concept of generativity to describe how a limited number of linguistic elements and rules can be used to produce an unlimited number of meanings (Corballis 1992). A third example comes from psychology, where generativity describes a particular life stage in which people become concerned with cultivating the next generation (Erikson 1950). Finally, at a more general level, Bhaskar (2008: 37) refers to generative mechanisms as structurally imbedded causalities that generate "the flux of phenomena that constitute the actual."

While scholars have mapped and described different forms of co-production and co-creation, they have not paid sufficient attention to the forms of "generative governance" that allow co-production, co-creation, and other forms of collaborative governance to emerge. Hence, we must explore how generative governance can facilitate resource mobilization, foster cross-boundary collaboration, expand processes of creative problem-solving, and ultimately produce public value outcomes. On a general level, generative governance can be defined as forms of governance that facilitate and enable the emergence and consolidation of productive interaction among distributed actors (Ansell & Torfing 2021). There are various types of generative governance, but the focus here is on generative institutions, which are rule-bound infrastructures that support and facilitate the emergence, adaptation, and multiplication of different forms of co-production and co-creation. Two generative governance institutions are particularly important: platforms and arenas.

As already explained in Chapter 3, platforms are relatively permanent opportunity structures that support the formation of collaborative partnerships, networks, and projects through the provision of dedicated but reusable templates, competences, and resources. Platforms may be physical or digital hubs that help to attract relevant and affected actors and urge them to collaborate in order to solve a particular problem or carry out a specific task. They may also facilitate sustained communication among the participants, offer organizational templates that help to structure their interaction and workflow and enable distributed actors to keep track of decisions, outputs, and outcomes. Platforms will sometimes offer valuable knowledge and information, access to administrative assistance and advice, and perhaps even financing for new solutions. Finally, they may contain pre-described procedures for evaluation and accountability. In short, platforms help make it easier to collaborate by lowering the transaction costs of sustained interaction.

Issues That Unite is an example of a physical platform allowing local citizens to raise questions and issues about how to enhance the quality of urban life in the Danish city of Aarhus and to form collaborative working groups around the issues that gather general support and are worth investigating. In the US, Streetwyze is an adaptable digital platform that allows public organizations and citizens to gain distributed access to the local community, search and share information, come together and create solutions that help to build healthier, wealthier, and more just, equitable, diverse, and sustainable neighborhoods.

Whether physical or digital, platforms scaffold the formation of arenas that are temporary institutional spaces for participation, communication, and joint action that are guided by self-regulated norms, rules, and procedures that help to stabilize the interaction and drive the process to conclusion. One platform can facilitate the emergence, adaptation, and consolidation of numerous co-creation arenas that are enabled but not determined by the platform. Hence, co-creation arenas are self-governing in the sense that they set their own agenda, regulate the pattern of participation, and make their own decisions that may either involve dissolving the co-creation arena when the problem is solved or extending it by redefining its purpose or redefining the problem. Co-creation arenas may also spill over into the creation of new arenas that have different goals and a different composition but are supported by the same platform.

The Gentofte Municipal Council designed a new platform that supported the formation of multiple arenas that bring elected councilors and local citizens together in co-creation processes fostering new policy solutions to pressing problems. The platform is part of the new Local Governance Ordinance that contains procedures for creating and supporting a range of so-called "Task Committees" and ensuring that the new policy proposals are discussed, amended, and endorsed by the Municipal Council before they are implemented by the administration (Sørensen & Torfing 2019).

ENHANCING CO-PRODUCTION AND CO-CREATION

Co-production and co-creation offer a possible escape from the crossfire between growing expectations for the public sector and the scarcity of public resources. The idea of mobilizing societal resources and making citizens, communities, and private businesses active partners in delivering much-needed governance solutions may seem attractive to public managers and public employees who are fed up with not having the resources to solve pressing problems and challenges, and with being met with a wall of resistance and opposition when they try to make do with their limited resources. Co-production and co-creation may also appeal to elected politicians who need input from local citizens and stakeholders to better understand the problems at hand and design new and better solutions in response to real needs. Inviting citizens and stakeholders in co-producing and co-creating public solutions may even help politicians to bridge the longstanding gulf between those politicians who favor public solutions and those who favor private solutions by insisting that collaboration between public and private actors will create solutions that are better than both bureaucratic and market-based solutions. This optimistic assessment begs the question of how to mainstream and scale co-production and co-creation to produce a real impact in the future.

Co-production and co-creation are everywhere and nowhere (Ansell & Torfing 2021); examples of both can be found in almost all countries and policy areas, but few public organizations have mainstreamed and scaled co-production and co-creation to all of the relevant parts of the organization. For this to happen, three things are needed.

First, the current experiments with spurring the co-production of public services and the co-creation of public policy and governance must be carefully evaluated, the positive experiences must be communicated across the entire organization and the negative outcomes must be scrutinized in order to discover the problems and barriers leading to disappointment and failure and to find constructive ways of preventing or mitigating such problems and barriers in the future. Ideally, local experimentation can help to identify the scope conditions for reaping the fruits of co-production and co-creation and to

develop strategies for coping with the dilemmas that arise when the new practices collide with entrenched practices from the public governance orthodoxy.
Collaboration between researchers and practitioners often proves important in
this respect.

Second, the bottom-up processes through which distributed actors learn
new and important lessons about co-production and co-creation must be
translated into strategic management that can set a new direction for the entire
organization and integrate co-production and co-creation into the organizational mission and vision. Ideally, the strategic management exercised by
executive leaders will nurture local efforts to reap the fruits of co-production
and co-creation that will feed back into the overall organizational strategy by
prompting leaders to reflect on how the local efforts can be supported and
barriers to success can be removed (Ongaro et al. 2021).

Third, the expansion of co-production and co-creation as a core strategy for
public organizations requires the creation of a new interface between public
organizations and their external environment, or perhaps even a dissolution or
weakening of the boundaries between the inside and outside of public organizations. Focusing on problems and tasks rather than organizational strategies
and forming teams of relevant and affected actors around these problems and
tasks may be a good way of stimulating interaction between public and private
actors, including lay actors such as citizens, neighborhoods, and civil society
organizations. The formation of platforms and arenas may support the opening
up of public organizations to relevant and affected actors (Ansell & Gash
2018).

It may take a while for a public organization that is curious about the
benefits of co-production and co-creation to begin to experiment with and
promote new practices systematically. Overcoming inertia, obstacles, and outright resistance takes even longer, and the goal of mainstreaming and scaling
co-production and co-creation cannot be reached before elected politicians,
public employees, and external societal actors all initiate co-production and
co-creation. Hence, co-creation is not merely about promoting citizen involvement in government affairs, but also about involving public actors in social
affairs. In short, co-creation effectively blurs the demarcation between the
public and private sectors. This blurring is legitimized by the discovery that
public value is not merely a task for public managers and their employees,
since manifold public and private actors can contribute to the production of
public value outcomes (Sørensen & Torfing 2019).

REFERENCES

Ahire, S. L., Landeros, R. & Golhar, D. Y. (1995). Total Quality Management: A Literature Review and an Agenda for Future Research. *Production and Operations Management*, *4*(3), 277–306.

Alford, J. (2009). *Engaging Public Sector Clients: From Service-Delivery to Co-Production*. Basingstoke: Palgrave Macmillan.

Alford, J. & Yates, S. (2016). Co-Production of Public Services in Australia: The Roles of Government Organizations and Co-Producers. *Australian Journal of Public Administration*, *75*(2), 159–75.

Alonso, J. M., Clifton, J. & Díaz-Fuentes, D. (2015). The Impact of New Public Management on Efficiency: An Analysis of Madrid's Hospitals. *Health Policy*, *119*(3), 333–40.

Amirkhanyan, A. A., Kim, H. J. & Lambright, K. T. (2007). Putting the Pieces Together: A Comprehensive Framework for Understanding the Decision to Contract Out and Contractor Performance. *International Journal of Public Administration*, *30*(6–7), 699–725.

Ansell, C. & Gash, A. (2018). Collaborative Platforms as a Governance Strategy. *Journal of Public Administration Research and Theory*, *28*(1), 16–32.

Ansell, C. & Torfing, J. (2021). *Public Governance as Co-Creation: A Strategy for Revitalizing the Public Sector and Rejuvenating Democracy*. Cambridge: Cambridge University Press.

Bel, G. & Fageda, X. (2007). Why Do Local Governments Privatise Public Services? A Survey of Empirical Studies. *Local Government Studies*, *33*(4), 517–34.

Bhaskar, R. (2008). *A Realist Theory of Science*. London: Routledge.

Boardman, A. E. & Hewitt, E. S. (2004). Problems with Contracting Out Government Services: Lessons from Orderly Services at SCGH. *Industrial and Corporate Change*, *13*(6), 917–29.

Brandsen, T. & Honingh, M. (2016). Distinguishing Different Types of Coproduction: A Conceptual Analysis Based on the Classical Definitions. *Public Administration Review*, *76*(3), 427–35.

Brandsen, T. & Pestoff, V. (2006). Co-Production, the Third Sector and the Delivery of Public Services: An Introduction. *Public Management Review*, *8*(4), 493–501.

Brandsen, T., Steen, T. & Verschuere, B. (2018). *Co-Production and Co-Creation: Engaging Citizens in Public Services.* New York: Routledge.

Brandsen, T., Steen, T. & Verschuere, B. (2019). Public Administration into the Wild: Grappling with Co-Production and Social Innovation. In Massey, A. (Ed.), *A Research Agenda for Public Administration* (63–78). Cheltenham: Edward Elgar Publishing.

Brown, T. L., Potoski, M. & Slyke, D. M. (2006). Managing Public Service Contracts: Aligning Values, Institutions, and Markets. *Public Administration Review*, *66*(3), 323–31.

Bryson, J., Sancino, A., Benington, J. & Sørensen, E. (2017). Towards a Multi-Actor Theory of Public Value Co-Creation. *Public Management Review*, *19*(5), 640–54.

Citrin, J. (1979). Do People Want Something for Nothing? Public Opinion on Taxes and Government Spending. *National Tax Journal*, *32*(2S), 113–29.

Corballis, M. C. (1992). On the Evolution of Language and Generativity. *Cognition*, *44*(3), 197–226.

Davies, S. (2008). Contracting Out Employment Services to the Third and Private Sectors: A Critique. *Critical Social Policy*, *28*(2), 136–64.

Domberger, S. & Jensen, P. (1997). Contracting Out by the Public Sector: Theory, Evidence, Prospects. *Oxford Review of Economic Policy*, *13*(4), 67–78.

Erikson, E. H. (1950). *Childhood and Society*. New York: Norton.

Esping-Andersen, G. (1990). *The Three Worlds of Welfare Capitalism*. Princeton, NJ: Princeton University Press.

Gaebler, T. & Osborne, D. (1993). *Reinventing Government: How the Entrepreneurial Spirit Is Transforming the Public Sector*. Reading, MA: Addison-Wesley.

Giddens, A. (1994). *Beyond Left and Right: The Future of Radical Politics*. Cambridge: Polity Press.

Green-Pedersen, C. (2002). *The Politics of Justification: Party Competition and Welfare-State Retrenchment in Denmark and the Netherlands from 1982 to 1998*. Amsterdam: Amsterdam University Press.

Heimburg, D. V., Ness, O. & Storch, J. (2021). Co-Creation of Public Values: Citizenship, Social Justice, and Well-Being. In Thomassen, A. O. & Jensen, J. B. (Eds.), *Advances in Public Policy and Administration: Processual Perspectives on the Co-Production Turn in Public Sector Organizations* (20–41). Hershey, PA: IGI Global.

Hofstad, H., Sørensen, E., Torfing, J. & Vedeld, T. (2021). Leading Co-Creation for the Green Shift. *Public Money & Management*, 1–10. DOI: 10.1080/09540962.202 1.1992120.

Janamian, T., Crossland, L. & Wells, L. (2016). On the Road to Value Co-Creation in Health Care: The Role of Consumers in Defining the Destination, Planning the Journey and Sharing the Drive. *Medical Journal of Australia*, *204*(S7), S12–14.

Kelman, S. J. (2002). Contracting. In Salamon, L. M. (Ed.), *The Tools of Government: A Guide to the New Governance* (282–318). New York: Oxford University Press.

Kristensen, O. P. (1980). The Logic of Political–Bureaucratic Decision-Making as a Cause of Governmental Growth: Or Why Expansion of Public Programs is a "Private Good" and Their Restriction is a "Public Good." *European Journal of Political Research*, *8*(2), 249–64.

Levy, J. D. (1999). Vice into Virtue? Progressive Politics and Welfare Reform in Continental Europe. *Politics & Society*, *27*(2), 239–73.

Loeffler, E. & Bovaird, T. (2016). User and Community Co-Production of Public Services: What Does the Evidence Tell Us? *International Journal of Public Administration*, *39*(13), 1006–19.

Lowery, D. (1998). Consumer Sovereignty and Quasi-Market Failure. *Journal of Public Administration Research and Theory*, *8*(2), 137–72.

Mathie, A. & Cunningham, G. (2003). From Clients to Citizens: Asset-Based Community Development as a Strategy for Community-Driven Development. *Development in Practice*, *13*(5), 474–86.

Mazzucato, M. (2013). *The Entrepreneurial State: Debunking Public vs. Private Sector Myths*. London: Anthem Press.

Needham, C. (2008). Realizing the Potential of Co-Production: Negotiating Improvements in Public Services. *Social Policy and Society*, *7*(2), 221–31.

Ongaro, E., Sancino, A., Pluchinotta, I., Williams, H., Kitchener, M. & Ferlie, E. (2021). Strategic Management as an Enabler of Co-Creation in Public Services. *Policy & Politics*, *49*(2), 287–304.

Osborne, S. P. & Brown, L. (2011). Innovation in Public Services: Engaging with Risk. *Public Money and Management*, *31*(3), 4–6.

Osborne, S. P. & Strokosch, K. (2013). It Takes Two to Tango? Understanding the Co-Production of Public Services by Integrating the Services Management and Public Administration Perspective. *British Journal of Management*, *24*(S1), 31–47.

Osborne, S. P., Strokosch, K. & Radnor, Z. (2018). Co-Production and the Co-Creation of Value in Public Services: A Perspective from Service Management. In Brandsen, T., Steen, T. & Verschuere, B. (Eds.), *Co-Production and Co-Creation: Engaging Citizens in Public Services* (18–26). New York: Routledge.

Ostrom, E. (1978). Citizen Participation and Policing: What Do We Know? *Journal of Voluntary Action Research*, *7*(1–2), 102–8.

Ostrom, E. (1996). Crossing the Great Divide: Coproduction, Synergy, and Development. *World Development*, *24*(6), 1073–87.

Ostrom, E., Parks, R. B. & Whitaker, G. P. (1977). *Policing Metropolitan America.* Washington, DC: National Science Foundation.

Patton, M. Q. (2010). *Developmental Evaluation: Applying Complexity Concepts to Enhance Innovation and Use*. New York: The Guilford Press.

Petersen, O. H., Hjelmar, U. & Vrangbæk, D. K. (2015). *Is Contracting Out Still the Great Panacea? A Meta-Analysis of International Studies on Costs and Service Quality*. Paper presented at International Conference on Public Policy in Milan, Italy.

Pierson, P. (1994). *Dismantling the Welfare State?* Cambridge: Cambridge University Press.

Radnor, Z. & Osborne, S. P. (2013). Lean: A Failed Theory for Public Services? *Public Management Review*, *15*(2), 265–87.

Radnor, Z., Holweg, M. & Waring, J. (2012). Lean In Healthcare: The Unfilled Promise? *Social Science & Medicine*, *74*(3), 364–71.

Røiseland, A. & Lo, C. (2019). Samskaping: nyttig begrep for norske forskere og praktikere? *Norsk statsvitenskapelig tidsskrift*, *35*(1), 51–8.

Rudra, N. (2008). *Globalization and the Race to the Bottom in Developing Countries: Who Really Gets Hurt?* Cambridge: Cambridge University Press.

Sclar, E. D. (2000). *You Don't Always Get What You Pay For: The Economics of Privatization.* Ithaca, NY: Cornell University Press.

Sørensen, E. & Torfing, J. (2019). Designing Institutional Platforms and Arenas for Interactive Political Leadership. *Public Management Review*, *21*(10), 1443–63.

Torfing, J., Sørensen, E. & Røiseland, A. (2019). Transforming the Public Sector into an Arena for Co-Creation: Barriers, Drivers, Benefits, and Ways Forward. *Administration & Society*, *51*(5), 795–825.

United Nations SDG Partnership Platform (2021). https://sustainabledevelopment.un .org/partnership.

Wilson, J. Q. (2021). *Political Organizations*. Princeton, NJ: Princeton University Press.

Womack, J. P. & Jones, D. T. (1996). Beyond Toyota: How to Root Out Waste and Pursue Perfection. *Harvard Business Review*, *74*(5), 140–51.

7. From unicentric to pluricentric coordination

Planning and coordination were key features of postwar public bureaucracy. Central government agencies aimed to predict the future to control it. They often developed a grand masterplan and then sought to subject policymaking and the development of administrative operations to its core principles and targets. Hence, coordination took the form of centralized control and the imposition of a particular design on local and distributed actors. The result was popular resistance, administrative opposition and a good deal of decoupling, and failure to adjust to new trends and developments on the ground.

The growing criticism of the centralized planning system and the hierarchical coordination of the rapidly expanding and increasingly differentiated polity gradually led to the abandonment of comprehensive planning and a growing appreciation of market competition as a decentered coordination mechanism that aims to replace a priori coordination based on predetermined political goals with ex post coordination depending on market forces. However, this new type of market-based coordination often spins out of control, thus leading to an undersupply of common goods and negative externalities. The results often go against key political goals and values.

Now, in an attempt to avoid both government and market failure, we have seen growing interest in pluricentric coordination aimed at aligning a plethora of sectors, organizations, and initiatives through collaborative interaction in order to mitigate conflicts, create synergies and joint problem-solving, and prevent gaps and overlaps in regulation, the provision of infrastructure and the delivery of services that tend to take place in increasingly turbulent environments. This chapter paints a broad picture of the rise of unicentric coordination within modern bureaucracies and its link to centralized planning. It then proceeds to show why and how unicentric coordination gives way to pluricentric coordination (Pedersen et al. 2011), which aims to produce a flexible coherence and alignment between empowered actors aiming to adapt to changing contexts while holding each other to account for joint and individual achievements. Finally, it shows how governance networks can provide a framework for pluricentric coordination in the face of turbulence.

THE RISE OF UNICENTRIC COORDINATION IN PUBLIC BUREAUCRACY

The need for coordination is intrinsically linked to the rise of bureaucratic specialization. The bureaucratic governance model adopted in the postwar era by most public sector organizations aimed to enhance the efficiency and effectiveness of public agencies by creating an elaborate, fine-grained division of labor that allowed the public employees within a particular sector or bureau to specialize in carrying out a particular set of tasks, thereby becoming experts in what they were doing along the way. Specialization is an important tool for complexity reduction as it allows public employees to focus on a limited number of political goals, legal and administrative rules, and operational tasks. However, specialization without coordination is centrifugal in the sense of creating a situation where agencies pursue their own goals and agendas that may conflict with and counteract each other (Bouckaert et al. 2016). Specialized agencies often have no knowledge about what other agencies are doing, and this mutual ignorance may produce service gaps, policy failures, and planning disasters. Hence, what seems to work well from the point of view of a single autonomous agency may be highly problematic from a whole-of-government perspective.

In public bureaucracy, coordination undertaken by a central government agency with the authority to impose some degree of coherence and order provides the solution to the risk of flux and chaos in highly compartmentalized and specialized public organizations. Coordination may either be horizontal or vertical. Horizontal coordination between different public line agencies occurs when a higher-level authority or an appointed lead agency aims to ensure some degree of consistency and/or complementarity between the ideas, goals, actions, and resource deployment of relatively autonomous public agencies in order to produce effective governance solutions that square with the overall government priorities. An example would be the effort to make all government departments contribute to realizing the government's climate goals and emission reduction targets. In Oslo, such climate policy coordination has created a climate budget that allocates emission reduction targets for each department and monitors their attainment.

Vertical coordination between public agencies at different levels of local, regional, and national government occurs when an agency at the apex of government aims to ensure that everyone is on the same page and making decisions that contribute to realizing overall government objectives. This type of coordination is particularly important in federal systems where regional states and local governments enjoy considerable decision-making autonomy and there is no guarantee that government decisions made at different levels point in the same direction and subscribe to the same goals. There is great need for vertical coordination in the multi-level governance system created by the European Union (EU) (Bolleyer & Börzel 2014), since the distance from Brussels to the local governments in the various member states appears quite long, and local conditions for policy implementation tend to vary. Short of powers to impose specific policy goals and governance practices on local and regional authorities in the member states, the EU is forced to work through national governments or involve lower-level government actors in more loose forms of coordination based on voluntary standards, as we have seen in the case of the Open Method of Coordination (Armstrong 2010).

Whether horizontal or vertical, policy coordination is important since the success of one policy often depends on the successful implementation of other policies and since complex policy problems often cut across the administrative division of labor in public bureaucracy (Peters 2018). Getting unemployed people back into the labor market is not simply a question of local job centers encouraging them to search and apply for new work, as many unemployed people lack training, have health problems, face language barriers, or need daycare for their children to be able to return to active employment. Hence, the services of other public agencies are often crucial for successful re-entry into the labor market, and the different agencies must find ways to coordinate their efforts. Likewise, problems such as the COVID-19 pandemic cut across the efforts of multiple agencies to contain the spread of the infectious disease, reorganize public service provision in line with new health regulations, help people suffering from lockdown-induced distress and loneliness, create new jobs for those who are laid off and so on. When multiple agencies are facing the same cross-cutting problem, inter-agency coordination is paramount to avoid gaps, redundancies, contradictory strategies, and negative spillovers.

Policy coordination may also occur between different programs within the same policy area or between different service delivery units. Programs for homeless people in a major city should be based on the same principles and convey the same basic message to the homeless to avoid creating confusion or false expectations. Educational institutions such as high schools, community colleges and universities should offer programs and services that facilitate student mobility and allow students to flexibly combine different education programs. Finally, we should avoid creating situations where the same social client is presented with and expected to adhere to numerous social action plans produced by different social policy agencies. In Denmark, there are examples of public authorities developing seventeen different action plans for a single social client facing different but related problems.

Coordination is equally important for governments, citizens, and individual service users. Governments want to avoid policy and governance failures triggered by uncoordinated government action that undermines the efficiency and effectiveness of policy delivery. Citizens expect consistency between and predictability in government programs, and individual service users want to avoid running helter-skelter between different agencies to get the help that they need and deserve.

We have already talked at length about the need for coordination without defining the term. Here, we define coordination as the attempt to foster a relatively harmonious functioning of different parts of government to ensure effective results of public governance. Hence, coordination occurs when decisions made in one unit, program, or organization consider those made in other relevant units, programs and organizations and are adjusted in an attempt to avoid or reduce their potentially adverse consequences (Lindblom 1965; Peters 2018). The degree and frequency of mutual adjustment may vary to produce different levels of coordination, ranging from independent decision-making in relatively autonomous agencies, via strategic agreements on overall goals and the arbitration of disputes, to the formulation of integrated government strategies based on top-down control (Metcalfe 1994).

Central agencies such as ministries of finance, budget offices, personnel offices, and the like play a key role in fostering coordination within the public sector, but public managers at lower levels of government also undertake important coordination functions. The instruments for spurring unicentric coordination within public bureaucracies include: (1) centralized budget systems that create rules and incentives that tie public resources to the attainment of particular goals and ensure that each administrative unit contributes to overall government goals (and are penalized for not doing so); (2) intensive communication that helps to make administrative agencies familiar with the goals and tasks of other agencies and to align their action; (3) the creation of super-ministries (e.g., the Department of Homeland Security) that allocate tasks and resources and promote inter-agency knowledge-sharing and collaboration; (4) government-led cabinet committees, task forces, or work groups that facilitate the design of joint strategies for implementing overall government objectives while avoiding conflicts and facilitating joint problem-solving; (5) the formulation and mainstreaming of government objectives that help to ensure that all public agencies contribute to the production of desirable outcomes; (6) the publication of performance data through the creation of joint dashboards that make it possible for agencies to see themselves and subsequently act as part of a joint operation; and (7) the appointment of czars, which allocates a personal responsibility to specific individuals in charge of making a particular policy work in the face of organizational fragmentation and competing jurisdictions (Løgreid et al. 2014; Peters 2018).

Unicentric coordination is based on hierarchical power and authority and involves the imposition of ideas, goals, tasks, and concerns defined by central government agencies on the public agencies and private stakeholders subjected to coordination. Coordination based on the top-down imposition of demands flies in the face of the organizational autonomy that most bureaucratic agencies (and private organizations) expect to have and strive for, and it may prevent them from taking into account and flexibly exploiting local conditions and developments because they must follow orders from above. More importantly, coordination drawing on the imperative force of centralized hierarchical authority will tend to hamper mutual learning, as horizontal interaction is often scarce. Top-down imposition also tends to produce a limited sense of ownership of the coordination process and its outcomes, since the agencies whose actions are subjected to coordination will have limited influence and are merely expected to fall in line.

Other limitations to coordination based on top-down imposition include ignorance, turf protection, professional and ideological differences, and the role of politics. Hence, attempts made by central authorities to coordinate the actions of decentralized agencies may fail because of the ignorance of local agencies, which may turn a deaf ear to the messages from central government either because they are too busy with their daily operations or because the demands for changed behavior drown in the noise from over-crowded communication channels. Concerns for protecting the organizational turf against what may be seen as intrusion and unnecessary concessions may also make top-down coordination efforts unsuccessful. In addition, the presence of different professional methods and values and conflicting administrative ideologies can prevent local agencies from aligning themselves with other agencies. Finally, public agencies at the local or regional level may be controlled by other political parties than those controlling the national ministries—which may open up for political party-related opposition to coordination from above.

One of the key explanations for why public bureaucracies around the world have held on to unicentric coordination for so long despite its many problems and limitations is that it fits so well with the centralized planning model (Warren 1973). Rational comprehensive planning theory, which dominated the public sector after the Second World War and up to the early 1970s, saw planning as an engineering exercise through which planning experts collect quantitative data, forecast future needs and developments, define goals, identify and compare different policy designs and planning strategies, make optimizing decisions, and implement them through a multi-level governance system based on centralized coordination (Hartmann & Geertman 2022). The planning function was usually located in the executive and/or legislative branches of government and embraced all areas of interest to the public. The comprehensive planning system produced blueprints that were to be effectively implemented all the way down to the local level and across all sectors and policy areas. The key tool for securing success was coordination. The actions of multiple actors at different levels and in different sectors and policy areas had to fit the overall scheme and contribute to the realization of the central planning objectives. In sum, the strong postwar faith in social engineering and comprehensive planning made unicentric coordination a preferred strategy.

THE INTRODUCTION OF MARKET-BASED COORDINATION AND THE MOVE TOWARD AGENTIFICATION

Top-down coordination is prompted by inter-organizational specialization but may reduce this very specialization and the benefits derived from it by forcing all the agencies to apply the same standards and pursue the same goals. Since unicentric coordination is highly intrusive and directly seeks to constrain, correct, and change the behavior of those subjected to coordination by forcing them to act in accordance with the goals, priorities and guidelines of a comprehensive plan, attempts have been made since the late 1970s to shift from unicentric to multicentric coordination in order to facilitate coordination while safeguarding specialization (Kersbergen & Waarden 2004).

New Public Management (NPM) aims to shift the balance between imperative ex ante coordination through hierarchical forms of organization and anarchic ex post coordination through market exchange in favor of the latter (Jessop 1998). Privatization, contracting out and the commercialization of the remaining public sector introduced a new form of market-based coordination whereby an almost infinite number of sellers and buyers exploit the procedural rules of a "free" market to compete in order to maximize their revenue (sellers) and quality for money (buyers). In theory, multicentric market governance eventually leads to the formation of equilibrium prices and an optimal allocation of resources that emerges as a result of competition between a large number of individual, autonomous, and relatively specialized actors who are not subjected to government pressure. Hence, coordination is provided by the invisible hand of the market rather than the iron fist of government. In reality, however, examples of market failure are abundant because of imperfect information, incomplete markets and the presence of externalities and public goods (Stiglitz 2008; Salamon 2021). Still, NPM and its neoliberal advocates continue to recommend that a growing number of public services should be outsourced to private contractors and that the governance of social and economic life should be deregulated and "marketized."

Arguments about asset specificity (Walker & Weber 1984) recognized the limits to the introduction of market-based coordination, which raised questions about how to coordinate action within the part of the public sector that was not marketized. NPM suggested that large public organizations were to be disaggregated into smaller single- or special-purpose agencies and led by professional public managers empowered to use their budget, employees and organization flexibly to achieve a specific set of goals. These managers were to be held to account for their performance through an incentive-based system of performance management (Christensen 2012). Hence, the pendulum swung from ex ante coordination based on top-down imposition to ex post coordination based on performance assessment and the use of incentives.

This pendulum swing created a paradox right in the center of the new public governance orthodoxy, which aims at combining classical forms of bureaucratic governance with elements of NPM. Hence, while bureaucracy insists on the importance of policy coordination based on top-down control, NPM enhanced the autonomy of private contractors through the introduction of market-based coordination, and it empowered decentralized agencies and local public managers through an ongoing agentification of the public sector (Peters & Savoie 1996).

JOINED-UP GOVERNMENT AND PARTNERSHIPS AS STEPPING-STONES TO PLURICENTRIC COORDINATION

NPM replaced the rigid top-down coordination mechanisms with market-based coordination whereby public and private service providers and quasi-autonomous public agencies were empowered to deliver results in the best possible way and subsequently rewarded or penalized for their achievements. While the empowerment of specialized service providers and agencies may have helped to unleash the entrepreneurial spirit of agency managers that bureaucracy had been accused of suppressing and may have improved the quality of public solutions while enhancing the productivity of public employees, these achievements were obtained at high cost. The new, less intrusive, NPM-inspired and multicentric forms of coordination contributed to a furthering of the fragmentation of the already fragmented public sector, which supported the centrifugal forces that make policy coordination exceedingly difficult (if not impossible). A case in point is the new active labor market policies aimed at training and motivating unemployed individuals in different ways so that they can find gainful employment. In most European countries, the new workfare policies recruited a large number of private contractors and created numerous quasi-autonomous agencies in charge of training, counseling and pushing different target groups, the result being a fragmented governance landscape in which coordination is hardly possible.

The pendulum had apparently swung too far in the direction of the empowerment and autonomy of public and private agencies; in response, governments aimed to reassert the importance of unicentric coordination. To illustrate, the government of New Zealand launched a program to "restore the center." However, there were also some new and interesting responses that did not aim to bring central government authorities back into their role as top-down coordinators.

Prime ministers such as Britain's Tony Blair called for a more "joined-up" government (Ling 2002; Bogdanor 2005), and the same idea emerged in other countries, albeit sometimes under other names (Hagen & Kubicek 2000; OECD 2001, 2009; Six 2004). According to Pollitt (2003), joined-up government denotes the aspiration to achieve horizontal as well as vertical coordination in order to eliminate inter-agency tensions, make better use of scarce resources, create synergies and free-flowing ideas and provide citizens with more seamless service offers. One of the new features of joined-up government includes an attempt to blur the lines of demarcation between policy formulation and policy implementation, which constitute two sides of the same coin and mutually affect each other. Another interesting feature is that the coordination process is decentered in the sense that different actors along the horizontal and vertical axes are expected to contact each other and collaborate with each other in order to jointly contribute to goal attainment. Finally, coordination does not only involve collaboration between public actors but also includes relevant private for-profit and non-profit actors. There is even an ambition to empower citizens to participate in both policy formulation and service delivery (Pollitt 2003).

The inclusion of private actors (e.g., businesses, interest organizations, civil society actors, neighborhoods, and citizens) in the new joined-up coordination practices stimulates interest in partnerships as a tool for coordination. Partnerships are widely seen as a viable strategy for coordinating the decisions and actions of relevant and affected actors in the face of organizational fragmentation and environmental complexity (Lowndes & Skelcher 1998; Mitchell & Shortell 2000; Keast & Brown 2002). Successful partnerships are difficult to build (Hudson & Hardy 2002), but when interdependent public and private actors are brought together in trust-based interaction, they may aspire to share knowledge and information, engage in mutual adjustment of ideas, strategies and activities, and design joint solutions to common problems and challenges. Interestingly, empirical studies suggest that trust and access to relevant resources are more important than shared beliefs when actors decide to coordinate with others in collaborative partnerships (Calanni et al. 2010). Hence, diversity does not seem to prevent decentered and distributed coordination in partnerships.

That said, coordination through joined-up government or collaborative partnerships is not without problems. Hence, performance management becomes more difficult because the participating public actors will tend to have different and competing goals and targets, which are almost impossible to merge, and because the private actors may object to the idea of having their activities measured and assessed. There will also be problems with accountability, as the more the actors collaborate and integrate their operations, the more difficult it will be to determine who has contributed how much to which target. Finally, it is often unclear who takes the initiative to form and build a partnership with the purpose of enhancing coordination and not clear how well-known collective action problems can be avoided.

Partnerships aiming to coordinate policymaking and service delivery do not necessarily have to be as tight and formal as the public–private partnerships involved in managing major infrastructure projects, but a diverse set of actors must come together and be willing to listen to each other and adjust their ideas and actions—and that requires some form of leadership. This is confirmed by the empirical analysis of primary care partnerships in Victoria, Australia, which brings together national and regional authorities, local governments, hospitals, general practitioners, and community organizations. The analysis reveals how the independent staff acting as coordinators for the partnership played a key role in holding it together and facilitating interaction that contributed to fulfilling the goal of improving local health and well-being (Lewis et al. 2008).

PLURICENTRIC COORDINATION: FORMS, PROBLEMS AND MERITS

Joined-up government and the formation of coordination partnerships introduces a new kind of pluricentric coordination that is neither controlled by the apex of government nor involving an infinite number of competing actors operating in more or less free markets. Different public and private actors involved in policymaking and/or service delivery interact within a structure that is flatter than a traditional bureaucratic hierarchy, more focused on joint problem-solving than competitive markets and characterized by a high degree of self-management, albeit not without dedicated leadership.

The Ostroms talked about polycentric rather than pluricentric coordination, but "poly" and "pluri" both refer to the co-existence of multiple organizational centers within a system aiming to facilitate coordination to solve a problem or task. In the original formulation, polycentricity refers to:

> many centers of decisionmaking that are formally independent of each other. Whether they actually function independently, or instead constitute an interdependent system of relations, is an empirical question in particular cases. To the extent that they take each other into account in competitive relationships, enter into various contractual and cooperative undertakings or have recourse to central mechanisms to resolve conflicts, the various political jurisdictions in a metropolitan area may function in a coherent manner with consistent and predictable patterns of interacting behavior (Ostrom et al. 1961: 831–2).

Although multiple centers may simultaneously engage in competition, arbitration facilitated by higher-level authorities or cross-boundary collaboration, polycentric systems are seen as an alternative to state- and market-based coordination because the different actors are purposely connected and aim to coordinate their actions to achieve a particular goal, such as the preservation of common pool resources (Ostrom 2010).

Empirical research conducted since the 1970s has suggested that the complex interaction between several organizational centers involved in metropolitan governance did not lead to chaos, but rather to high performance based on inter-agency coordination (Ostrom & Whitaker 1973; Ostrom et al. 1993; Ostrom & Parks 1999; Andersson & Ostrom 2008). These results helped to convince many researchers and practitioners of how performance-improving coordination could potentially emerge in settings where many different actors worked alongside each other to produce outcomes.

Coming from economic theory based on individual utility maximization, Ostrom takes a rational choice approach to analyzing the interactions between public and private actors involved in polycentric coordination. Although institutionally situated actors may only have a bounded rationality, they tend to calculate the net costs and benefits of potential outcomes (Ostrom 2005, 2010). As such, the institutional analysis and development framework is based on what March and Olsen (1989, 1995) describe as a logic of consequentiality that presumes that actors are motivated by the individual gains that may derive from the outcome of a particular action.

More recently, researchers have developed an alternative theory of pluricentric coordination (Pedersen et al. 2011) that tends to view coordination as being conducted in interactive arenas promoting communication between a plurality of situated actors, each of whom has their own rule and resource base and acts in accordance with their own interpretation of the institutional prescriptions for appropriate action (March & Olsen 1989, 1995). In this perspective, action is scripted rather than calculated. This assumption has an important consequence, as it undermines the foundation of coordination in the rationalistic, comprehensive planning scheme; coordination becomes less an auxiliary tool for implementing a planned blueprint and more an essentially collaborative activity that supports an incomplete and emerging plan aimed at integrating different goals and articulating dissimilar practices (Innes & Booher 2010).

Another important consequence of the adoption of an interpretive institutionalist perspective is that it enables the explanation of why and how actors adjust their views, actions, and activities through communicative interaction. Actors are not equipped with exogenous preferences that only allow them to make concessions based on hard-nosed bargaining and compromise formation; rather, they have endogenous preferences that are formed by their interpretation of institutional logics of appropriate action and are shaped and reshaped through deliberation and mutual learning taking place in interactive arenas of networked coordination.

Finally, since coordination is predicated on the modification of the positions, views and discourses of the involved actors, it becomes difficult to distinguish between negative and positive coordination (Scharpf 1994); that is, coordination that reduces mutual externalities (negative coordination) versus coordination that serves to identify and promote collective goals (positive coordination). The endogenous character of the preferences and views of the actors means that coordination based on communicative interaction will always lead to more than negative coordination as the logics, strategies and interests of the involved actors are reshaped through deliberation and mutual learning. Likewise, positive coordination is always constrained by the ambiguous and competing interpretations of the common good, which only exists in and through particular hegemonic constructions.

In their award-winning article, Pedersen, Sehested and Sørensen (2011) map the gradual emergence of a pluricentric understanding of coordination in public administration theory, organization theory and planning theory, and they draw the contours of a pluricentric theory of coordination based on interpretive institutionalism. The pluricentric approach to coordination assumes that coordination takes place in an unstable and undecidable terrain of institutional fragmentation and power battles. In this context, the modest coordination ambition is to create a partially fixed understanding of goals, tools, and activities and how they may supplement, support, and overlay each other. The provisional acceptance of a common yet ambiguous storyline will tend to be self-reinforcing, as the actors may adjust their interpretations, ideas, and actions, thus creating temporal alignment across the involved actors. The idea of coordination as relying on the contingent articulation of the relative fixation of meaning, purpose, and roles that are deemed appropriate in the particular context and situation may sound excessively modest and perhaps even slightly pessimistic; it is at least far away from the idea of coordination based on a planned blueprint for action. However, all that coordination needs to work well is to facilitate the temporal construction of a common ground that allows the actors to reflect on and revise their goals and actions in the light of partially fixed discourse, which is bound to be challenged and dislocated by new and changing events. From this point of view, coordination is essentially about "striking the right balance between fixation and flexibility, between control and autonomy, between unity and diversity, and between simplicity and complexity" (Pedersen et al. 2011: 388).

The authors go on to argue that pluricentric coordination is a result of the interaction between three overlapping realms: (1) interaction in collaborative networks and partnerships; (2) construction of meaning and storylines; and (3) formal institutions and metagovernance. The overlap between realms 1 and 2 facilitates communication and the construction of shared meaning. The overlap between realms 2 and 3 allows the particular public agencies to frame the construction of meaning. Finally, the overlap between realms 1 and 3 facilitates a particular structuring of networked interaction.

When it works well and is successful, pluricentric coordination constructs "dynamic, decentered, interactive, situated, and overlapping linkages that promote communication between otherwise disconnected stories and practices" (Pedersen et al. 2011). The coordination linkages must be *dynamic* because coordination always takes place within changing contexts. The linkages must also be *decentered* in order to leave sufficient room for autonomous maneuvering and self-management for the actors involved at different levels and in different sectors and policy areas. The linkages must be *interactive* to ensure a continuous exchange of understandings, viewpoints, knowledge, and resources among relevant and affected actors. The pluricentric approach furthermore calls for *situated* modes of coordination in order to replace the traditional search for standardized solutions with tailor-made solutions. Finally, the linkages produced in and through pluricentric coordination must be overlapping, since, in the absence of an overarching template, actors must be connected through overlapping worldviews that are stabilized by different storylines.

PLURICENTRIC COORDINATION IN PRACTICE

There are many empirical examples of pluricentric coordination at the local, regional, and national levels (Sørensen et al. 2015; Harada & Jørgensen 2016; Jensen 2017; Klenk et al. 2021). In my own research on the governance of the green transition, I stumbled across an interesting case in Gentofte Municipality in Denmark. Here, the climate issue has previously been handled in a project-by-project manner, and mostly by the technical and environmental department. Hence, the idea behind the formation of a new intra-municipal climate network is to ensure cross-cutting knowledge-sharing, mainstreaming and coordination throughout the municipality around climate policy goals and the current efforts to achieve these goals. The internal mainstreaming of climate policy will in turn ensure that the municipality plays the role as the local climate leader in relation to the city's citizens, businesses, and civil society. The initiative regarding the formation of the new climate network stems from the municipal chief executive officer (CEO), who took cues from a collaborative process in and around a local task force involving elected councilors and local citizens. The appointed head of the climate network further developed the idea and received support and financing from the board of administrative directors in the municipality.

The participants in the internal climate network include administrative chiefs from three thematically organized municipal departments (social welfare, culture and leisure, and technical and environmental) and three cross-cutting administrative units (purchasing, communications, and human resources). Later, mid-level managers will also become involved and there are already regular dialogue meetings with administrative actors from outside the core group. There are no external stakeholders as the task of creating internal alignment is given top priority. The interdependence between different administrative silos in delivering climate goals is well understood, and there is general agreement about the politically endorsed strategic climate goals, although there is a great need to translate strategic goals into practice and, vice versa, to translate practical challenges into a language that can be meaningfully integrated with strategic reflections. Here, the key is to find creative ways of integrating climate policy issues into already existing tasks to avoid overburdening local agencies by urging them to invent new climate tasks.

The main driver of the pluricentric climate policy coordination is the intense media attention around climate policy, which has helped to create a broad consensus in the Municipal Council around the importance of the issue. In turn, this consensus has created a common understanding within the administration of having to create a shared implementation effort. However, the complexity of the municipal organization and the relatively high degree of organizational and political independence of each administrative silo render it difficult to create alignment, although there are clusters of actors with overlapping ideas and values.

The Paris Agreement and the ambitious climate goals of the Danish government provide a distant framing of the local climate policy efforts; otherwise, it is the aforementioned local taskforce involving local councilors and citizens that frames the collaborative processes in the climate network.

The core group, consisting of six administrative chiefs, the program manager, and a highly energetic development consultant, collectively leads the coordination efforts, with the rest of the organization becoming involved when relevant, but the program manager and development consultant are the lead actors and act as boundary spanners via-à-vis the rest of the organization. The network leaders spend most of their time facilitating meetings in the core group and dialogue meetings with different groups within the municipal organizations. The latter is a tool for conflict mediation and cultural transformation. Catalyzing innovation is also important, and two events stand out in this regard. One event is a dialogue meeting with the CEO of a private company, who explained how the company had integrated working with the Sustainable Development Goals into the daily practice of the company. Another event was a presentation by a well-known climate scientist and government advisor to the entire group of 1,300 municipal employees.

In terms of results, climate goals have become streamlined into communication in all policy areas. Beyond this, changes are hard to measure, but there is a shared sense that things are moving forward. There is a communication effort underway to communicate "small data" in terms of administrative success stories from everyday life. There is also an attempt to connect climate efforts to non-climate benefits (e.g., a better work environment resulting from climate-neutral solutions).

This illustrative case shows how formal institutions and political goals frame the networked interaction between manifold administrative agents that produce overlapping storylines that promote alignment and mutual adjustments to agency objectives and practices. Pluricentric coordination is revealed as a distributed practice in which boundary spanning is a central activity. At the same time, there seems to be no doubt that pluricentric coordination takes place in the shadow of hierarchy (Scharpf 1994), as political and administrative leaders are overseeing the coordination process and its results, and they are ready to step in and make corrections if necessary.

STUDYING PLURICENTRIC COORDINATION

After a long spell of unicentric coordination and a much briefer experiment with multicentric coordination, and partly inspired by new forms of joined-up government and coordination in partnerships, we have seen the emergence of new forms of pluricentric coordination offering a new approach to coordination based on the interplay of formal institutions, network structures and collective sense-making. The decentered pluricentric coordination process engages relevant and affected actors from the public and perhaps even the private sector in the multi-level negotiation of meaning aimed at fostering alignment and mutual adjustment vis-à-vis overlapping storylines. When it works best, it may help in striking a constructive balance between fixation and flexibility, control and autonomy, unity and diversity, and simplicity and complexity.

The diffusion and practical usage of pluricentric coordination throughout different policy sectors and levels of government is prompted by the limitations of hierarchical ex ante coordination based on imposition that fails to promote mutual learning and to build the ownership of processes and results. Pluricentric coordination may also be spurred by the limitations of market-related ex post coordination based on competition that makes it difficult to align actors and promote overall policy objectives. However, although pluricentric coordination provides a welcome alternative to state- and market-led coordination, the different forms of coordination will tend to co-exist, and pluricentric coordination will tend to be predicated on the exercise of political and administrative leadership by central government agencies, although these agencies may have lost their privileged status and governing in subtler and more indirect ways than previously.

Despite the growth of pluricentric coordination, there is still a dearth of studies focusing on how coordination can be achieved through distributed action in networks and partnerships. In the future, engaged scholarship based on interaction with public sector practitioners may provide much-needed knowledge that can inspire and guide multiple forms of pluricentric coordination.

One set of research questions deserving further attention relates to the form and functioning of pluricentric coordination. How are coordination networks organized and how do they facilitate the negotiation of meaning, consensus formation and mutual adjustment? What is the role of power differentials and hierarchy in pluricentric coordination? How are meaning formation, network structures and the role of formal institutions co-evolving over time?

Another set of questions revolves around the exercise of leadership in collaborative arenas aiming to enhance coordination. Who is initiating and framing processes of pluricentric coordination? What is the relation between external and internal leadership practices, and between executive leadership and leadership through boundary spanning? When and how is the shadow of hierarchy becoming more than a shadow?

A final set of questions concerns the drivers and barriers to pluricentric coordination and the conditions for success. What are the contextual, situational, institutional and political factors that support and drive pluricentric coordination? What are the factors that hamper collaboration and prevent mutual adjustment? How do we measure the results of pluricentric coordination? What will "best practice" pluricentric coordination look like?

REFERENCES

Andersson, K. P. & Ostrom, E. (2008). Analyzing Decentralized Resource Regimes from a Polycentric Perspective. *Policy Sciences, 41*(1), 71–93.
Armstrong, K. A. (2010). *Governing Social Inclusion: Europeanization through Policy Coordination*. Oxford: Oxford University Press.
Bogdanor, V. (Ed.) (2005). *Joined-Up Government*. Oxford: Oxford University Press.
Bolleyer, N. & Börzel, T. A. (2014). Balancing Integration and Flexibility in the European Union: Constitutional Dispositions and Dynamics of Coordination. *Comparative European Politics, 12*(4), 384–403.
Bouckaert, G., Peters, B. G. & Verhoest, K. (2016). *Coordination of Public Sector Organizations*. London: Palgrave Macmillan.
Calanni, J., Leach, W. D. & Weible, C. (2010). Explaining Coordination Networks in Collaborative Partnerships. *Western Political Science Association 2010 Annual Meeting Paper*.
Christensen, T. (2012). Post-NPM and Changing Public Governance. *Meiji Journal of Political Science and Economics, 1*(1), 1–11.

Hagen, M. & Kubicek, H. (2000). *One-Stop-Government in Europe: An Overview*. Bremen: University of Bremen.

Harada, Y. & Jørgensen, G. (2016). Area-Based Urban Regeneration Comparing Denmark and Japan. *Planning Practice & Research, 31*(4), 359–82.

Hartmann, T. & Geertman, S. (2022). Planning Theory. In Ansell, C. & Torfing, J. (Eds.), *Handbook on Theories of Governance*, 2nd edn (57–66). Northampton, MA: Edward Elgar Publishing.

Hudson, B. & Hardy, B. (2002). What Is a "Successful" Partnership and How Can It Be Measured? In Glendinning, C. (Ed.), *Partnerships, New Labour and the Governance of Welfare* (51–65). Bristol: Policy Press.

Innes, J. E. & Booher, D. E. (2010). *Planning with Complexity: An Introduction to Collaborative Rationality for Public Policy*. London: Routledge.

Jensen, K. R. (2017). *Leading Global Innovation: Facilitating Multicultural Collaboration and International Market Success*. Basingstoke: Palgrave Macmillan.

Jessop, B. (1998). The Rise of Governance and the Risks of Failure: The Case of Economic Development. *International Social Science Journal, 50*(155), 29–45.

Keast, R. & Brown, K. (2002). The Government Service Delivery Project: A Case Study of the Push and Pull of Central Government Coordination. *Public Management Review, 4*(4), 439–59.

Kersbergen, K. V. & Waarden, F. V. (2004). "Governance" as a Bridge between Disciplines: Cross-Disciplinary Inspiration Regarding Shifts in Governance and Problems of Governability, Accountability and Legitimacy. *European Journal of Political Research, 43*(2), 143–71.

Klenk, T., Cacace, M. & Ettelt, S. (2021). The Public Health Service in the Corona Crisis: Between Hierarchy, Loose Coupling and Pluricentric Coordination. *dms–der moderne staat–Zeitschrift für Public Policy, Recht und Management, 14*(2), 7–8.

Lewis, J. M., Baeza, J. I. & Alexander, D. (2008). Partnerships in Primary Care in Australia: Network Structure, Dynamics and Sustainability. *Social Science & Medicine, 67*(2), 280–91.

Lindblom, C. E. (1965). *The Intelligence of Democracy: Decision Making through Mutual Adjustment*. New York: The Free Press.

Ling, T. (2002). Delivering Joined-Up Government in the UK: Dimensions, Issues and Problems. *Public Administration, 80*(4), 615–42.

Lægreid, P., Randma-Liiv, T., Rykkja, L. H. & Sarapuu, K. (2014). Introduction: Emerging Coordination Practices in European Public Management. In Lægreid, P., Randma-Liiv, T., Rykkja, L. H. & Sarapuu, K. (Eds.), *Organizing for Coordination in the Public Sector* (1–17). London: Palgrave Macmillan.

Lowndes, V. & Skelcher, C. (1998). The Dynamics of Multi-Organizational Partnerships: An Analysis of Changing Modes of Governance. *Public Administration, 76*(2), 313–33.

March, J. G. & Olsen, J. P. (1989). *Rediscovering Institutions*. New York: The Free Press.

March, J. G. & Olsen, J. P. (1995). *Democratic Governance*. New York: The Free Press.

Metcalfe, L. (1994). International Policy Co-ordination and Public Management Reform. *International Review of Administrative Sciences, 60*(2), 271–90.

Mitchell, S. M. & Shortell, S. M. (2000). The Governance and Management of Effective Community Health Partnerships: A Typology for Research, Policy, and Practice. *The Milbank Quarterly, 78*(2), 241–89.

OECD (2001). *Local Partnerships for Better Governance*. Paris: OECD Publishing.

OECD (2009). *Breaking Out of Silos: Joining Up Policy Locally.* Paris: OECD Publishing.

Ostrom, E. (2005). Doing Institutional Analysis: Digging Deeper Than Markets and Hierarchies. In Ménard, C. & Shirley, M. M. (Eds.), *Handbook of New Institutional Economics* (819–48). Boston, MA: Springer.

Ostrom, E. (2010). Beyond Markets and States: Polycentric Governance of Complex Economic Systems. *American Economic Review, 100*(3), 641–72.

Ostrom, E. & Parks, R. B. (1999). Neither Gargantua nor the Land of Lilliputs: Conjectures on Mixed Systems of Metropolitan Organization. In McGinnis, M. D. (Ed.), *Polycentricity and Local Public Economies: Readings from the Workshop in Political Theory and Policy Analysis* (284–305). Ann Arbor, MI: University of Michigan Press.

Ostrom, E. & Whitaker, G. (1973). Does Local Community Control of Police Make a Difference? Some Preliminary Findings. *American Journal of Political Science, 17*(1), 48–76.

Ostrom, E., Schroeder, L. & Wynne, S. (1993). Analyzing the Performance of Alternative Institutional Arrangements for Sustaining Rural Infrastructure in Developing Countries. *Journal of Public Administration Research and Theory, 3*(1), 11–45.

Ostrom, V., Tiebout, C. M. & Warren, R. (1961). The Organization of Government in Metropolitan Areas: A Theoretical Inquiry. *American Political Science Review, 55*(4), 831–42.

Pedersen, A. R., Sehested, K. & Sørensen, E. (2011). Emerging Theoretical Understandings of Pluricentric Coordination in Public Governance. *American Review of Public Administration, 41*(4), 375–94.

Peters, B. G. (2018). The Challenge of Policy Coordination. *Policy Design and Practice, 1*(1), 1–11.

Peters, B. G. & Savoie, D. J. (1996). Managing Incoherence: The Coordination and Empowerment Conundrum. *Public Administration Review, 56*(3), 281–90.

Pollitt, C. (2003). Joined-Up Government: A Survey. *Political Studies Review, 1*(1), 34–49.

Salamon, L. M. (2021). Market Failure. In Ott, J. S. & Dicke, L. A. (Eds.), *The Nature of the Nonprofit Sector*, 4th edn (228–9). New York: Routledge.

Scharpf, F. W. (1994). Games Real Actors Could Play: Positive and Negative Coordination in Embedded Negotiations. *Journal of Theoretical Politics, 6*(1), 27–53.

Six, P. (2004). Joined-Up Government in the Western World in Comparative Perspective: A Preliminary Literature Review and Exploration. *Journal of Public Administration Research and Theory*, 14(1), 103–38.

Sørensen, E., Lidström, A. & Hanssen, G. S. (2015). Conditions for Political Leadership in Pluricentric Scandinavian Regions. *Scandinavian Journal of Public Administration, 19*(4), 111–30.

Stiglitz, J. E. (2008). Government Failure vs. Market Failure: Principles of Regulation. In Balleisen, E. J. & Moss, D. A. (Eds.), *Government and Market: Towards a New Theory of Regulation* (13–51). Cambridge: Cambridge University Press.

Walker, G. & Weber, D. (1984). A Transaction Cost Approach to Make-or-Buy Decisions. *Administrative Science Quarterly, 29*(3), 373–91.

Warren, K. F. (1973). Review of Political Bureaucracy, by L. C. Mainzer. *Administrative Science Quarterly, 18*(3), 424–6.

8. From national- to multi-level governance

In the postwar era, nation-states were largely in control of the regulation of social and economic policies seeking to regulate the relatively closed national economies and to provide citizen welfare. Giving rise to uneven patterns, successive waves of devolution of political and administrative tasks to local and regional authorities, and the rise of supranational, international, and global organizations, undermined the centralized powers of the nation-state, which were displaced downwards and upwards. In tandem with this development, the rise of policy and governance networks displaced state power outwards to non-majoritarian decision-making arenas populated by private stakeholders. This combined development resulted in a three-way hollowing out of the state (Jessop 2002). In the emerging system of multi-level governance, executive and regulatory power is distributed across levels, sectors, and policy actors, the effect being that the participating actors tend to become both policy-takers and policymakers.

In the emerging multi-level governance system, the mutual adjustment of goals, tools and actions across levels, sectors and actors becomes highly important. Communication between the different levels is sometimes difficult, however, as the discussion partners at other levels appear to be elusive and difficult to engage in joint conversations. Moreover, the surge of nationalism tends to drive a wedge between the national and transnational forms of governance. A re-articulation of the Catholic subsidiarity principle stipulating that public governance tasks should be carried out at the lowest possible level may help to solve this problem in the future by recognizing the current trend toward localism, regionalism, and nationalism and seeking to delimit the higher-level public authorities, such as the European Union (EU). However, strengthening local-, regional, and national-level governance is no easy task in turbulent times in which one crisis after another calls for supranational and international policy initiatives. Indeed, we seem to have reached an impasse, where centrifugal powers threaten to pull the multi-level governance system in different directions. Metropolitan areas increasingly act like small states, while the EU and federal governments insist on the precedence of macro-level policymaking and regulation. The centrifugal local, regional, national, and supranational

forces were the very reason why the multi-level governance system was established in the first place, but they are now threatening its very functioning.

A possible strategy for ending this unfortunate tug of war is for researchers and policymakers to focus less on the multiple levels and distribution of
authority between these levels and more on the tangled connections linking
them. This new, systemic focus may become institutionalized in different
ways. One would be to enhance the efforts to bring actors from different levels
together in cross-cutting governance networks, while another way is for the
local and regional levels of governance to better exploit their embeddedness
in national and supranational governance; for example, realizing that the
different levels of governance are all present and a part of localized territorial
governance. The two forms of institutionalized connectivity are interlinked.
To illustrate: cities have emerged as potent vehicles for the promotion of green
transformations, but their actions are prompted and conditioned by national
and supranational governance and thus rely on constant efforts to align actors
across levels through formal or informal governance networks. The virtual
and/or real presence of the actors from different levels in local territorial
efforts to build infrastructures for sustainable transport and energy production
facilitates coordination and joint problem-solving.

To shed light on these attempts to rethink multi-level governance, this
chapter begins by accounting for the demise of the nation-state and the rise of
multi-level governance. It then discusses the limits and barriers to multi-level
governance, and next turns to consider how multi-level governance networks
can help to connect different governance levels and how the local level of territorial governance may gain importance through its recognition and exploitation of its multi-level embeddedness. The chapter also considers a more
flexible (and thus robust) approach to multi-level governance that relies on
a continuous up- and down-scaling of governance, depending on the problem
at hand. The conclusion sets out an agenda for further research.

THE DEMISE OF THE NATION-STATE AND THE RISE OF MULTI-LEVEL GOVERNANCE

Earlier modes of statehood, including city-states, empires, the medieval state
system, absolutism, and modern imperial-colonial blocs, gradually gave way
to the formation of nation-states based on the territorialization of political
power and the construction of a system of sovereign states with fixed borders.
The Westphalian Peace Treaty was the formal expression of the rise of the
nation-state and triggered efforts to form a protective national army, bind
together the national territory through a network of railroads, create a unifying
national identity and improve the welfare of the population. In northwestern
Europe, North America, Australia, and New Zealand, the postwar era saw the

expansion of economic and social policies. The national political and administrative system took control over economic policies and deployed different versions of Keynesian economics to steer free of economic crisis and secure a non-inflationary full employment. The principal tool was the regulation of public consumption and investment. Since periodic unemployment and socio-economic hardship proved impossible to eradicate by means of economic policies and high economic growth rates alone, social welfare policies were expanded based on different mixes of charity, social insurance, and tax-financed welfare programs. Central government actors were in charge of developing and guiding Keynesian economic policies and social welfare policies that were pursued within a historically specific strategic framework provided by the relatively closed national economy and territorially demarcated nation-state. Local and regional states were merely considered as vehicles for the implementation of government policies and were not expected to make any independent contribution to public governance. Except for participation in corporatist negotiations, private market actors played a limited role in public governance, although liberal welfare states left a considerable role for private welfare providers. Hence, the state was seen as the chief supplement and corrective to the private market forces in a mixed economy. Civil society organizations also had limited impact on public governance beyond their complementary charity work. In sum, the Keynesian welfare state, which supported and regulated the life of a relatively well-integrated citizenry, was both essentially national and state-centered (for a fuller account of this development, see Jessop 2013).

The heyday of the Keynesian welfare national state ended in the 1970s with the arrival of the deep economic stagflation crises and the erosion of the Fordist system of mass production and mass consumption, which was responsible for the high economic growth rates in the postwar era. State finances came under pressure, and the nation-states suddenly appeared unable to solve pressing socio-economic problems. The world was also being transformed by new technologies, the globalization of the capitalist economy, new lines of social and political conflict, the empowerment of citizens through the educational and anti-authoritarian revolutions, and new and emerging threats, such as environmental problems, climate change, terrorism, and the security vacuum emerging in the wake of the collapse of the Soviet Union.

In this new and rapidly changing world, the old nation-state appeared to be losing steam. A growing number of academic and political commentators thought that it had "become too small to solve the world's big problems and too big to solve its little ones" (Jessop 2013: 11). At the same time, a growing number of social and political actors beyond the usual suspects of big business and peak labor-market organizations sought to influence policy decision and contribute to public governance by deploying their own resources. In response to these developments, the architecture of public governance started to change. International and supranational governance institutions were strengthened (Sweet & Sandholtz 1998; Zürn 2004), and national, political, and administrative power was devolved to regional and local authorities (Rodríguez-Pose & Gill 2003). Simultaneously, public and private actors formed networks and partnerships aiming to solve pressing societal problems (Kickert et al. 1997).

Jessop (2013) captures the gradual transformation of public governance with his notion of the three-way hollowing out of the state that designates a process through which national governmental powers are being transferred *upwards* to supranational, international, or even global governance institutions, *downwards* to regional and local states, and *outwards* to networks, partnerships, and alliances engaging public and private actors aiming to deal with a variety of governance problems and having a variable geographical basis. The first two processes lead to a de-nationalization of statehood as the link between national sovereignty, and the performance of key state functions is severed and a new set of organizations is undertaking typical state functions, such as policy formulation and regulatory governance based on a delegated, pooled, and negotiated sovereign. Similarly, the last process leads to the de-statification of politics and public governance as the state loses its near-monopoly on public governance through the displacement of power to governance networks, public–private partnerships, regional strategic alliances, cross-border regions, and global compacts.

While the nation-state has undoubtedly lost some of its previous powers and prerogatives, the de-nationalization of statehood and de-statification of politics and governance does not necessarily create a zero-sum game in which the nation-state loses power every time actors at other levels or in other sectors become more powerful (Jessop 2013). Nation-states may play a new and crucial role in distributing decision-making power between different levels, metagoverning governance processes taking place at other levels and involving other sectors and combining and integrating governance efforts between multiple levels and scales. Indeed, nation-states remain the ultimate arbiters of the allocation of decision rights within the new system of multi-level governance (Schakel et al. 2015). Hence, the scope of the exercise of power carried out by nation-states is widening while their political and regulatory power shrinks.

The result of the three-way hollowing out of the nation-state is the creation of a complex system of multi-level governance (Hooghe & Marks 2001). In contrast to what we might refer to as a system of multi-level govern*ment*, this particular construct involves more than merely a formal delegation of power to intergovernmental arenas and local and regional governments. Hence, multi-level governance is characterized by relatively self-organized interactions between interdependent public and private actors at different levels and scales but also *across* these levels and scales (Bache & Flinders 2004; Tortola

2017). The interactions may be structured by either formal and constitutional rules or more flexible and adaptable ad hoc designs (Hooghe & Marks 2004).

While a huge literature on multi-level governance now exists, a key point of ambiguity remains concerning the empirical referent of the concept. Hence, although the EU is clearly seen as the vanguard of the transformations described above, the multi-level governance concept also seems to capture similar transformations in other parts of the world, and perhaps even the functioning of federal political systems (Tortola 2017). Decentralization is a strong trend in most parts of the world, the number of regional economic (and political) structures is rapidly increasing and many international organizations have become more supranational by introducing decision-making based on super-majorities (Schakel et al. 2015).

Whereas functionalist theories explain the rise of multi-level governance with reference to the benefits accruing from governance beyond the nation-state and across multiple levels and scales, and sometimes also with reference to its foundation in norms and values of a particular community, post-functionalist theories perceive multi-level governance as a political construction that simultaneously shapes the identity of social communities and the rules for inter-scalar governance interaction. The latter perspective is particularly helpful as it allows us to understand the tension inherent to multi-level governance between the institutionalization of shared rules for coordination among multiple actors at different levels and scales, who help us to create public value and the limits on self-rule imposed on participating groups and actors (Hooghe & Marks 2020).

LIMITS TO MULTI-LEVEL GOVERNANCE IN THE EU

Although the changing treaty base seems to have strengthened the supranational decision-making in the European Council, Commission, and Court of Justice, conflict continues between the supranationalism within the Commission and the Court of Justice and the intergovernmentalism in the Council. In fact, the literature mentions a "new intergovernmentalism" based on the introduction of new policy areas that are not subject to supranational decision-making as well as on a new legislative activism in the EU member states (Bickerton et al. 2015). Some EU scholars even suggest that a new parliamentarism is on the rise (Schmidt 2016). The conflicts at the apex of the EU and the complicated procedures for balancing the influence of its core institutions may hamper the effectiveness of policymaking and crisis management, as we saw with the "corona-nationalism" toward the end of the COVID-19 crisis (Bouckaert et al. 2020).

The multi-level EU governance system combines relatively fixed, all-purpose constitutional structures that create a particular jurisdictional distribution of powers between levels that are neatly nested within each other with more flexible special-purpose policy processes with a variable and polycentric geometry. While the two types of multi-level governance may complement each other (Hooghe & Marks 2004), they may also clash, undermine each other, and create ambiguities that reduce governance effectiveness.

Multi-level policy formation will also tend to be hampered by the problems of ensuring constructive communication and dialogue between a plethora of public and private actors located at different levels. Identifying relevant actors at other levels of governance and engaging them in a discussion about societal problems and possible solutions is not always easy, and it is notoriously difficult to ensure that information flows unhindered up and down the multi-level governance system and that relevant decision-makers receive the policy feedback they need to make wise decisions. To illustrate, local governments are invited to discuss local experiences with climate policy at the European level, but the conclusions emerging from discussions in Europe-wide committees rarely reach those who make the new policy decisions. A related problem is the failure to ensure that the involvement of stakeholders from the economy and civil society lead to effective participation in European governance. The EU struggles to make itself relevant to citizens and include the voices of local people in governance processes, although the European Citizen Initiative has managed to broaden the EU policy agenda based on citizen participation (Greenwood 2019).

Moreover, if long implementation chains with many veto points are a problem for the implementation of public policy in a national context (Pressman & Wildavsky 1973), the problem is even bigger in the context of multi-level EU governance. Long, vertical implementation chains tend to create problems with execution and compliance, and the political diversity of the EU member states (and the political conflicts between them) may exacerbate the problem. Although there does not seem to be an increase in non-compliance when controlling for the increasing number of policies and changing enforcement strategies (Börzel 2001; Gogokhia 2018; Börzel & Buzogány 2019), a number of infringement cases still exist, concentrated in a handful of countries.

Speaking of implementation, there is a considerable social, economic, and political diversity at the local level across the EU member states, meaning that highly standardized solutions are of little use. There is no one size that fits all localities, meaning that policy designs must be flexible and implementation processes adaptive (Glachant 2001). While flexibility and adaptability are a must in EU policy formulation and implementation, this raises the problem of how to avoid goal displacement in local implementation processes (Blom-Hansen 2005).

When policies are eventually implemented at different levels of the multi-level EU system, legitimacy problems may arise. When EU policies hit their mark and produce desirable results, they may create output legitimacy, but the lack of opportunity for citizens to inform and influence decisions and the opaque and convoluted EU decision-making procedures tend to result in low input and throughput legitimacy. Low throughput legitimacy is a particularly serious problem as it tends to raise questions regarding input and output legitimacy (Schmidt 2013). A related problem is the apparent lack of democratic legitimacy resulting from the lack of transparency, the uncoupling of EU governance from representative institutions, the selective participation bias in the more or less secluded EU committees and the "multi-levelness" itself that triggers a complex blame avoidance game when things go wrong (Papadopoulos 2010).

While many of the above problems are standard in political-administrative systems, two of them seem to be more fundamental and might therefore threaten the cohesion of the multi-level EU governance system. The first problem is the clear and visible clashes between the politically constructed ideas and values of the EU and those of particular member states. The EU aims to propagate ideas and values about democracy, equal rights, the rule of law, and legal fairness. As we have seen, however, Poland and Hungary have repeatedly breached these fundamental ideas and values, thereby raising doubts about their continued EU membership. The second problem is even more serious, as conflicting views seem to exist about the distribution of power between the top and bottom of the multi-level EU governance system. On the one hand, Europe is seeing a surging localism, regionalism, and nationalism: local and regional governments want more autonomy, governance discretion, and political influence; a growing number of national governments are protesting the ever-increasing EU budgets; and populist movements are criticizing the technocratic governance coming from Brussels (Katz & Nowak 2018; Schakel 2020; Reiser & Hebenstreit 2020; Huddy et al. 2021). On the other hand, the central EU decision-makers are calling for stronger EU governance in crisis-prone policy areas, such as health, migration, financial regulation, and climate change mitigation, and stronger EU governance often means more top-down governance and security through directive- and standard-setting. The top and bottom levels of the multi-level governance system are pulling in different directions, putting national governments in the ambiguous position of simultaneously being advocates for stronger EU-level governance and for national policy choices made by sub-national regional and local governments.

The subsidiarity principle may help to solve this intra-EU tug of war. This principle, which is enshrined in the Treaty of the European Union, says that the EU should not take action (except in the areas falling within its exclusive competence) unless its action proves to be more effective than action taken at the national, regional, or local level. A higher level of governance must therefore be able to demonstrate the necessity of its actions in the areas where competences are shared to justify these actions. Ideally, the subsidiarity principle should ensure that decisions are taken as closely as possible to the citizens, but it comes with several limitations. First, the local and sub-national regional levels are not even mentioned as part of the subsidiarity principle, which merely deals with the relation between the EU and its member states. This reflects how it is up to the member states to allocate domestic governance tasks between different levels of governance. Second, national parliaments have had limited success using the Early Warning Mechanism (EWM) to block unwanted legislation initiated by the Commission, thus causing it to be rejected, withdrawn, or permanently deferred. The national parliaments have had some success in using the EWM to engage in policy dialogue with EU institutions, but they have only drawn the yellow card three times between 2009 and 2017 and been overruled twice (Cooper 2019). Finally, yet most importantly, the subsidiarity principle mainly creates a battleground for competing claims about where and how different problems and challenges should be solved. Hence, there is no legal or rational basis for adjudication; it is reduced to a political power game in which different levels tend to insist that they should be the primary level of regulation and problem-solving. Hence, the tug of war goes on within the subsidiarity principle framework.

BRIDGING THE DIVIDES THROUGH THE FORMATION OF MULTI-LEVEL GOVERNANCE NETWORKS

A key idea behind the political development of the multi-level EU governance system is to fully exploit the competences and capacities of each level, sector, and actor by flexibly distributing tasks along the vertical and horizontal axes in ways that reflect the nature of the problem or challenge at hand and the context in which it emerges and must be solved. The tug of war between the different levels may prevent the development of anything near an optimal allocation of tasks because each of the involved actors are inclined to fight for their particular domain and maximize their interest in taking more or less governing responsibility without paying much attention to input from actors at other levels or from other sectors.

Competition, struggles, and conflicts in complex governance systems are renowned for being overcome by the promotion of collaboration that allows the actors to develop common understandings, create synergies, and solve common problems through networking. A large body of literature sings the praises of the role of governance networks in turning political antagonisms into a constructive management of differences (Kickert, Klijn & Koppenjan 1997;

Sørensen & Torfing 2007; Klijn & Koppenjan 2015). Moreover, there seems to be general agreement that the EU is a networked polity (Kohler-Koch 1999; Ansell 2000). Fragmented supranational institutions, state agencies, and societal associations are linked through formal and informal networks characterized by strong lateral communication and coordination that crosses functional boundaries within and between organizations. Governance networks seem to be ubiquitous in the EU. They are found in and around the influential EU committees, where directives are presented and negotiated. They are formed as part of the structural and social development programs, where goals are determined and resources allocated through networked negotiations and projects are funded on the basis of the formation of local and regional partnerships. Finally, governance networks are an integral part of the Open Method of Coordination, where relevant and affected actors are invited to develop voluntary policy standards and monitor national, regional, and local compliance.

The network mode of governance is ubiquitous, but most of the governance networks within the multi-level EU governance systems are formed at a particular level of governance, and the participants come from that particular level as well, or perhaps from two different levels at most (e.g., from the national and supranational levels). While the formation of national/supranational networks reflects the need to align member states with each other as well as with the core EU institutions, the networks formed at the local, regional, and national levels reflect the need to create some degree of consensus around particular policy and governance initiatives through the involvement of relevant and affected actors (Marcussen & Torfing 2007). A case in point is the networked governance of the active employment policy in Europe, where governance networks are formed at the local, regional, national, and supranational levels. These networks play different roles: the supranational networks define goals and standards and secure a broad ownership to them among the key European players; the national networks align the EU goals with national context and policy priorities and write national assessment reports to the EU; the regional networks coordinate and monitor the local efforts to promote active employment policies; and the local networks coordinate the efforts of public and private actors.

The horizontal, single-level governance networks play a crucial role in policy delivery at their particular level, not least because they involve relevant and affected actors in the formulation, coordination, and evaluation of policy action. However, there is a strong need for vertical multi-level governance networks involving actors from the local, regional, national, *and* sub-national levels. Good examples of such networks exist, such as in relation to the structural and social funds in the EU (Heinelt et al. 2003) and in the efforts to curb the climate crisis (Betsill & Bulkeley 2006), but more of this type of network is required that can help to: (1) define problems and challenges and develop joint solutions based on experiences and ideas of highly distributed actors; (2) identify, mobilize, and flexibly deploy resources and capacities of actors from different levels and sectors; (3) facilitate pluricentric coordination between the involved actors; and (4) enhance upward and downward accountability by raising questions about results, institutional support, and resource allocation.

The formation of governance networks spanning several levels of governance is troublesome, since identifying and attracting knowledgeable and well-motivated actors from all levels of governance can be quite difficult, not to mention creating sustained, intense communication between them. However, three favorable conditions may help to spur the formation of multi-level governance networks. First, low-level actors want to influence higher-level actors, who are seen to be more powerful and capable of influencing the conditions for governance at the lower levels. Second, high-level actors need input in terms of information, knowledge, and credible assessment from lower-level actors to design effective policy and governance solutions. Finally, the COVID-19 pandemic has taught us to use online meetings as a tool to bring together dispersed actors and overcome geographical distance in a time-efficient manner.

There has been some skepticism regarding the effectiveness of multi-level governance networks. It has been pointed out that there is a considerable risk of the highly distributed actors becoming "veto players" who block consensus formation or spur the formation of unpopular compromise (Scharpf 1988). However, this pessimistic approach has since been qualified. In the EU, policy stalemate in multi-level governance networks can be prevented through "subterfuge" and "escape routes" (Héritier 1999) based on cooperation between the most relevant actors. Still, interactive governance structures have been argued to be less suitable for rapid adjustment in the face of crisis and societal turbulence than traditional government structures (Papadopoulos 2005). This problem is of little importance, however, since this is about the contribution of multi-level networks to effective routine governance based on information gathering, continuous evaluation, planning, and coordination.

Vertical multi-level governance networks are driven by interdependencies, the search for valuable resources and commonality in terms of interest and objectives, and egalitarian policy interaction between actors coming from different levels of governance (Torfing et al. 2012). In contrast, vertical multi-level government tends to take the form of a series of principal–agent relations based on delegation and control, which are used to secure the implementation of policies developed at the apex. The sharp contrast between multi-level governance networks and multi-level government should not lead us to overlook the fact that governments at different levels may play a crucial role in the performance of multi-level metagovernance (Jessop 2004). While the European Council will exercise political metagovernance, the Commission will exercise a more administrative and technocratic metagovernance in relation to multi-level governance networks. Their combined efforts will include agenda-setting, storytelling, network design, conflict mediation, resource allocation, and so forth. Similarly, both democratically elected governments and their administrative aides at the national, regional, and local levels will be involved in orchestrating multi-level network governance by identifying, motivating and supporting participants, providing political input to multi-scalar negotiations, reforming public policies, and administrative procedures to fit new Europe-wide policies, and so on.

The metagovernance of multi-level governance networks is important to maintain the primacy of politics and to ensure that the interactive policy processes that cut across levels and sectors are anchored in accountable governments. But the problem remains: who is to blame if the metagovernance of multi-level governance networks fails and the Europe-wide network delivers poor results? To avoid metagovernance failure, coordination between the metagoverning agencies at multiple levels is crucial. A joint forum for strategic reflection and proactive metagovernance will often be necessary and should function and operate parallel to the multi-level governance network.

REDISCOVERING THE LOCAL IN ITS MULTI-LEVEL EMBEDDEDNESS

Multi-level governance networks are essential for establishing collaborative connections between different agencies and sectors all the way up and down the multi-level EU governance system. In the absence of such connections, the wholeness of the multi-level governance system disappears, and it risks degenerating into a multi-level government system in which higher-level principals delegate tasks to lower-level agents and control their performance, thus triggering resistance, counterstrategies and conflicts.

There is another way to avoid the tug of war between the top and bottom of multi-level governance systems: examining how the different levels are implicated in producing local territorial governance. Cities and provincial regions are becoming increasingly active and self-confident governance actors who are setting their own agenda, developing their own policy strategies, and coming up with their own tailor-made responses to key societal problems and challenges. In so doing, they draw on regional, national, and supranational resources, tools, guidelines and frameworks. This "local turn" in multi-level governance can help us to move beyond the zero-sum game between the various levels and appreciate the interlacing and mutual support for governance advanced by multiple levels (Zapata-Barrero et al. 2017). Unlike the supranational and intergovernmental level of governance, the local and sub-national regional levels provide an arena where the governance efforts of all levels in the multi-level governance system tend to be present and interact with each other. The local and regional co-existence of multi-level governance efforts is not merely a result of non-exclusive jurisdictions, meaning that several levels aim to govern the same territorial space, but also a result of the political and institutional embeddedness of local and sub-national regional governance in governance structures provided by the national and supranational levels.

EU immigration policy provides examples of how both local- and regional-level governance draw upon and combine a range of different multi-level governance efforts. Myrberg (2017) shows how local and national governance intersect in Danish and Swedish municipalities, also revealing how not all levels of governance are contributing to the production of local governance outcomes in the field of immigration policy. Campomori and Caponio (2017) show how multi-level governance efforts shape immigration policy at the regional level in Italy, and they identify a range of contextual, organizational, and political factors shaping the articulation of the different governance efforts.

Another policy area in which the local turn in multi-level governance is particularly clear is climate policy. Here, the goals set by the Paris Agreement and the targets and policy issues by national governments frame local and regional climate change mitigation actions involving a broad range of public and private actors (Sørensen & Torfing 2020; Hofstad et al. 2021). A study of the implementation of climate protection policies in Newcastle upon Tyne and Cambridgeshire finds that local sustainability planning efforts are shaped by forms of governance that stretch across geographical scales and beyond the boundary of the urban spaces (Bulkeley & Betsill 2005). The study offers an alternative approach to the analysis of sustainable cities, which begins to blur the idea of a nested multi-level governance system by meshing the global and the local in the presence of the nation-state. The UN Local Agenda 21 has spurred local climate action that is drawing on national planning policy guidance.

Another study of climate change mitigation by Corfee-Morlot et al. (2009) argues that the concentration of the populations, productive activities, and infrastructures in cities creates large opportunities for urban climate governance, but it also emphasizes how a multi-level approach helps to avoid policy gaps and promote policy learning. The interlacing of local, regional, national, and global climate policy initiatives facilitates bottom-up policy formulation and top-down capacity-building through the design of enabling frameworks that empower local and regional actors. Hence, the local arena for multi-level governance may produce much-needed synergies.

The simultaneity of multi-level governance efforts at the local, sub-national, and regional levels gives rise to good synergies, but we should not blind ourselves to the political conflicts and struggles that may arise when government actors from different levels and with different political leanings come together with private actors with different interests to produce seamless governance. Myrberg (2017) shows how local governments contest national government policies in the field of immigration policy, and Bulkeley and Betsill (2005) draw on a multi-level governance framework to describe how political struggles erupt in local climate planning.

THE IMPORTANCE OF SCALING IN MULTI-LEVEL GOVERNANCE

Not all governance in Europe will necessarily involve all levels of governance in a joint effort to solve pressing problems and challenges through cross-cutting networks or a local interlacing of interventions. Much depends on the policy problem or policy ambition. Some policy areas (e.g., immigration, recycling, climate change) require action close to the citizens and local stakeholders, while other areas (employment, health regulation, infrastructure, protection of workers' rights) call for action at many different levels. Other areas, such as patent rights regulation, rules for service contraction and fisheries, are more top-heavy. The nature of the policy problem or policy goals plays a key role in determining which levels, sectors, and actors are mobilized within a multi-level governance system, but things might change over time because of internal dynamics in the governance process; what might begin as a local and regional effort to increase the number of chargers for electric cars may end up being politicized and involve actors at the national as well as supranational levels. And conversely, a policy strategy developed through interaction between the Commission and EU member states may end up trickling down to the local and regional levels when it comes to implementation. Hence, policy efforts are not statically located at a given set of levels and involving a particular set of actors from particular sectors; rather, they are subject to scaling, defined as the dynamic processes through which collaborative forms of governance move from one scale to another. The scaling of collaborative governance upwards, downwards, and outwards is crucial, since the failure of scaling can become a major source of policy failure (Ansell & Torfing 2018).

Scaling is a multidimensional concept referring to the *membership* of a collaborative governance arena that may be limited or wide; the *level* at which the members interact that may be local, regional, nation, supranational, or global; and the *strategic horizon* of the collaborative governance processes. Each of these scaling dimensions can be combined with temporal, geographical, and functional dimensions to produce a nuanced framework for analyzing the scaling of governance networks (Ansell & Torfing 2018: 5). The general expectation is that the impact of collaborative governance will increase when the scale is enhanced, but also that the complexity and challenges encountered will grow and increase the demand for multi-level metagovernance.

The reasons for scaling collaborative governance up or down vary across the different scaling dimensions (Ansell & Torfing 2018: 10). Scaling up membership can be motivated by the need to mobilize further resources, competences, and forms of expertise, maintain wider support over a longer period of time or diffuse governance efforts across geographical areas, whereas reasons for scaling down membership can include an interest in bringing together dedicated actors around a particular project, attempts to avoid overburdening members or the need to focus on a particular locality. Scaling up the level of governance can be motivated by a need for greater attention and support from higher-level authorities, an interest in speeding up a project and extending operations or enhancing policy learning and transforming central laws and directives, whereas scaling down the level of governance can be motivated by the need to implement local solutions, mobilize local resources, or focus resources on a few localities. Finally, scaling up the strategic horizon may be prompted by demands to solve trans-border problems, a need for long-term planning or the pursuit of economies of scale, whereas scaling down the strategic horizon can be motivated by a need to deal with localized problems, provide just-in-time services, engage in customization, or enhance innovation through local experimentation.

In terms of the empirical analysis of scaling, Farr-Wharton and Keast (2018) have explored how local networks of Australian workers in creative industries, who are often subject to precarious labor conditions and risk exploitation, have scaled up their network activities to obtain access to regional, national, and international resources to improve their conditions. The opposite movement is analyzed by Ansell (2018), who has studied how global health networks seek to eradicate major global diseases by stimulating collaboration among United Nations agencies, donor organizations, and the global public health community while simultaneously scaling down to national and local levels of governance to deliver health solutions robustly to target groups.

Scaling helps us to appreciate the dynamic changes in the size and endurance of governance networks and their extension to different levels, sectors, and actors. Multi-level governance networks may shrink or expand over time, and the number of levels supporting and conditioning local and regional governance efforts may also vary. The variations are likely to affect the ability of multi-level governance networks and the local interlacing of multi-level governance efforts to reduce conflict and competition between the different scales in multi-level governance systems.

FURTHER RESEARCH IN THE FIELD OF MULTI-LEVEL GOVERNANCE

Multi-level governance has existed in limited forms for many decades and is by no means a new phenomenon. For example, local and regional authorities have collaborated in the field of planning, and nation-states have collaborated with supra- and international organizations to establish trade regimes. Nevertheless, the recent expansion of the EU has created a prime example of multi-level governance combining formal and informal institutions and processes. The multi-level EU governance system works well in many respects and has managed to overcome problems and setbacks while rapidly including new member states. However, the multi-level system risks being torn apart by the conflict between the ever-strengthening localism, regionalism, and nationalism and the self-accelerating strengthening of supranational powers fueled by the need to act collectively and in unison in an increasingly turbulent world.

This chapter has "discovered" and discussed two ways of easing the tension between the top and bottom of the multi-level EU governance system: (1) the formation and strengthening of multi-level governance networks linking the different levels in joint discussions through which innovative solutions with a common ownership may emerge; and (2) the local turn in multi-level governance, which urges us to focus on and exploit the co-presence of governance efforts from multiple levels of governance at the local level, where public services are delivered and social and economic actors are regulated.

As we have seen above, new and interesting research has highlighted the importance of these two institutional governance designs, but more research is needed to understand their condition of emergence, the drivers and barriers affecting their functioning, and, ultimately, their impact on the conflicts and tension in the multi-level EU governance system. Empirical studies of the Europe-wide attempts to cope with the COVID-19 pandemic in a robust and efficient manner seem to provide an obvious case for learning more about how tensions in multi-level governance can be ameliorated. Early in the pandemic, we saw several instances of corona-nationalism and regional and local exceptionalism; at the same time, the EU sought to launch a unified, top-down strategy for fighting the pandemic and dealing with its consequences. Gradually, the different governance levels began working together and good results were produced. However, it would be interesting to study multi-level governance from a local perspective to see how the local, regional, national, and supranational governance efforts came together and supported each other—possibly clashing—and also how the different levels of governance communicated to spur policy learning and compliance through the formation of multi-level governance networks.

REFERENCES

Ansell, C. (2000). The Networked Polity: Regional Development in Western Europe. *Governance*, *13*(2), 279–91.

Ansell, C. (2018). When Collaborative Governance Scales Up: Lessons from Global Public Health about Compound Collaboration. In Ansell, C. & Torfing, J. (Eds.), *How Does Collaborative Governance Scale?* (95–116). Bristol: Policy Press.

Ansell, C. & Torfing, J. (Eds.) (2018). *How Does Collaborative Governance Scale?* Bristol: Policy Press.

Bache, I. & Flinders, M. (Eds.) (2004). *Multi-Level Governance*. Oxford: Oxford University Press.

Betsill, M. M. & Bulkeley, H. (2006). Cities and the Multilevel Governance of Global Climate Change. *Global Governance*, *12*, 141–59.

Bickerton, C. J., Hodson, D. & Puetter, U. (Eds.) (2015). *The New Intergovernmentalism: States and Supranational Actors in the Post-Maastricht Era*. Oxford: Oxford University Press.

Blom-Hansen, J. (2005). Principals, Agents, and the Implementation of EU Cohesion Policy. *Journal of European Public Policy*, *12*(4), 624–48.

Börzel, T. A. (2001). Non-Compliance in the European Union: Pathology or Statistical Artefact? *Journal of European Public Policy*, *8*(5), 803–24.

Börzel, T. A. & Buzogány, A. (2019). Compliance with EU Environmental Law: The Iceberg Is Melting. *Environmental Politics*, *28*(2), 315–41.

Bouckaert, G., Galli, D., Kuhlmann, S., Reiter, R. & Van Hecke, S. (2020). European Coronationalism? A Hot Spot Governing a Pandemic Crisis. *Public Administration Review*, *80*(5), 765–73.

Bulkeley, H. & Betsill, M. (2005). Rethinking Sustainable Cities: Multilevel Governance and the Urban Politics of Climate Change. *Environmental Politics*, *14*(1), 42–63.

Campomori, F. & Caponio, T. (2017). Immigrant Integration Policymaking in Italy: Regional Policies in a Multi-Level Governance Perspective. *Revue Internationale des Sciences Administratives*, *83*(2), 309–27.

Cooper, I. (2019). National Parliaments in the Democratic Politics of the EU: The Subsidiarity Early Warning Mechanism, 2009–2017. *Comparative European Politics*, *17*(6), 919–39.

Corfee-Morlot, J., Kamal-Chaoui, L., Donovan, M. G., Cochran, I., Robert, A. & Teasdale, P. (2009). Cities, Climate Change and Multilevel Governance. OECD Environmental Working Papers No. 14. Paris: OECD Publishing.

Farr-Wharton, B. & Keast, R. L. (2018). Scaling Up Networks for Starving Artists. In Ansell, C. & Torfing, J. (Eds.), *How Does Collaborative Governance Scale?* (139–56). Bristol: Policy Press.

Glachant, M. (2001). The Need for Adaptability in EU Environmental Policy Design and Implementation. *European Environment*, 11(5), 239–49.

Gogokhia, G. (2018). Non-Compliance of EU Directives: Past Experience or Ongoing Challenge. *Public Goods & Governance*, *3*(2), 25–31.

Greenwood, J. (2019). The European Citizens' Initiative: Bringing the EU Closer to Its Citizens? *Comparative European Politics*, *17*(6), 940–56.

Heinelt, H., Kopp-Malek, T., Lang, J. & Reissert, B. (2003). Policy-Making in Fragmented Systems: How to Explain Success. In Kohler-Koch, B. (Ed.), *Linking EU and National Governance* (135–53). Oxford: Oxford University Press.

Héritier, A. (1999). Elements of Democratic Legitimation in Europe: An Alternative Perspective. *Journal of European Public Policy*, *6*(2), 269–82.

Hofstad, H., Millstein, M., Tønnesen, A., Vedeld, T. & Hansen, K. B. (2021). The Role of Goal-Setting in Urban Climate Governance. *Earth System Governance*, *7*, 100088.

Hooghe, L. & Marks, G. (2001). *Multi-Level Governance and European Integration*. Lanham, MD: Rowman.

Hooghe, L. & Marks, G. (2004). Contrasting Visions of Multi-Level Governance. In Bache, I. & Flinders, M. V. (Eds.), *Multi-Level Governance* (15–30). Oxford: Oxford University Press.

Hooghe, L. & Marks, G. (2020). A Postfunctionalist Theory of Multilevel Governance. *The British Journal of Politics and International Relations*, *22*(4), 820–6.

Huddy, L., Del Ponte, A. & Davies, C. (2021). Nationalism, Patriotism, and Support for the European Union. *Political Psychology*, *42*(6), 995–1017.

Jessop, B. (2002). *The Future of the Capitalist State*. Cambridge: Polity Press.

Jessop, B. (2004). Multi-Level Governance and Multi-Level Metagovernance. In Bache, I. & Flinders, M. (Eds.), *Multi-Level Governance* (49–74). Oxford: Oxford University Press.

Jessop, B. (2013). Hollowing Out the "Nation-State" and Multi-Level Governance. In Kennett, P. (Ed.), *A Handbook of Comparative Social Policy*, 2nd edn. Cheltenham: Edward Elgar Publishing.

Katz, B. & Nowak, J. (2018). *The New Localism: How Cities Can Thrive in the Age of Populism*. Washington, DC: Brookings Institution Press.

Kickert, W. J. M., Klijn, E. H. & Koppenjan, J. F. M. (1997). *Managing Complex Networks: Strategies for the Public Sector*. London: Sage Publications.

Klijn, E. H. & Koppenjan, J. (2015). *Governance Networks in the Public Sector*. Abingdon: Routledge.

Kohler-Koch, B. (1999). The Evolution and Transformation of European Governance. In Kohler-Koch, B. & Eising, R. (Eds.), *The Transformation of Governance in the European Union* (13–34). Abingdon: Routledge.

Marcussen, M. & Torfing, J. (Eds.) (2007). *Democratic Network Governance in Europe*. Basingstoke: Palgrave Macmillan.

Myrberg, G. (2017). Local Challenges and National Concerns: Municipal Level Responses to National Refugee Settlement Policies in Denmark and Sweden. *Revue Internationale des Sciences Administratives*, *83*(2), 329–46.

Papadopoulos, Y. (2005). Taking Stock of Multi-Level Governance Networks. *European Political Science*, 4(3), 316–27.

Papadopoulos, Y. (2010). Accountability and Multi-Level Governance: More Accountability, Less Democracy? *West European Politics*, *33*(5), 1030–49.

Pressman, J. L. & Wildavsky, A. (1973). *Implementation*. San Francisco, CA: University of California Press.

Reiser, M. & Hebenstreit, J. (2020). Populism versus Technocracy? Populist Responses to the Technocratic Nature of the EU. *Politics and Governance*, *8*(4), 568–79.

Rodríguez-Pose, A. & Gill, N. (2003). The Global Trend towards Devolution and Its Implications. *Environment and Planning C: Government and Policy*, *21*(3), 333–51.

Schakel, A. H. (2020). Multi-Level Governance in a "Europe with the Regions." *The British Journal of Politics and International Relations*, *22*(4), 767–75.

Schakel, A. H., Hooghe, L. & Marks, G. (2015). Multilevel Governance and the State. In Leibfried, S., Huber, E., Lange, M., Levy, J. D. & Stephens, J. D. (Eds.),

The Oxford Handbook of Transformations of the State (269–85). Oxford: Oxford University Press.

Scharpf, F. W. (1988). The Joint-Decision Trap: Lessons from German Federalism and European Integration. *Public Administration, 66*(3), 239–78.

Schmidt, V. A. (2013). Democracy and Legitimacy in the European Union Revisited: Input, Output and "Throughput." *Political Studies, 61*(1), 2–22.

Schmidt, V. A. (2016). The New EU Governance: New Intergovernmentalism, New Supranationalism, and New Parliamentarism. Istituto Affari Internazionali IAI Working Papers.

Sørensen, E. & Torfing, J. (2007). *Theories of Democratic Network Governance.* London: Palgrave Macmillan.

Sørensen, E. & Torfing, J. (2020). Radical and Disruptive Answers to Downstream Problems in Collaborative Governance? *Public Management Review, 23*(11), 1590–611.

Sweet, A. S. & Sandholtz, W. (Eds.) (1998). *European Integration and Supranational Governance.* Oxford: Oxford University Press.

Torfing, J., Peters, B. G., Pierre, J. & Sørensen, E. (2012). *Interactive Governance: Advancing the Paradigm.* Oxford: Oxford University Press.

Tortola, P. D. (2017). Clarifying Multilevel Governance. *European Journal of Political Research, 56*(2), 234–50.

Zapata-Barrero, R., Caponio, T. & Scholten, P. (2017). Theorizing the "Local Turn" in a Multi-Level Governance Framework of Analysis: A Case Study in Immigrant Policies. *International Review of Administrative Sciences, 83*(2), 241–6.

Zürn, M. (2004). Global Governance and Legitimacy Problems. *Government and Opposition, 39*(2), 260–87.

9. From hard to soft power

Public governance has traditionally depended on laws and rule-based regulations and compliance secured by means of auditing, administrative and legal sanctioning—and ultimately the exercise of legitimate violence. To this legal governance regime, New Public Management (NPM) has added the use of incentive-based inducements, both when regulating external societal actors, such as private contractors, and when ensuring the compliance of public agencies and employees. Legal impositions and inducements are both examples of "hard power" aimed at forcing subordinate actors to comply with legal rules and deliver expected outputs. Today, with the rise of collaborative governance in networks and partnerships and new forms of multi-level governance, the classical legal and political authority on which the exercise of hard power rests is eroding. This does not mean that the exercise of state power is diminishing, but rather that the form of state power is transformed. Hence, new forms of "soft power" based on voluntary norms and standards, ongoing dialogue and jointly formulated discourse seem to be gaining ground. This raises timely and important questions about what soft power is, how it is exercised, how efficient it is and what its limits are.

This chapter will explore the conditions for soft power to deliver the desired results and the need to combine soft and hard power in the exercise of smart power. First, it discusses the use of hard power in public governance and administration. Next, it accounts for the emergence of the notion of soft power in international relations theory and then proceeds to discuss the changing face of public governance and the growing importance of soft power. Drawing on Foucault's (1991) governmentality theory and the dual notions of "technologies of agency" and "technologies of performance," it scrutinizes how public health campaigns mobilize citizens as active and self-responsible agents who are caring for their own health by behaving in accordance with public standards for healthy living. This analysis is followed by a study of crime prevention that illustrates how soft and hard power can be combined in the exercise of smart power. The conclusion reflects on avenues for future research on hard, soft, and smart power in the field of public administration and governance.

THE ROLE OF HARD POWER IN PUBLIC ADMINISTRATION AND GOVERNANCE

The unfortunate split between political science on the one hand and public administration and governance research on the other tends to produce a flawed image of the latter as being devoid of politics and power (Peters et al. 2022). Hence, public administration and governance are sometimes assumed to be preoccupied with studying the depoliticized "administration of things" rather than the politicized "government of men" (Saint-Simon 1975). As such, political science seems to have monopolized the study of politics and power, thus relegating public administration and governance research to merely studying the effective functioning and operation of administrative organizations and the role of the exercise of public management therein. This apparent division of labor between the two disciplines is regrettable, since administrative decisions and attempts to govern society and the economy are in reality imbued with politics and power (Peters et al. 2022). Not only is public administration and governance taking place within a politically governed organization, but the very act of administration and governance is also an act of power, since it creates a strategic field of force relations that tends to realize one set of solutions at the expense of others, which gives rise to resistance and opposition (Foucault 1976).

Power is an elusive and essentially contested concept, but there is broad agreement that it involves a certain capacity to affect outcomes, either through the actions of social and political agency or the shaping of the discursive, institutional, and structural contexts for action (Clegg 1989; Torfing 2009). Agency-based power may involve the use of particular strategies and resources to prevail over opponents in concrete decision-making processes, the ability to control the agenda through non-decision-making and/or attempts to shape how other actors perceive their interests so that they are aligned with one's own interests (Lukes 1974). Structural power invokes institutional and organizational biases that tend to narrow down the choices that social and political agents can make, possibly even providing a discursive scripting of their actions. Usually, however, power is exercised by situated agents who are drawing upon or exploiting a particular structural, institutional, and/or discursive context to affect outcomes. To illustrate: public employees with limited formal power resources may succeed in convincing the administrative municipal chief executive officer to put "employee well-being" high on the agenda because the government has launched a campaign about "attractive public workplaces" to ensure the future recruitment of relevant personnel.

Structure and agency may be combined in the exercise of power in many different ways, and the mechanisms through which power is exercised may vary over a continuum ranging from coercion to the acceptance of the implications of what appears to be a shared norm or belief, although the latter may reflect an asymmetrical distribution of resources and capacities (Rothman 2011). In the public sector, administration and governance have typically relied on power mechanisms close to the coercive end of the continuum, where we find coercion, threats, discipline, and inducement based on the conditional use of pecuniary and non-pecuniary rewards and punishments (carrots and sticks) (Nye 2008). Exercising power in this manner is referred to as hard power, and it aims to secure compliance with the rules and demands of the political and administrative system as well as its leaders, managers, and professionally trained employees by means of making subordinates fear that they will be hit by negative sanctions or not receive positive ones.

The public sector is based on the rule of law. All public decisions must be based on a judicial hierarchy of legal rules and rulings that are formal, explicit, and transparent. The number of laws and legal regulations is astronomical and ever increasing; for example, the legal rules governing Danish employment policy amount to several thousand pages. No wonder that the local job centers struggle to make agile decisions and to prevent employees and clients from suffering administrative burdens placed upon them by the thick layers of legal regulations that are motivated by concerns for eliminating fraud. The laws regulating public service production and the governance of society and the economy used to be very detailed, thus specifying the exact rules applying to different groups of clients, citizens, and business firms in particular situations. This has changed over the years, and many laws are now instead specifying the overall purpose and legal framework, then delegating the responsibility for making discretionary decisions within this framework to professional frontline staff.

The principle of legality is worth little if there is no system to ensure compliance with the many legal rules. In pre-modern times, the sovereign political leader could choose, more or less arbitrarily, to decapitate criminal offenders, serious wrongdoers, and enemies of the state. Today, we have an elaborate system of independent and impartial courts and judges that can impose legal sanctions such as fines, sentences, and confinement on those who have failed to comply with constitutional and public laws, legal statutes, public regulations, and legally grounded administrative rules. Small administrative breaches of rules in the public sector are either neglected or dealt with by public managers using a variety of corrective and disciplinary measures. The legal and administrative sanctioning of unlawful action is important, but administrative compliance is usually ensured by the discipline imbedded in daily procedures and routines and by the threat of sanctions in the case of clear and visible transgressions.

Public managers and employees are well aware of the consequences of major rule breaches, but compliance based on the anticipation of negative sanctions of unwanted behavior also works for the majority of the citizens and most socio-economic actors, with notorious tax evaders, criminal gangs and drug cartels as major exceptions. In fact, government may have its way by threatening to pass new legislation or issue new regulations if a particular group of social and economic actors does not change its behavior or fails to self-regulate its activities. Even citizens may be threatened to change their behavior by the prospect of new laws and sanctions. As such, if they are capable thereof, parents may work harder to provide care for their children if they know the next step is losing custody.

Building on a calculative approach to ensuring compliance, NPM has focused more on inducements than coercion. Assuming that people calculate the costs and benefits of their actions, the public sector should define clear goals and norms, monitor performance and provide pecuniary and non-pecuniary rewards and punishment. Hence, unemployed benefit recipients who are committed to reentering the labor market may gain access to training and education, whereas those who fail to demonstrate their willingness to work by applying for jobs and going to job interviews may face cuts to their benefits. Moreover, private contractors delivering services to citizens on behalf of the public sector are governed through the use of a combination of bonuses and penalties that are carefully described in elaborate contracts. Finally, public employees are subjected to transactional leadership that uses pecuniary incitements (e.g., bonus wages, promotion/demotion, further education opportunities) and non-pecuniary incitements, such as praise or scorn, to motivate public employees to deliver what is expected from them in terms of hard work, commitment to the organization, wise decisions, service-mindedness, and so on.

Since it aims to influence the rational calculations of different subjects, inducements can be seen as providing a less blunt instrument than the straightforward coercion provided by laws and courts backed by the public monopoly on legitimate violence. Inducements should nevertheless be classified as hard power, since the negative sanctions or loss of positive ones can ultimately have serious consequences: unemployed individuals may lose their benefits, contracts may be terminated, and public employees may be dismissed.

In sum, legally based coercion, discipline, and threats, together with pecuniary and non-pecuniary inducements, have played a central role in securing order and stability in modern society and public bureaucracy. This has worked well at a time when most people accepted this type of hard power but may not continue to work so well as more people and actors become increasingly competent, assertive, and critical and demand respect and possibilities to influence societal decisions and their own living conditions without the threat of coercion or strong inducements that limit their autonomy.

In the light of this development, the major limitation of hard power is that the exercise of power remains external to the subject. The subject is facing an external force of laws, legal rules, threats, and inducements that it must obey without necessarily understanding or being in agreement with its normative foundation, without being able to discuss its premises and implementation, and without any real opportunity to influence its form or function. Hard power demands to be accepted without question, which is becoming harder and harder for most people and actors to swallow, and which in turn is prompting the search for soft-power alternatives. Many people will continue to accept hard power, but a growing number will not. Over time, that will tend to enhance the transaction costs associated with hard power and thus make it less efficient.

THE RISE OF SOFT POWER IN INTERNATIONAL RELATIONS THEORY

Nye (1990) famously discovered the use of soft power in international relations theory. In the international sphere, there is no global government, only loosely coupled collaboration between sovereign nation-states that are pursuing their national interests through constant rivalry. Conflicts are bound to flare up and lead to mutual warnings, threats, and sanctions, and ultimately to war. International conflicts will not only be military but also related to economic trade and access to markets. Here, compliance with the rules of international organizations and regional trade regimes may provide economic benefits, while non-compliance will incur a loss for the national economy. Hence, hard power based on coercion and inducements has been the rule of the game.

In his original post-Cold War article (later published in book form), Nye (2004) observes that the US remains a relatively uncontested superpower while also contending that military and economic strength no longer enables the US to control the political environment and secure desirable outcomes at the global level (Nye 1990). The problem is not so much the rising challenge of another major power (i.e., China), but rather the general diffusion of power. Nation-states are not only becoming more powerful on average and thus less difficult to control, but new interdependencies in economic markets, technology development, global communications, and human aspirations are also emerging and tend to make global society more complex. Not only nation-states but also big corporations and international organizations are caught up in the new webs of interdependency. At the same time, national security goals are supplemented with more or less shared economic goals, social developmental goals, and environmental goals.

In this new world of distributed and shared power, the exercise of hard power is less conducive to securing desired outcomes. While military power remains important for national security and economic power can still provide inducements for other nation-states to adhere to a particular economic regime, new means of power are necessary to control the political environment and ensure particular outcomes. Military aggression, political threats, and economic blackmail will not fare well in the global world of multi-dimensional interdependencies. Nye argues that the hard command power must give way to a soft co-optive power aimed at setting the agenda, defining common norms and ideas, and structuring the situations so that they lead other actors in a particular direction. As power becomes softer, the resources become more intangible and may include cultural norm diffusion, ideological discourse, and international institutions. The joint development of common norms, ideas, and values may even create a common sense of ownership of their realization, whereas collaboration with actors with opposing norms and ideas may undermine one's political and moral-intellectual leadership in the world.

In a later book on public leadership, Nye (2008) asserts that soft power is ultimately about winning the hearts and minds of those you aim to lead through institutional control, agenda-setting, and the framing of decisions and actions. Since generating attractive and influential ideas is not the same as mobilizing people, leaders must engage with their followers and spur participation, dialogue, and collaboration through the exercise of horizontal and distributed leadership. Through constant interaction, leaders must develop and mold ideas that attract their followers. Soft power is the power of attraction, although the followers may also provide important feedback that makes leaders revise their ideas and visions. Indeed, critical and competent followers have the power to resist, criticize, or lead their leaders, and by doing so they may end up empowering their leaders if they are responsive and listen to their followers (Nye 2008: 32–7).

The distinction between hard and soft power is a matter of degree, as leadership behavior often contains elements of both forms of power and can be ordered along a continuum ranging from harder to softer forms of power that depend on different military, economic, institutional, and rhetorical resources (Rothman 2011). In real life, the combined use of more or less hard and soft power tends to vary over time and between situations. The combination of hard and soft forms of power also varies with the position of public leaders: "those without formal positions tend to rely more on soft power, whereas those in formal positions are better placed to mix hard and soft power" (Nye 2008: 38). The use of inducements, threats, and coercion must be backed by some formal authority.

Soft power is not necessarily a good thing, as nobody likes to be persuaded or manipulated to accept ideas put forward by transformative leaders. Moreover, soft power can be used for good and bad purposes depending on the eye of the beholder (see Zeitoun et al. 2011). Nevertheless, soft power may be more effective in situations where a distributed set of competent and interdependent actors form horizontal networks aiming to govern society and the economy. In today's network society, leaders often try to avoid using hard power because they expect strong opposition to attempts at imposing their will by means of coercion. That said, soft power cannot stand alone. Communication with followers may not always be persuasive and foster agreement, and some situations require leaders to cut to the chase and make unpopular decisions to remain on course and deliver results. Hence, while hard power may be out of fashion, it is still needed—but it must be used sparingly and dosed correctly. As Nye (2008: 43) concludes: "the ability to combine hard and soft power into an effective strategy is *smart power*." The smart power idea has received considerable attention from scholars and practitioners alike, and it is often pre-understood that the combined use of both hard and soft power can yield superior results compared to relying exclusively on one kind of power or another (Nossel 2004; Wilson 2008).

The international and national political spheres have all become less amenable to Hobbesian and Machiavellian brutes and more amenable to enlightened and reflexive leaders who are sensitized to the use of soft power based on engagement and attraction. Nevertheless, there are some important limitations on the use of softer forms of power (Gallarotti 2011). The effects of soft power are often indirect and long term, whereas hard power aims to produce a more immediate effect. Moreover, leaders sometimes underestimate their soft resources and are more focused on the hard resources and how they can be used to achieve results. Finally, the use of soft power presupposes that actors are open to reasoning and will bow to the better argument or to norms and values allegedly benefiting all nations, organizations, and employees. However, we do find social antagonisms and hard-nosed interest conflicts that limit the use of soft power. To illustrate, a strong clash between the respective national identities and interests of Russia and Ukraine may produce an immunity to soft power, hence the focus on economic sanctions and military aid to Ukraine.

Despite these limitations, the conceptual couplet of hard and soft power has received considerable scholarly attention (see Baldwin 2002; Ferguson 2003; Berenskoetter & Williams 2007; Kurlantzick 2007; Gallarotti 2011; Petrone 2019), and the hard–soft power debate is also mirrored in similar discussions of hard and soft law (Trubek & Trubek 2005), and hard and soft governance (Maggetti 2015).

THE CHANGING FACE OF PUBLIC GOVERNANCE AND THE USE OF SOFT POWER

While Nye (1990, 2004) was originally studying the exercise of power on the global scene and the complex web of international relations, he later extended the scope of his study to public leadership involving formal as well as informal political leaders aiming to govern our present network society. As we shall see, this discussion can be extended beyond presidents and prime ministers to cover all public leaders, including administrative leaders who must lead their organization and staff or some collaborative governance network or partnership aiming to bring about innovation and societal transformation.

If administrative leaders in the public bureaucracy heyday could rely solely on command and control when leading their employees, organization, and environment, this is hardly the case today. Public employees are no longer the submissive and allegiant breed they used to be; they are better trained and educated, more competent, and empowered by new public narratives about entrepreneurship and innovation and experiments with self-managing teams, networks, and organizations in which leaders are facilitators of communication and dialogue. Moreover, public service organizations tend to compete to attract good and competent employees, and they have growing concerns with the well-being of their employees that do not go well together with the exercise of hard power. NPM strengthened the leadership role of public managers who should "steer rather than row" and distance themselves from their employees to be able to exercise power based on sticks and carrots (Schillemans 2013). However, the new managerial leadership focused on entrepreneurship in a deregulated public sector, and the transactional leadership of public employees soon gave way to transformational leadership based on the formation, communication and maintenance of organizational goals, missions, and visions (Jensen et al. 2019).

The creation of a growing number of single- or special-purpose agencies as part of the NPM attempt to reduce complexity and avoid sub-optimizing behavior fragmented the organizational landscape of public governance and increased the need for an inter-organizational coordinative leadership. Here, public leaders ended up leading peers from other organizations for whom they were not formal leaders, which in turn eroded the basis for the use of hard power. External collaboration extended beyond the confines of the public sector and involved private contractors delivering outsourced services to citizens based on service contracts. Preparing, negotiating, and monitoring service contracts involves collaboration with a broad set of actors and leadership, which fosters trust to reduce performance-monitoring costs. Finally, public leaders often play the role of metagovernor in policy-specific governance networks in which the currency is soft rather than hard power. Horizontal network relations preclude the exercise of coercive power, although public authorities may threaten to take over and dictate a solution if the network fails to produce feasible results. The threat of overriding the governance networks is often subtle, however, and merely a way of spurring collaboration based on interdependency.

Hence, as further detailed in the previous chapters, the changing face of public administration and governance is shifting the balance from hard toward soft power. There are many examples of this development in both Western and non-Western societies. First, in a situation where national governments seem increasingly unwilling or unable to advance regulations and policy that tackle big global problems (e.g., climate change), cities find ways to act as autonomous and interdependent actors and develop their own effective governance solutions in alliance and collaboration with international organizations and together with other cities through global networks (e.g., C40, Eurocities). Since, compared with nation-states, cities lack political, economic, and institutional power, they can only succeed in shaping outcomes through soft power; that is, through their ability to attract people, money, innovations, and goods from around the world (Swiney 2020). Cities mobilize their citizens, engage with stakeholders, draw on their cultural values and democratic legitimacy, create visions and set targets, draw up bold investment plans, create innovation hubs, host international conferences, and support each other in a determined effort to attract attention, capital, and innovators while creating a strong local followership.

Second, domestic cultural policy in China has been undergoing a major shift that is seen to be related to the use of soft power (Zhang & Courty 2021). Initiated, subsidized, and partly controlled by the central government, the so-called "Chinese Museum Boom" has greatly expanded the number of small and big museums throughout the country while reducing admission fees, thus enhancing accessibility to local citizens. The growing number of museums is helping to conserve relics, display art, and promote cultural research and international cooperation. It is also part of a wider strategy to shape national identity and cultivate the vision of "harmonious society." As such, museums are playing a vital role in consolidating Chinese cultural identity and promoting cultural nationalism through the glorification of cultural heritage, interpretation of national history, and patriotic education (Denton 2014; Shelach-Lavi 2019). According to Varutti (2014), the use of soft power by the Chinese government is a response to the concern that "Communist ideology is no longer the main source of cohesion and public authority in Chinese society." Hence, "the government is turning to other tools to justify its authority and secure its power, both factual and symbolic. ... The immensely rich Chinese cultural heritage becomes a source of political legitimation insofar as the associations established with ancient cultural and artistic traditions contribute to inscribing the authority of the current government in a line of continuity harking back to imperial rule" (Varutti 2014: 2). While the Chinese case is very clear and highly illustrative of cultural policy as a soft-power tool, believing that the ideological use of museums is merely something going on in autocratic societies would be a mistake. A recent book by Lord and Blankenberg (2016) discusses the soft-power role of museums in a broad range of Western and non-Western countries.

A final example of soft power in public administration and governance comes from the field of education. Here, the Organisation for Economic Co-operation and Development (OECD) has increasingly gained power and is now regarded as an international authority in the field, particularly through its Programme for International Student Assessment (PISA), which is highly esteemed in many countries and seems to influence domestic education reforms (Bieber & Martens 2011). The external advice based on sound empirical data and presented in the comparative PISA reports has challenged existing domestic educational policies and propelled reforms in countries such as Denmark, Germany, Poland, and Switzerland (Bieber & Martens 2011; Białecki et al. 2017; Niemann et al. 2017). The attraction and policy effect of the PISA reports provides an interesting example of how international organizations can exercise soft power and drive domestic-level policy convergence.

Salamon (2002) was one of the first to register the ongoing revolution in public administration and governance, which has shifted the balance from the hard power of traditional public administration to the soft power of a new governance paradigm that provides a new set of tools that are more indirect, more collaborative, and more reliant on third parties to help provide public services and solutions. Hence, instead of using its authority to dictate solutions, government provides some overall goals and resources that attract private, societal actors and involves them in the provision of governance solutions based on networked collaboration and broadly accepted standards.

The new soft-power governance paradigm shifts the focus from the administrative unit responsible for a particular program to the tools and instruments through which public purpose is produced. The tools of governance and the choice between different tools is not merely a technical decision but also a political one. The choice of tools gives some actors—and therefore some particular perspectives and norms—an advantage in determining the form and outcomes of public policy (Salamon 2002: 11). With government as the main orchestrator, a variety of public agencies and third-party actors (e.g., private firms, civil society organizations, volunteer groups) collaborate through networks and partnerships formed on the basis of relations of interdependency. Hence, hierarchical principal–agent theories are discarded in favor of horizontal network theories focused on the interplay between the actors who are involved in operating a particular tool. The old insistence on government based on public authority is replaced by continuous interactions between public and private actors who are collaborating to use their complementary skills and competences rather than competing. Finally, and for our purposes most importantly, the new governance paradigm replaces command and control with negotiation and persuasion as the modus operandi of public programs and governance tools. Negotiation is not only instrumental in the implementation phase, where different actors work together to deliver services, regulations, and public solutions, but also encompasses the goals that public action aims to serve.

This new way of governing requires a new skill set, as public managers must have *activation skills* to attract actors and form a network around a particular tool, *orchestration skills* to get them to collaborate and coordinate with each other, and *modulation skills* combining persuasion with inducements to safeguard the focus on creating public purpose. Persuasion and the construction of joint ownership over ends and means is preferable, but the use of rewards and penalties is sometimes necessary as the lender of last resort.

This new type of "third-party government" that turns governance into a team sport helps to mobilize resources, enhances legitimacy, and breaks down implementation resistance (Salamon 2002: 602–3). The reliance on attraction, negotiation and persuasion aims to create a common ground for multi-party problem-solving instead of governing based on hard power aimed at forcing people to act in a certain way, break down their resistance, and create docile bodies that hardly contribute anything to the process except for compliance. The advantages of this new governance paradigm tendentially based on soft rather than hard power are obvious, but the fruits can only be properly reaped if the management and accountability challenges are solved through the development of new skills and designs and if the public purpose prevails over the risk of "third-party government" turning into "private interest government," where private, societal actors involved in governance use the resources to which they obtain access to pursue their own interests at the expense of the negotiated interpretation of the public interest.

TECHNOLOGIES OF AGENCY AND TECHNOLOGIES OF PERFORMANCE: THE CASE OF PUBLIC HEALTH CAMPAIGNS

Health is an increasingly salient policy area covering both occasional emergency health responses to pandemics, war and terror incidents, and natural catastrophes and the steady and long-lasting attempt to fight the negative health consequences of lifestyle diseases. Recently, we have seen an overwhelming and rather exceptional display of hard power to curb the COVID-19 pandemic: state- and city-wide lockdowns, mandatory testing, the quarantining of infected persons, and fines to those who do not follow the rapidly changing health regulations. Even here, however, soft power through appeals to good citizenship and solidarity with vulnerable population groups and persuasive encouragements to adopt healthy sanitation habits and norms about social distancing played a significant role.

The use of soft power is even more pronounced in the state-sponsored campaigns for healthy living that form part of the new preventive health policy. However, attempts at banning smoking and prohibiting underage drinking and the use of excise taxes to reduce the use of tobacco, alcohol, and sugary beverages are clear examples of hard power. Such measures have a high impact, but research shows that excise taxes must be very high to truly change people's behavior, and tax hikes tend to make government rather unpopular (Chaloupka et al. 2019). More importantly, hard power does not win over the population for the "good cause" of healthy living, which can reduce public health costs and enhance productivity and life quality. This is where soft power enters the picture.

Health promotion campaigns aiming to encourage people to eat healthily, reduce the use of unhealthy substances and exercise more are gaining ground. Studies show how campaigns aimed at eliciting fear are less effective than those describing the advantages of new healthy norms and habits (Soames Job 1988; Siegel 1998; Quattrin et al. 2015), although the latter may foster resistance, denial, and othering, which contribute to the stigmatization of disadvantaged groups (Thompson & Kumar 2011). A new kind of engaging health promotion strategy uses social media to get people to exercise (Edney et al. 2018).

Foucault's theories of power may help us to understand the tools used in health promotion campaigns (Torfing 2009). Toward the end of his authorship, Foucault (1986, 1991) began equating power with government, which he defined as "the conduct of conduct." Playing on the double meaning of the term "conduct" in both French and English, "the conduct of conduct" refers to the power-ridden practice through which the current and future actions of free and resourceful actors (conduct as "behavior") are mobilized and shaped in accordance with some overall goals (conduct as "regulation") (Foucault 1991). As such, Foucault's notion of government as "the conduct of conduct" clearly transgresses the classical understanding of government as the sovereign power exercised by elected politicians and executive administrators. According to Foucault (1991), government is basically a process of subjectivation; that is, a process whereby a person is turned into a subject in the dual sense of constituting a particular free subjectivity and of being subjected to a particular conception of normalized behavior; in other words, government is a soft, identity-producing power rather than a hard, prohibitive one.

In the words of Rose (1999), power involves the shaping of freedom. Unlike domination, power presupposes the freedom of subjects to act differently and aims to mobilize and shape this very freedom to ensure conformity to particular ideas, goals, and ideas (Foucault 1991). Hence, soft power is a governing practice combining "technologies of agency" with "technologies of performance" (Dean 1999: 165). Technologies of agency aim to mobilize the energies, wills, and capacities of free, self-responsible, and autonomous actors, whereas technologies of performance aim to shape their free action through the production of norms, standards, and targets that prescribe a particular performance. Soft power based on the mobilization of free and autonomous agents who use their free action to do the right thing is ubiquitous in the modern welfare state. It is also found in the private market economy, where the corporate social responsibility (CSR) discourse encourages private corporations to make socially responsible choices that protect the natural environment and improve the welfare of their employees, the local community and society at large. Socially responsible firms freely commit to abide by a set of societal expectations of corporate behavior, and they accept being evaluated against a set of CSR performance indicators (Carroll 2008).

COMBINING SOFT AND HARD POWER IN SMART CRIME PREVENTION

Many big cities around the world are tormented by drug-related gang wars that produce a general sense of unsafety and victims among gang members, their families, and innocent civilians. Preventing gang-related crime is a truly wicked problem, and it is difficult to prevent at-risk youth from joining criminal gangs and to get members to exit their gang, since criminal gangs tend to provide many of the things that youth in deprived and dangerous neighborhoods need, including extra income through criminal activities, access to material goods such as cars, drugs, and liquor, protection from other gangs, and thrills and excitement, together with a sense of belonging, pride, and solidarity. When people first become part of such a gang, exit is difficult because of the simultaneous loss of all of these attractions and the fear of being punished by the gang they are leaving (Jankowski 1991, 2008).

Hard power is a preferred strategy in many countries, where the maximum imprisonment for drug-related gang violence has been increased as part of "tough on crime" strategies. The hard-power strategy is often supplemented with soft-power strategies aiming to improve the neighborhood, reduce youth unemployment, provide leisure activities for at-risk youth, and recruit role models who can demonstrate that there is an alternative to crime and violence. However, these strategies often fail when pursued in isolation from other strategies. The problem with choosing either a hard or soft crime prevention strategy can be solved by smart power aimed at combining hard and soft power as part of an integrated strategy to curb gang-related violence.

Major US cities, such as Boston, Chicago, Cincinnati, and Oakland, have all used smart power as part of so-called "Call-Ins," which are hour-long meetings between the police, the city administration, and key gang members aimed at persuading the latter to exit their criminal activities, put down their guns and stop the gang- and drug-related shootings in their local neighborhoods (Braga et al. 2014; Engel et al. 2013; Kennedy 2011; Papachristos & Kirk 2015). Based on field studies and social network analysis, a group of fifteen to twenty gang members with a history of involvement in gunfire is carefully selected and called in for a joint meeting, if necessary with the help of parole and probation officers. Initially, the police tell them about how their activities are monitored and the punishment that is awaiting them the next time they are caught in criminal activities. After this focused deterrence message, the gang members are confronted with horrifying stories about the suffering of the victims of their shootings. Mothers and sisters of victims show pictures of their fallen sons and siblings while fighting back tears. Next, community members express their desire to help the gang members, emphasize their love for them, and invite them to participate in communal activities. Finally, a variety of public agencies offer to help them out of their addiction-related problems and into education and jobs that will enable them to raise a family without risking the lives of their family members. In sum, hard and soft power are combined to facilitate the exit of gang members from their criminal milieu.

Some cities have organized many such Call-Ins to change the dynamic in the streets, where rival gangs solve disputes by shooting each other. Throughout 2013, the Chicago Police Department held eighteen Call-Ins that reached 149 gang factions and 438 individual gang members. The results from research based on a quasi-experimental design suggest that the gang factions attending a Call-In experience a 23% reduction in overall shooting events and a 32% reduction in gunshot victims in the year after treatment compared to similar factions that did not attend a Call-In (Papachristos & Kirk 2015). Hence, smart power seems to work relatively well as a crime prevention strategy.

THE FUTURE OF HARD, SOFT, AND SMART POWER

This chapter has introduced and discussed the use and exercise of soft power in public administration and governance. The soft-power concept was developed in the field of international politics, but the concept may also be used at the level of national, regional, and local governance. In a way, the concept works better within the individual nation-state than between nation-states. Indeed, the idea of exercising power by means of attracting other actors is slightly problematic at the level of interstate relations because a nation-state holds many different public and private actors, some of which are attracted by a particular set of norms and ideas while others are not (Fan 2008). At the national, regional, or local level of governance, this problem is solved since the distributed actors can more easily be treated as unitary actors capable of either attracting or being attracted to other actors.

The use of soft power is necessitated by the emergence of a shared-power world of distributed action involving independent actors who tend to oppose and reject the use of hard power that dictates solutions instead of aiming to attract, persuade, and build a common ground for joint problem-solving. Soft power is efficient and effective, since it mobilizes valuable resources, enhances innovation through feedback from critical followers, and avoids spending valuable resources fighting lengthy battles with different opponents. Finally, it empowers its followers to act within the jointly formulated framework instead of having them plotting how to get rid of the Hobbesian or Machiavellian brute that has just steamrolled them. Nevertheless, as discussed above, there are limits to the exercise of soft power, and combining soft power with some element of hard power is sometimes a good idea, as long as the exercise of hard power does not undercut the ability to exercise soft power. When successful, soft and hard power work in tandem in the exercise of smart power.

Public administration and governance scholars could benefit from a stronger focus on the exercise of power and from a further embrace of the notion of soft power that captures how power is exercised in our network society. The soft-power concept requires further clarification via-à-vis competing notions of soft law and soft governance, and theory development should be encouraged since the concept of soft power is somewhat undertheorized. Studies of soft power are highly relevant for the exercise of public leadership but may also help to shed light on the form and functioning of the tools used when governing society and the economy or providing services to users and citizens. The mapping of different forms of soft power, identifying the scope conditions and studying their impact will help us to gain new knowledge about how power is exercised in the day-to-day governance of modern society. Finally, we need to study the conditions for combining soft and hard power in the exercise of smart power to see when persuasion is (not) furthered by a more or less explicit threat.

REFERENCES

Baldwin, D. (2002). Power and International Relations. In Carlsnaes, W., Risse-Kappen, T. & Simmons, B. A. (Eds.), *Handbook of International Relations* (177–91). London: Sage.

Berenskoetter, F. & Williams, M. J. (Eds.) (2007). *Power in World Politics*. London: Routledge.

Białecki, I., Jakubowski, M. & Wiśniewski, J. (2017). Education Policy in Poland: The Impact of PISA (and Other International Studies). *European Journal of Education, 52*(2), 167–74.

Bieber, T. & Martens, K. (2011). The OECD PISA Study as a Soft Power in Education? Lessons from Switzerland and the US. *European Journal of Education, 46*(1), 101–16.

Braga, A. A., Hureau, D. M. & Papachristos, A. V. (2014). Deterring Gang-Involved Gun Violence: Measuring the Impact of Boston's Operation Ceasefire on Street Gang Behavior. *Journal of Quantitative Criminology, 30*(1), 113–39.

Carroll, A. B. (2008). A History of Corporate Social Responsibility: Concepts and Practices. In Crane, A., Matten, D., McWilliams, A., Moon, J. & Siegel, D. S. (Eds.), *The Oxford Handbook of Corporate Social Responsibility* (1–20). Oxford: Oxford Handbooks Online.

Chaloupka, F. J., Powell, L. M. & Warner, K. E. (2019). The Use of Excise Taxes to Reduce Tobacco, Alcohol, and Sugary Beverage Consumption. *Annual Review of Public Health, 40*(1), 187–201.

Clegg, S. (1989). *Frameworks of Power*. London: Sage.

Dean, M. (1999). *Governmentality: Power and Rule in Modern Society*. London: Sage.

Denton, K. (2014). Museums in China: Power, Politics, and Identities. *The China Quarterly, 220*, 1166–9.

Edney, L. C., Haji Ali Afzali, H., Cheng, T. C. & Karnon, J. (2018). Estimating the Reference Incremental Cost-Effectiveness Ratio for the Australian Health System. *Pharmacoeconomics, 36*(2), 239–52.

Engel, R. S., Tillyer, M. S. & Corsaro, N. (2013). Reducing Gang Violence Using Focused Deterrence: Evaluating the Cincinnati Initiative to Reduce Violence (CIRV). *Justice Quarterly, 30*(3), 403–39.

Fan, Y. (2008). Soft Power: Power of Attraction or Confusion? *Place Branding and Public Diplomacy, 4*(2), 147–58.

Ferguson, N. (2003). Think Again: Power. *Foreign Policy, 134*, 18–24.

Foucault, M. (1976). *Discipline and Punish: The Birth of the Prison*. New York: Pantheon.

Foucault, M. (1986). *The Care of the Self: History of Sexuality*, vol. 3. New York: Pantheon.

Foucault, M. (1991). Governmentality. In Burchell, G., Gordon, C. & Miller, P. (Eds.), *The Foucault Effect* (87–104). Hemel Hempstead: Harvester Wheatsheaf.

Gallarotti, G. M. (2011). Soft Power: What It Is, Why It's Important, and the Conditions for Its Effective Use. *Journal of Political Power, 4*(1), 25–47.

Jankowski, M. S. (1991). *Islands in the Street: Gangs and American Urban Society*, vol. 159. Berkeley, CA: University of California Press.

Jankowski, M. S. (2008). *Cracks in the Pavement: Social Change and Resilience in Poor Neighborhoods*. Berkeley, CA: University of California Press.

Jensen, U. T., Andersen, L. B., Bro, L. L., Bøllingtoft, A., Eriksen, T. L. M., Holten, A. L., … & Westergård-Nielsen, N. (2019). Conceptualizing and Measuring Transformational and Transactional Leadership. *Administration & Society, 51*(1), 3–33.

Kennedy, D. M. (2011). Whither Streetwork: The Place of Outreach Workers in Community Violence Prevention. *Criminology & Public Policy, 10*(4), 1045–51.

Kurlantzick, J. (2007). *Charm Offensive: How China's Soft Power Is Transforming the World*. New Haven, CT: Yale University Press.

Lord, G. D. & Blankenberg, N. (2016). *Cities, Museums and Soft Power*. Washington, DC: Rowman & Littlefield.

Lukes, S. (1974). *Power: A Radical View*. Basingstoke: Macmillan.

Maggetti, M. (2015). Hard and Soft Governance. In Lynggaard, K., Manners, I. & Löfgren, J. (Eds.), *Research Methods in European Union Studies* (252–65). London: Palgrave Macmillan.

Niemann, D., Martens, K. & Teltemann, J. (2017). PISA and Its Consequences: Shaping Education Policies through International Comparisons. *European Journal of Education*, *52*(2), 175–83.

Nossel, S. (2004). Smart Power. *Foreign Affairs*, *83*(2), 131–42.

Nye, J. S. (1990). Soft Power. *Foreign Policy*, *80*, 153–71.

Nye, J. S. (2004). Soft Power and American Foreign Policy. *Political Science Quarterly*, *119*(2), 255–70.

Nye, J. S. (2008). *The Powers to Lead*. Oxford: Oxford University Press.

Papachristos, A. V. & Kirk, D. S. (2015). Changing the Street Dynamic: Evaluating Chicago's Group Violence Reduction Strategy. *Criminology & Public Policy*, *14*(3), 525–58.

Peters, B. G., Pierre, J., Sørensen, E. & Torfing, J. (2022). Bringing Political Science Back into Public Administration Research. *Governance: An International Journal of Policy, Administration, and Institutions*, *35*(4), 962–82.

Petrone, F. (2019). A Specter is Haunting the West (?): The BRICS and the Future of Global Governance. *The Rest: Journal of Politics and Development*, *9*(1), 20–32.

Quattrin, R., Filiputti, E. & Brusaferro, S. (2015). Health Promotion Campaigns and Mass Media: Looking for Evidence. *Primary Health Care: Open Access*, *5*(1), 1–7.

Rose, N. (1999). *Powers of Freedom: Reframing Political Thought*. Cambridge: Cambridge University Press.

Rothman, S. B. (2011). Revising the Soft Power Concept: What Are the Means and Mechanisms of Soft Power? *Journal of Political Power*, *4*(1), 49–64.

Saint-Simon, H. (1975). *Henri Saint-Simon (1760–1825): Selected Writings on Science, Industry and Social Organisation*. Teaneck, NJ: Holmes and Meier.

Salamon, L. M. (2002). *The Tools of Government: A Guide to the New Governance*. New York: Oxford University Press.

Schillemans, T. (2013). Moving beyond the Clash of Interests: On a Stewardship Theory and the Relationships between Central Government Departments and Public Agencies. *Public Management Review*, *15*(4), 541–62.

Shelach-Lavi, G. (2019). Archaeology and Politics in China: Historical Paradigm and Identity Construction in Museum Exhibitions. *China Information*, *33*(1), 23–45.

Siegel, M. (1998). Mass Media Antismoking Campaigns: A Powerful Tool for Health Promotion. *Annals of Internal Medicine*, *129*(2), 128–32.

Soames Job, R. F. (1988). Effective and Ineffective Use of Fear in Health Promotion Campaigns. *American Journal of Public Health*, *78*(2), 163–7.

Swiney, C. (2020). The Urbanization of International Law and International Relations: The Rising Soft Power of Cities in Global Governance. *Michigan Journal of International Law*, *41*(2), 227–78.

Thompson, L. & Kumar, A. (2011). Responses to Health Promotion Campaigns: Resistance, Denial and Othering. *Critical Public Health*, *21*(1), 105–17.

Torfing, J. (2009). Rethinking Path-Dependence in Public Policy Research. *Critical Policy Studies*, *3*(1), 70–83.

Trubek, D. M. & Trubek, L. G. (2005). Hard and Soft Law in the Construction of Social Europe: The Role of the Open Method of Co-ordination. *European Law Journal*, *11*(3), 343–64.

Varutti, M. (2014). *Museums in China: The Politics of Representation after Mao*, vol. 13. Woodbridge: Boydell Press.

Wilson, E. J. (2008). Hard Power, Soft Power, Smart Power. *The Annals of the American Academy of Political and Social Science*, *616*(1), 110–24.

Zeitoun, M., Mirumachi, N. & Warner, J. (2011). Transboundary Water Interaction II: Soft Power Underlying Conflict and Cooperation. *International Environmental Agreements*, *11*(2), 159–78.
Zhang, F. & Courty, P. (2021). The China Museum Boom: Soft Power and Cultural Nationalism. *International Journal of Cultural Policy*, *27*(1), 30–49.

10. From intra-organizational to inter-organizational leadership

Public bureaucracy tended to reduce the administrative role of public leaders to ensure public employees complied with legal and administrative rules. New Public Management (NPM) claimed that this focus on compliance was too narrow and recommended that public leaders exercised a clear, visible, and proactive leadership aiming to enhance the efficiency and effectiveness of public organizations. As such, multiple generations of public managers were taught to use a combination of transactional and transformational leadership to strengthen public employee motivation to deliver high-quality services at low cost. Hence, public leaders should lead downwards and inwards, focusing on the delivery of measurable results based on the mobilization of their own budget, organization, and employees. In sum, the public governance orthodoxy combines an internal leadership for compliance with an internal leadership for performance.

Today, there is growing awareness of how holistic service production in a fragmented public sector as well as the creation of innovative public value outcomes in response to wicked and turbulent problems require inter-organizational and cross-boundary collaboration. This new awareness prompts the development of new forms of distributive, horizontal, and integrative leadership aimed at involving a broad range of actors in undertaking important leadership tasks, facilitating the constructive management of difference in groups of peers and bringing public and private actors together in fruitful cooperation. These new forms of leadership give rise to a series of dilemmas that must be handled to further advance these new forms of inter-organizational leadership. Hence, a key challenge facing public leaders is to lead their own organizations while simultaneously leading collaborative processes that threaten to dissolve the boundary between their organization and its environment. Another challenge is to align horizontal, dialogue-based leadership with vertical, imposition-based leadership. Finally, the distribution of leadership tasks may conflict with the attempt to ensure accountability.

This chapter takes a closer look at the shift from the exclusive focus on intra-organizational leadership characterizing the public governance orthodoxy to a more encompassing focus on the inter-organizational leadership practiced in networks and partnerships in which a plethora of public and private actors aim to produce public value outcomes. First, it unravels the limitations of the so-called "managerial revolution" that advocated for a stronger and more proactive public leadership without ever really questioning the intra-organizational focus of public leaders. Next, it examines the discovery of wicked and turbulent problems and the need for collaborative governance that cuts across organizational and sectoral boundaries. These discussions pave the way for a new focus on inter-organizational leadership aiming to metagovern collaborative governance arenas based on distributional, horizontal, and integrative leadership. The overview of these and other forms of inter-organizational leadership is followed by discussion of the inherent dilemmas and the attempt to cope with them. The conclusion sets an agenda for future research in inter-organizational leadership.

THE MANAGERIAL REVOLUTION AND ITS LIMITS

Traditional forms of bureaucratic public administration relied on organizational structures, rules, and procedures to ensure compliance with legal and administrative rules. Democratically elected politicians made authoritative political decisions and delegated responsibility for the implementation of laws and regulations to public administration that allegedly would know how to pick the right tool to ensure goal attainment and could be trusted to serve their political principles based on an equal measure of loyalty and neutrality. Public managers would translate laws and regulations into administrative rules and routines and ensure that the lower echelons of public employees follow the rules. Centralized hierarchies, emphasis on written rules, bureaucratic virtues and well-established procedures for oversight, and auditing help public managers to ensure compliance without too much direct interference in the routinized behavior of public administrators. Indeed, the whole idea of Weberian bureaucracy is to create an organization in which the impact of "time" and "personalized leadership" is minimal (Derakhshan & Fatehi 1985).

NPM supporters were unconvinced that the tandem of bureaucratic virtues and organizational structures would effectively prevent opportunistic behavior on the part of public employees who are axiomatically assumed to pursue their own interests and seek to enhance their autonomy as public sector professionals. Moreover, even if compliance with rules and norms could be ensured, this is not enough since rule-following does not necessarily translate into desirable results such as the delivery of high-quality, low-cost solutions (Osborne & Gaebler 1993). The criticisms of the narrow focus on rule compliance rather than the production of measurable results call for a managerial revolution promoting professional, hands-on leadership in the public sector (Hood 1991). To motivate public employees to do their utmost to enhance both efficiency and effectiveness in service delivery, we need a clearer, more visible, and more proactive leadership exercised by dedicated public managers. Public management should be considered a profession in its own right, and public managers should be trained and educated to maximize their impact (Hood 1991). Performance information must be readily available as a tool for management, and room for exercising leadership should be expanded through a combination of devolution and deregulation. However, it is not enough to "let" managers manage, since we must also "make" them manage by creating incentive systems with wage bonuses and short-term contracts that encourage them to do so (Normann 2001). Finally, as political power and administrative responsibility are devolved to relatively autonomous public organizations, the top-level public managers must invest time and resources in strategic management that can set the course for middle managers and employees and gradually transform the organization to optimize goal achievement. Eventually, the tasks of public leaders and managers are further differentiated according to their position in the organizational hierarchy. While top-level leaders lead the entire organization, section heads and middle managers lead other managers, while frontline managers lead their staff.

The managerial revolution upgrades and expands the role of public managers, giving them a new mission to enhance the performance of public service organizations by providing clear goals and targets for service production, continuously monitoring, assessing results and using sticks, carrots, and sermons to motivate employees to further improve efficiency and effectiveness (Dooren et al. 2015). The renewed effort to enhance staff motivation combines transactional leadership that speaks to the extrinsic motivation of public employees with transformational leadership that speaks to their intrinsic task motivation and public service motivation (Jensen et al. 2019). This combination creates tension between the *Homo economicus* model that underpins transactional leadership and the more social constructivist assumptions concerning the shaping of values and identities that is implicit in transformational leadership. NPM seems to have become more pragmatic over the years, however, and is ready to pursue new leadership strategies to enhance motivation.

It goes without saying that public managers should continue to ensure compliance with political and administrative rules and laws in a more hands-off manner, but the emphasis is on hands-on performance management. In both cases, the exercise of leadership focuses on creating internal organizational structures and routines (compliance systems or performance management systems) and shaping public employee behavior (goal-setting, rule-making, monitoring, and conditional use of rewards and punishment). As such, the NPM-instigated managerial revolution does not transgress the boundaries of public service organizations. As explained in Chapter 7, there was a brief attempt at more joined-up government, but it was too little, too late and remained internal to the public sector. The bottom line is that public leadership is exercised from the top and down the bureaucratic chain of command, and it continues to have an inward focus as it is preoccupied with delivering rule-bound results based on the internal budget, organizational capacities, and employees. Thus, as mentioned in Chapters 6, 7, and 8, there is little focus within the public governance orthodoxy on how to mobilize external resources, how to promote pluricentric coordination, and how to facilitate multi-level governance. This might be because the focus is primarily on solving relatively simple problems through public service provision.

FROM SIMPLE TO WICKED AND TURBULENT PROBLEMS

After the Second World War, many Western countries expanded the public sector to solve a range of fairly simple problems. Young people needed daycare, education, and training before eventually entering the labor market. Those unable to sustain themselves as wage earners needed social benefits, unemployment benefits or retirement, and those who fell ill, became frail or suffered injury needed health care and hospital treatment. In a growing number of areas, the publicly financed welfare state provided services to meet citizens' needs. Services were standardized and produced in massive quantities, exploiting economies of scale. It was often a matter of predicting and providing: what would demographic development look like in the coming years, and how many citizens would need what kind of services?

In the 1960s and 1970s, researchers and practitioners discovered a new type of "wicked" problem that was particularly visible in public planning (Churchman 1967; Rittel & Webber 1973). Wicked problems are ill-defined, and closer scrutiny often reveals that they are symptoms of myriad other problems. There are often many stakeholders with different perspectives and interests, which leads to goal conflicts that preclude trial and error. There is no final solution because social systems are open and subject to change. Finally, there is frequently no room for error or delay in solving them. In short, wicked problems are cognitively and politically complex.

The conceptualization of wicked problems was important in terms of helping to explain why certain problems were difficult to solve and why there were so many examples of policy failures. Over the years, the new problem diagnosis has become so popular that we must caution ourselves that not all problems are wicked and that there are different degrees of wickedness (Alford & Head 2017; Peters 2017). Critics have pointed out a series of limitations and flaws in the wicked-problem concept, but they tend to admit that it makes sense to talk about wickedness in terms of a high level of unstructuredness or problematicity around a policy problem and an excess of wide and conflictual distances between stakeholders (Turnbull & Hoppe 2019). Other researchers have expanded the diagnosis of wicked problems and talk about super-wicked problems (Lazarus 2009; Levin et al. 2012). These are wicked problems where the time for solving them is running out, those seeking to solve the problems are causing them, government does not control the choices necessary to solve them, and the future is irrationally discounted as decision-makers make short-sighted choices. The current climate crisis offers a case in point.

New research emphasizes the temporal dimension of wicked problems and identifies turbulent problems that appear to be highly variable, inconsistent, unexpected, unpredictable, and potentially overwhelming, as well as being complex (Porte 2007; Ansell & Trondal 2017; Ansell et al. 2021). As witnessed by the tsunami of financial, refugee, nature, climate, and health crises we are confronting, we seem to be living in turbulent times in which unexpected, unpredictable, and wicked problems come and go and put pressure on government to design new, robust coping strategies. The COVID-19 pandemic has demonstrated both the turbulence and complexity of the governance challenges that call for collaboration between a broad array of public and private actors and the development of innovative and adaptive solutions (Ansell et al. 2021).

THE PROACTIVE USE OF NETWORKS AND PARTNERSHIPS IN PUBLIC GOVERNANCE

Although Daviter (2017) warns us that serious questions remain regarding the effectiveness of collaborative governance as a tool for solving wicked problems, there is widespread agreement that wicked and turbulent problems are best dealt with through collaboration in networks and partnerships. Roberts (2000) claims that collaborative strategies for solving wicked and unruly problems may work well when power is dispersed and actors recognize their interdependence—and thus the need to exchange and pool ideas and resources in pursuit of collaborative advantage (Huxham 1996). Collaborative strategies are at least better than hierarchical and competitive strategies. Weber and Khademian (2008) argue that wicked problems that are unstructured, cross-cutting and relentless are best solved in networks of actors engaged in sending, receiving, and integrating knowledge and ideas. Hence, the capacity to spur collective learning through the integration of disparate knowledge is key to solving wicked problems. Head and Alford (2015) contend that collaborative governance allows distributed actors to reduce conflict through dialogue and develop a shared understanding of the nature of the problem and the range of possible solutions. Network governance facilitates frame reflection, a more holistic inquiry into causes and impacts and a flexible adaptation of provisional solutions to emergent features and surprises. It also enhances the implementation of solutions based on shared contributions, coordinated actions, and joint ownership. The will to communicate among the involved actors and a basic level of trust in the other actors' competences and intentions are key enabling conditions. Hutter (2016) adds that collaborative engagement allows relevant and affected actors to deal with uncertainty and disruption through sense-making and the joint interpretation of events provided that the actors are committed to collaboration and public problem-solving. Finally, Hofstad and Torfing (2015, 2017) highlight the innovative capacity of collaborative networking. Wicked problems call for innovative solutions that disrupt common wisdom and habitual practices, and innovation is stimulated by processes of mutual learning, risk-sharing, and the development of joint ownership over new and bold solutions.

Collaborative forms of governance are by no means new (Kenis & Schneider 1991). Pluralists such as Bentley (1967) and Truman (1971) studied public policymaking based on collaboration, which constitutes the backbone of corporatism and neo-corporatism (Cawson 1978). Heclo (1978) discovered the role of sector-specific policy networks in the US Congress that linked politicians, administrators, and interest organizations. The focus in the growing literature on policy networks (Marsh & Rhodes 1992), however, was more on interest mediation and policy alignment than on complex problem-solving. Hence, it is asserted that collaboration leads to consensus, compromise, or agreement, thereby allowing for stable governance.

The new literature on governance networks (Mayntz 1993; Kickert et al. 1997; Koppenjan & Klijn 2004; Sørensen & Torfing 2007) goes a step farther by viewing collaborative networking as a tool for solving complex problems in fragmented polities. Governance networks bring together a broad range of interdependent public and private actors who explore problems, exchange ideas and resources, engage in mutual learning, and coordinate their efforts to contribute to implementation. Participation goes beyond the infamous "iron triangles" to include a broad range of knowledgeable and competent actors who aim to solve problems that none of them can solve on their own. While inclusive participation helps to enhance input legitimacy, the contribution to complex problem-solving helps to enhance output legitimacy.

Ultimately, the notion of governance networks is a structural concept highlighting the self-regulated creation of interrelations between a particular set of social and political actors that allow them to exchange or pool ideas and resources. As such, much of the research on governance networks focuses on the inclusion and exclusion of actors, the building of trust relations, the patterns of interaction, the formation of coalitions, and so on. While the participating actors are assumed to be collaborating to explore problems and develop joint solutions, the process of collaboration through which actors work together to transform a joint object while constructively managing their differences (Gray 1989) is not always at the forefront of governance network research.

This lacuna spurred the rise of collaborative governance research (Ansell & Gash 2008; Emerson et al. 2012) that focuses less on the structure of the interrelations between the manifold governance actors and more on the contextual conditions, the institutional design, the forms of leadership and the inherent dynamics that support collaborative processes and the production of outputs and outcomes. Parts of the research on collaborative governance have a tendency to focus on collaborative processes that are initiated and managed by public agencies to enhance their reach into wider society and based on interaction between more or less well-organized actors, such as public agencies, interest organizations, private businesses, civil society organizations, researchers, and so on. New research studying co-creation as a tool for public governance tends to emphasize the distributed participation and leadership and highlights the role of lay actors, such as users, citizens, and neighborhoods (Ansell & Torfing 2021). Compared to the parent concept of collaborative governance, the notion of co-creation also highlights the attempt to find innovative solutions to wicked problems rather than merely aligning actors around a particular set of solutions.

Whether one looks at policy networks, governance networks, collaborative governance, or co-creation, the key idea is that collaboration between relevant and affected actors will usually help to clarify complex problems and develop shared solutions. In other words, complex problems are best addressed by complex networks of collaborating actors. This begs the question of how to lead and manage collaborative networks (Sørensen & Torfing 2009) and how to characterize the impact of collaborative leadership and management (Klijn et al. 2010).

THE NEW FORMS OF INTER-ORGANIZATIONAL LEADERSHIP

Confronted with the ubiquitous networks of collaborating actors aiming to solve wicked and unruly problems in the field of public planning, climate change, or crisis management, public leaders and managers realize that downward and inward leadership practices are not particularly helpful, since the challenge is to lead a group of horizontally related actors that come from different organizations, sectors, and parts of society (Kramer et al. 2019). Hence, intra-organizational leadership must be replaced with inter-organizational leadership (see Müller-Seitz 2012).

An eye-opener stressing the importance of inter-organizational leadership is provided by the efforts to lead and manage the mandated governance networks responsible for the adaptation of the Danish active labor-market policy to local conditions (the so-called "Local Employment Councils"). The local networks bring together representatives from the municipal job center, the employers' organization, local trade unions, the disabled people's association, and so on, and they are led and managed by the mayor with the support of experienced public managers. Studies based on quantitative and qualitative data from a series of case studies show that inter-organizational leadership plays a key role in promoting the effective and democratic governance of local active employment policy and that concrete forms of leadership and management are more important than institutional governance designs in shaping outcomes (see Damgaard & Torfing 2010, 2011). Other studies confirm the positive impact of inter-organizational leadership on network outcomes (Klijn et al. 2010; Ysa et al. 2014).

Leadership in and of inter-organizational networks differs significantly from leadership in individual organizations (Silvia & McGuire 2010). The network actors are both *interdependent*, insofar as they need to exchange ideas and resources to solve common problems, and *independent* in the sense that they each have their different rule and resource base and participate in network activities on a voluntary basis. The independence of the network actors means that they are unlikely to accept traditional bureaucratic forms of command-and-control leadership. The network actors are also likely to oppose leadership based on performance management, sticks and carrots and transformative leadership, where particular goals, values, and visions are imposed on the network rather than being developed through deliberative interaction; in networks, public leaders should not present solutions to the actors—they should involve them in making them.

The notion of metagovernance aims to capture the attempts of public leaders to influence the process and outcomes of collaborative networking without reverting too much to hierarchical forms of imposition (Jessop 2002; Sørensen & Torfing 2009; Torfing et al. 2012). Other research contributions explore facilitative leadership and network management (Ansell & Gash 2008; Koppenjan & Klijn 2004). In this new literature on inter-organizational leadership, it is common to draw a distinction between hands-off network design and hands-on process management. Hands-off network design involves the formulating of mandates and remits for collaborative networks, allocating budget frames, recruiting actors, building trust relations, defining ground-rules for interaction, setting up a communication infrastructure, planning activities, defining milestones and deadlines, and so on. Hands-on process management involves the motivation of actors, clarification of interdependencies, facilitation of collaboration, mediation of conflict, stimulation of learning, catalyzation of innovation, support of decision-making, evaluation of progress toward goal attainment, and so on. While network structuring through institutional design and collaborative process management is equally important, the work in hand will examine the latter more closely.

There are a number of different contributions to understanding what hands-on process management in inter-organizational settings entails. Here, we shall briefly review a few important ideas about distributed leadership, horizontal leadership, and integrative leadership.

First, leadership in collaborative arenas is often *distributed* in the sense that public managers, public employees, non-governmental organizations, volunteer coordinators, commercial enterprises, social entrepreneurs, or even resourceful citizens are all, to a greater or lesser extent, contributing to the exercise of leadership, which breaks down the traditional leader–follower dichotomy (Bolden 2011). Distributed leadership is not done by an individual to other actors but rather is a result of interactions between a broad range of actors (Bennett et al. 2003). These interactions may take the form of a joint discussion of goals, plans, and procedures, but they may also involve the distribution of leadership tasks to different actors. As for the latter, Spillane (2006) distinguishes between: (1) collaborated distribution, where two or more individuals work together to execute a particular leadership task; (2) collective distribution, where two or more individuals work separately but interdependently to carry out a leadership task; and (3) coordinated distribution, where two or more individuals work in sequence to complete a leadership task.

This kind of decentered, non-heroic leadership associated with distributed leadership works well in governance networks in which the ability of a single leader to lead through the imposition of their will on the rest of the actors is limited. Distributed leadership is advantageous in that it tends to enhance the overall leadership capacity by involving competent and well-motivated actors in the exercise of shared leadership, but the risk is that leadership becomes somewhat diffuse and nobody is ready to assume responsibility when things go wrong. This problem can be overcome by cultivating the norm that all network leaders refer to a lead actor or an appointed leadership group that assumes overall responsibility for coordinating the exercise of inter-organizational leaderships and ensuring that core leadership tasks are fulfilled by competent, engaged, and accountable actors.

Second, leadership will tend to be *horizontal* in collaborative networks where the facilitator and the different participants are peers and therefore share the same general status. Horizontal leadership aims to empower the members of the "team," delegate power to team members, and facilitate their self-management while securing high-intensity, all-to-all communication, and creating a shared socio-cognitive space (Yu et al. 2018; Drouin et al. 2021). Horizontal leadership co-exists with vertical leadership aimed at giving direction to the collaborative endeavor and ensuring progress toward the achievement of common goals. The literature points to the importance of balancing horizontal and vertical leadership.

Relational coordination is the core of horizontal leadership. It proposes that "shared goals, shared knowledge, and mutual respect help to support frequent, timely, accurate, problem-solving communication, and vice versa, enabling stakeholders to effectively coordinate their work across boundaries" (Bolton et al. 2021: 290). Relational coordination is facilitated by boundary spanners who are translating meaning across boundaries and lifeworlds; shared information and knowledge systems allowing everyone to access updated material; and shared accountability and reward systems that encourage actors to work together while reducing collective action problems.

Relational coordination in horizontal teams seems to work well in relatively homogenous groups (e.g., work groups, task forces) but may not work as well in governance networks where the actors have different characteristics and interests and do not really know each other (Hoch et al. 2010). At the very least, a great deal of work may be required on the part of horizontal leaders to turn a loosely coupled network of governance actors into a problem-solving team.

Third, integrative leadership is cross-boundary leadership aiming to develop networks and partnerships that *integrate* actors across organizational, sectoral, and/or jurisdictional borders in order to solve problems and achieve a common good (Crosby & Bryson 2010; Morse 2010). Drawing on Mary Parker Follett's (1924) ideas about integration as a social process that unites different views, interests, or forms of knowledge in ways that satisfy all of the involved parties, integrative leadership aims to catalyze the collaboration between actors relevant for public problem-solving. This is achieved by exploiting initial conditions, enabling structures, past experiences, and contingencies that generate opportunities and a sense of urgency and necessity (Bryson et al. 2006), and through the use of boundary objects (e.g., maps, reports, physical models, forecasts) and boundary-spanning activities (e.g., roundtables, workshops, video conferences, town walks). The latter may be initiated and orchestrated by boundary organizations that serve as intermediaries and brokers linking different groups, communities, and organizations (Morse 2010). Integrative leaders connect relevant and affected actors who together can solve public problems through structured collaboration. As Crosby and Bryson (2010) point out, however, integrative leaders are not merely a medium for networked collaboration but also active agents and instigators who play the roles of champions and sponsors. Champions are tireless, process-savvy organizers and promoters of change efforts who provide visionary ideas, prompt action, and bring enthusiasm to a project. Sponsors are less involved in the change process but deploy authority, money, or connections to move the change effort forward and protect the integrity of the process. Both sponsors and champions will need to see the problem as significant and to envision a solution to the problem, but they should not be too wedded to specific problem definitions or solutions, as that will deprive them of the ability to enroll diverse stakeholders in collaborative problem-solving and to bridge the differences between them. Integrative leaders do not only act as champions and sponsors bringing actors together in problem-solving networks and partnerships. They must also build trust, manage conflicts, equalize power differentials, deal with shocks, build supportive governance structures, and track results in order to ensure accountability (Crosby & Bryson 2010).

Theories of distributed leadership, horizontal leadership and integrative leadership tend to overlap, and it is not always easy to see the differences between them; although distributed leadership is primarily concerned with the leader–follower relations, horizontal leadership focuses on facilitating good teamwork, while integrative leadership is predominantly concerned with the catalyzing role of leadership. Together, the three theories of inter-organizational leadership aim to shift the focus of leadership thinking from how to motivate individual employees ("leading through others") to how to build and sustain collaborative relations between manifold actors ("leading with others"). Hence, leadership in a world of dispersed and shared powers should focus less on compliance and performance and more on mobilizing the knowledge, expertise, and resources of different actors and securing a constructive and fruitful exchange between them. In so doing, leaders must give up their heroic, commanding role in favor of a more modest role as the facilitator of collaborative interaction. As facilitators, they must create space for other actors and let them take the lead within the overall framework guiding the collaboration.

In reality, the exercise of a distributed, horizontal, and integrative leadership is very difficult, and success is by no means guaranteed. Endres and Weibler (2019) studied two similar inter-organizational networks to explore the conditions for the emergence of some kind of shared leadership. They found that the development of a joint motivational network identity, which includes a collectivistic network identity, joint network motivation, and a largely value-laden attitude toward network participation, is conducive to the development of shared leadership. In the network where such an identity was absent, the collaborative governance process remained leaderless. Thus, inter-organizational leadership is not only a function of the skills of the leaders but also conditioned by the identity of the network actors.

DILEMMAS AND COPING STRATEGIES

As collaborative governance in networks and partnerships is becoming a prominent tool for dealing with wicked and unruly problems, the need for inter-organizational leadership increases. Silvia and McGuire (2010) find a stark difference between inter-organizational leadership in network contexts and intra-organizational leadership in single-agency contexts. Leaders in network contexts focus much more on people-oriented leadership behaviors, such as treating everybody equally, building mutual trust, and sharing leadership tasks, than do leaders in single-agency settings. This reflects the ambition of inter-organizational leaders to build and sustain collaborative interaction.

We need to train future leaders in inter-organizational leadership, since this type of leadership will take up a growing amount of their time and energy. Future leaders must be taught a new skill set, but they should also be encouraged to reflect on the dilemmas arising from an increasing emphasis on inter-organizational leadership that embraces the ideas of distributional, horizontal, and integrative leadership.

A first dilemma emerges because public leaders and managers continue to have a clear and formal responsibility for leading their own organizations and employees while, simultaneously, they must lead collaborative processes that threaten to dissolve the boundary between their organization and its environment. This raises questions about the loyalty and commitment of public leaders: should they give priority to the intra-organizational leadership and seek to protect the integrity of their own organization and pursue its organizational interests in the network setting? Or should they prioritize the inter-organizational leadership of the network by supporting the collaborative process and the joint production of public value outcomes? Leaders who invest a lot of time and energy in inter-organizational leadership may be accused of neglecting or even undermining their own organizations. Conversely, leaders who merely have an eye for their own organization, its interests and its survival may be criticized for failing to create collaborative advantage. Organizations may cope with this dilemma by having leaders who specialize in either intra- or inter-organizational leadership. The resulting risk of conflict between the two types of leadership may be solved by creating leadership teams with mixed and shifting roles and competences.

A second dilemma arises between a horizontal leadership aimed at facilitating dialogue in a group of peers and a vertical leadership that imposes a particular agenda or insists on a particular type of solution. While vertical leadership is needed to provide direction, mandate, and legitimacy, there is always a risk of vertical leadership becoming too heavy-handed and either generating fierce opposition or demotivating the participants in networked collaboration. At the same time, the absence of vertical leadership may lead to mission drift or create frustration among the participants because of unclear framework conditions for collaboration. Hence, the balancing of vertical and horizontal leadership is called for. One way to try to achieve a balance is to ensure an ongoing dialogue between champions and sponsors catalyzing and framing collaboration and the horizontal leaders who are facilitating, supporting, and driving the interaction in the group of peer stakeholders. Continuous dialogue can help to ensure that vertical leadership is neither too strong nor too weak, and thus that the horizontal leadership of collaborative networks takes place in the shadow of hierarchy (Scharpf 1994).

A final dilemma is between the distributed leadership in collaborative problem-solving processes and the need to ensure some kind of accountability for overall performance. It is notoriously difficult to ensure accountability in collaborative settings, where the "many-hands" problem prevents the identification of responsible actors (Schillemans & Bovens 2011). This problem is exacerbated when not only action but also leadership is distributed. It is easier to hold hierarchical leaders to account for governance failures but giving up distributed leadership will reduce the aggregate leadership capacity in networks and may foster resentment toward the hierarchical leadership. One way of coping with this dilemma is to insist on holding the entire network to account by forcing it to produce regular, non-technical accounts of its work that can be assessed by both higher-level authorities and relevant constituencies affected by the governance solutions.

THE FUTURE OF INTER-ORGANIZATIONAL LEADERSHIP

While the research on wicked problems and the need for collaborative governance in networks and partnerships is well established, the research on inter-organizational leadership is relatively new. Hence, although important inroads have been made, much more research is still required in this area.

Theoretically, we need closer scrutiny of the different theories of inter-organizational leadership and their distinctiveness and overlaps. Such a research exercise may serve as a prelude to the development of an integrated theoretical framework capable of guiding future studies and perhaps leading to the formulation of different theoretical models.

Empirically, we need more in-depth knowledge of the concrete forms and tools of inter-organizational leadership and how they are deployed by administrative and/or political leaders or perhaps by professional facilitators who are hired for the occasion. Conflict mediation is important in multi-actor governance but seems to be neglected by theories of distributed, horizontal, and integrative leadership that only pay scant attention to the risk that collaborative governance may foster destructive conflicts leading to stalemate. Having drawn up an inventory of the tools that inter-organizational leaders can use, the next step will be to study which tools are used in different contexts and how different combinations of tools may impact efficiency, effectiveness, resilience, democratic legitimacy, and other outcomes.

Further studies of inter-organizational leadership should also pay attention to the interaction between hands-on leadership and hands-off institutional design to assess the joint impact of different forms and combinations of metagovernance. One area where such a study is urgent is green transition and the achievement of the Sustainable Development Goals that the UN describes as a result of collaboration in networks and partnerships. We urgently need to find the "holy grail" in terms of the competing constellations of governance and leaderships tools that can spur the co-creation of green solutions.

A final point concerns the (re-)training of public managers. After many years of leadership training with a strong emphasis on intra-organizational leadership focused on compliance and employee performance, we need new training programs based on a new curriculum that can teach public leaders how to lead inter-organizational collaboration in networks and partnerships where the focus is on solving complex and unruly problems and accomplishing grand societal missions.

REFERENCES

Alford, J. & Head, B. W. (2017). Wicked and Less Wicked Problems: A Typology and a Contingency Framework. *Policy and Society*, *36*(3), 397–413.

Ansell, C. & Gash, A. (2008). Collaborative Governance in Theory and Practice. *Journal of Public Administration Research and Theory*, *18*(4), 543–71.

Ansell, C. & Torfing, J. (2021). *Public Governance as Co-Creation: A Strategy for Revitalizing the Public Sector and Rejuvenating Democracy*. Cambridge: Cambridge University Press.

Ansell, C. & Trondal, J. (2017). Governing Turbulence: An Organizational-Institutional Agenda. *Perspectives on Public Management and Governance*, *1*(1), 43–57.

Ansell, C., Sørensen, E. & Torfing, J. (2021). The COVID-19 Pandemic as a Game Changer for Public Administration and Leadership? The Need for Robust Governance Responses to Turbulent Problems. *Public Management Review*, *23*(7), 949–60.

Bennett, N., Wise, C., Woods, P. A. & Harvey, J. A. (2003). *Distributed Leadership: A Review of Literature*. Nottingham: National College of School Leadership.

Bentley, A. F. (1967). *The Process of Government: A Study of Social Pressure*. Cambridge, MA: Harvard University Press.

Bolden, R. (2011). Distributed Leadership in Organizations: A Review of Theory and Research. *International Journal of Management Reviews*, *13*(3), 251–69.

Bolton, R., Logan, C. & Gittell, J. H. (2021). Revisiting Relational Coordination: A Systematic Review. *The Journal of Applied Behavioral Science*, *57*(3), 290–322.

Bryson, J. M., Crosby, B. C. & Stone, M. M. (2006). The Design and Implementation of Cross-Sector Collaborations: Propositions from the Literature. *Public Administration Review*, *66*(s1), 44–55.

Cawson, A. (1978). Pluralism, Corporatism and the Role of the State. *Government and Opposition*, *13*(2), 178–98.

Churchman, C. W. (1967). Guest Editorial: Wicked Problems. *Management Science*, *14*(4), B141–B142.

Crosby, B. C. & Bryson, J. M. (2010). Integrative Leadership and the Creation and Maintenance of Cross-Sector Collaboration. *Leadership Quarterly*, *21*(2), 211–30.

Damgaard, B. & Torfing, J. (2010). Network Governance of Active Employment Policy: The Danish Experience. *Journal of European Social Policy*, *20*(3), 248–62.

Damgaard, B. & Torfing, J. (2011). The Impact of Metagovernance on Local Governance Networks: Lessons from Danish Employment Policy. *Local Government Studies*, *37*(3), 291–316.

Daviter, F. (2017). Coping, Taming or Solving: Alternative Approaches to the Governance of Wicked Problems. *Policy Studies*, *38*(6), 571–88.

Derakhshan, F. & Fatehi, K. (1985). Bureaucracy as a Leadership Substitute: A Review of History. *Leadership & Organization Development Journal*, *6*(4), 13–16.

Dooren, W. V., Bouckaert, G. & Halligan, J. (2015). *Performance Management in the Public Sector*. London: Routledge.

Drouin, N., Müller, R., Sankaran, S. & Vaagaasar, A. L. (2021). Balancing Leadership in Projects: Role of the Socio-Cognitive Space. *Project Leadership and Society*, *2*, 100031.

Emerson, K., Nabatchi, T. & Balogh, S. (2012). An Integrative Framework for Collaborative Governance. *Journal of Public Administration Research and Theory*, *22*(1), 1–29.

Endres, S. & Weibler, J. (2019). *Plural Leadership: Eine zukunftsweisende Alternative zur One-Man-Show*. Berlin: Springer-Verlag.

Follett, M. P. (1924). *Creative Experience*. New York: Longmans, Green & Co.

Gray, B. (1989). *Collaborating: Finding Common Ground for Multiparty Problems*. San Francisco, CA: Jossey-Bass Publishers.

Head, B. W. & Alford, J. (2015). Wicked Problems: Implications for Public Policy and Management. *Administration & Society*, *47*(6), 711–39.

Heclo, H. (1978). Issue Networks and the Executive Establishment. *Public Administration Concepts Cases*, *413*(413), 46–57.

Hoch, J. E., Pearce, C. L. & Welzel, L. (2010). Is the Most Effective Team Leadership Shared? The Impact of Shared Leadership, Age Diversity, and Coordination on Team Performance. *Journal of Personnel Psychology*, *9*(3), 105–16.

Hofstad, H. & Torfing, J. (2015). Collaborative Innovation as a Tool for Environmental, Economic and Social Sustainability in Regional Governance. *Scandinavian Journal of Public Administration*, *19*(4), 49–70.

Hofstad, H. & Torfing, J. (2017). Towards a Climate-Resilient City: Collaborative Innovation for a "Green Shift." In Fernandez, R. A. C., Zubelzu, S. & Martínez, R. (Eds). *Oslo Carbon Footprint and the Industrial Life Cycle* (221–42). Cham: Springer.

Hood, C. (1991). A Public Administration for All Seasons? *Public Administration*, *69*(1), 1–19.

Hutter, G. (2016). Collaborative Governance and Rare Floods in Urban Regions: Dealing with Uncertainty and Surprise. *Environmental Science & Policy*, *55*(P2), 302–8.

Huxham, C. (Ed.) (1996). *Creating Collaborative Advantage*. London: Sage.

Jensen, U. T., Andersen, L. B., Bro, L. L., Bøllingtoft, A., Eriksen, T. L. M., Holten, A. L., ... & Westergård-Nielsen, N. (2019). Conceptualizing and Measuring Transformational and Transactional Leadership. *Administration & Society*, *51*(1), 3–33.

Jessop, B. (2002). *The Future of the Capitalist State*. Cambridge: Polity Press.

Kenis, P. & Schneider, V. (1991). Policy Networks and Policy Analysis: Scrutinizing a New Analytical Toolbox. In Marin, B. & Mayntz, R. (Eds.), *Policy Networks* (25–59). Frankfurt-am-Main: Campus Verlag.

Kickert, W. J. M., Klijn, E. H. & Koppenjan, J. F. M. (Eds.) (1997). *Managing Complex Networks*. London: Sage.

Klijn, E. H., Steijn, B. & Edelenbos, J. (2010). The Impact of Network Management on Outcomes in Governance Networks. *Public Administration, 88*(4), 1063–82.

Koppenjan, J. & Klijn, E. H. (2004). *Managing Uncertainties in Networks: A Network Approach to Problem Solving and Decision Making*. Abingdon: Routledge.

Kramer, M. W., Day, E. A., Nguyen, C., Hoelscher, C. S. & Cooper, O. D. (2019). Leadership in an Interorganizational Collaboration: A Qualitative Study of a Statewide Interagency Taskforce. *Human Relations, 72*(2), 397–419.

Lazarus, R. J. (2009). Super Wicked Problems and Climate Change: Restraining the Present to Liberate the Future. *Cornell Law Review, 94*(5), 1153–234.

Levin, K., Cashore, B., Bernstein, S. & Auld, G. (2012). Overcoming the Tragedy of Super Wicked Problems: Constraining Our Future Selves to Ameliorate Global Climate Change. *Policy Sciences, 45*(2), 123–52.

Marsh, D. & Rhodes, R. A. W. (Eds.) (1992). *Policy Networks in British Government*. Oxford: Oxford University Press.

Mayntz, R. (1993). Governing Failure and the Problem of Governability: Some Comments on a Theoretical Paradigm. In Kooiman, J. (Ed.), *Modern Governance* (9–21). London: Sage.

Morse, R. S. (2010). Integrative Public Leadership: Catalyzing Collaboration to Create Public Value. *The Leadership Quarterly, 21*(2), 231–45.

Müller-Seitz, G. (2012). Leadership in Interorganizational Networks: A Literature Review and Suggestions for Future Research. *International Journal of Management Reviews, 14*(4), 428–43.

Normann, R. (2001). *Service Management*, 3rd edn. Chichester: Wiley.

Osborne, D. & Gaebler, T. (1993). *Reinventing Government: How the Entrepreneurial Spirit Is Transforming the Public Sector*. Reading, MA: Addison-Wesley.

Peters, B. G. (2017). What Is So Wicked about Wicked Problems? A Conceptual Analysis and a Research Program. *Policy and Society, 36*(3), 385–96.

Porte, T. R. L. (2007). Critical Infrastructure in the Face of a Predatory Future: Preparing for Untoward Surprise. *Journal of Contingencies and Crisis Management, 15*(1), 60–64.

Rittel, H. W. & Webber, M. M. (1973). Dilemmas in a General Theory of Planning. *Policy Sciences, 4*(2), 155–69.

Roberts, N. C. (2000). Wicked Problems and Network Approaches to Resolution. *International Public Management Review, 1*(1), 1–19.

Scharpf, F. W. (1994). Games Real Actors Could Play: Positive and Negative Coordination in Embedded Negotiations. *Journal of Theoretical Politics, 6*(1), 27–53.

Schillemans, T. & Bovens, M. (2011). The Challenge of Multiple Accountability. In Dubnick, M. J. & Frederickson, H. G. (Eds.), *Accountable Governance: Problems and Promises* (3–21). New York: Routledge.

Silvia, C. & McGuire, M. (2010). Leading Public Sector Networks: An Empirical Examination of Integrative Leadership Behaviors. *The Leadership Quarterly, 21*(2), 264–77.

Sørensen, E. & Torfing, J. (Eds.) (2007). *Theories of Democratic Network Governance*. London: Palgrave Macmillan.

Sørensen, E. & Torfing, J. (2009). Making Governance Networks Effective and Democratic through Metagovernance. *Public Administration, 87*(2), 234–58.

Spillane, J. P. (2006). Towards a Theory of Leadership Practice: A Distributed Perspective. In Westbury, I. & Milburn, G. (Eds.), *Rethinking Schooling* (208–42). London: Routledge.

Torfing, J., Peters, B. G., Pierre, J. & Sørensen, E. (2012). *Interactive Governance: Advancing the Paradigm*. Oxford: Oxford University Press.

Truman, D. (1971). *The Governmental Process*. New York: Knopf.

Turnbull, N. & Hoppe, R. (2019). Problematizing "Wickedness": A Critique of the Wicked Problems Concept, from Philosophy to Practice. *Policy and Society*, *38*(2), 315–37.

Weber, E. P. & Khademian, A. M. (2008). Wicked Problems, Knowledge Challenges and Collaborative Capacity Builders in Network Settings. *Public Administration Review*, *68*(2), 334–49.

Ysa, T., Sierra, V. & Esteve, M. (2014). Determinants of Network Outcomes: The Impact of Management Strategies. *Public Administration*, *92*(3), 636–55.

Yu, M., Vaagaasar, A. L., Müller, R., Wang, L. & Zhu, F. (2018). Empowerment: The Key to Horizontal Leadership in Projects. *International Journal of Project Management*, *36*(7), 992–1006.

11. From stability and continuous improvement to innovation

Public bureaucracy tends to prioritize stability over change. When change is needed, it is better for it to be incremental to avoid the hazards of over-ambitious goal-setting and the lack of adequate means to reach said goals. There is no particular premium on innovation in public bureaucracy. New Public Management (NPM) accused public bureaucracies of being too big and ossified (Downs 1967) and therefore incapable of pursuing the goal of continuous service improvement. For public bureaucracies, the solution to the problem of the lack of dynamism was to focus on goals and results rather than rules, to strengthen the role of public managers and to introduce new forms of market-based competition into the public sector. Indeed, NPM aimed to spur organizational innovation by strengthening the capacity for strategic management and expanding the entrepreneurial role of local managers within a deregulated public sector, but the emphasis on performance control, compliance with given standards, efficiency, and budget discipline appears to have undermined the attempt to boost public innovation capacity. Hence, what stands out is the attempt of the public governance orthodoxy to improve service quality incrementally while continuously cutting costs.

Today, however, the cross-pressure of increasing citizen expectations for the ability of the public sector to solve pressing problems and deliver high-quality services, together with the continued shortage of public resources, has created a strong need for public innovation and for rethinking and transforming governance in ways that support public innovation. Innovation is not always called for; the failure rate is high and incremental change tends to gain the upper hand vis-à-vis more disruptive innovation strategies. However, opening up the public sector for inputs from external actors, creating a flatter bureaucracy, drilling holes in the administrative silos and building a new design-focused innovation culture in public organizations may help to turn the public sector into a serial innovator that constantly asks itself how innovative services, policies, and governance solutions can create value for citizens and society at large.

Supportive public sector reforms must be underpinned by new research on public innovation. While there has been plenty of research on private sector innovation, the interest in public sector innovation is relatively recent and sustained by the discovery of the innovative capacity of the public sector (Mazzucato 2013). Matching the need for public innovation with research on how innovation is produced, what the drivers and conditions are, and which institutional designs and forms of leadership may spur innovation could help us to create a public sector capable of providing both stable and predictable services when needed and improving and innovating these services and solving big, complex problems through radical innovation.

This chapter takes a closer look at the transition from a public sector focused mainly on incremental change and continuous improvement to a public sector that is more geared toward innovation. It begins by explaining the preference of the public governance orthodoxy for incrementalism and continuous improvement and then considers the growing demand for public innovation. It provides examples of public innovation and discusses how public sector innovation can be enhanced by collaboration between a plethora of public and private actors engaged in mutual learning. Finally, it looks at how it is possible to spur innovation in the future.

FROM STABILITY VIA INCREMENTAL CHANGE TO CONTINUOUS IMPROVEMENT

According to Weber (1922), bureaucracy is the preferred organizational model in modern societies based on rational-legal authority. Bureaucratic organizations are technically superior over other organization types because of their efficiency, pertinence, and continuity, which is ensured by their hierarchical, specialized, professional, and rule-based organization and decision-making processes. Stable rules, regulations, and procedures are important features of Weberian bureaucracy as they help to ensure core values such as legality, transparency, equity, and predictability. Stable laws and rules are more the result of rational decision-making than the whims of charismatic leaders, and administrative compliance is ensured through a combination of hierarchical control and professional norms.

The stable legal and administrative framework that guides administrative decisions in public bureaucracies is ill-adapted to the new conditions, demands and expectations that tend to generate a need for change (Crozier 1964). When change is particularly urgent in bureaucratic administration, there is a strong preference for incremental changes that only marginally modify existing procedures, programs, and policies. Incremental change reduces the risks associated with radical reforms that tend to raise expectations beyond what can be achieved and may lead to disruptive failures and destructive blame games if the new designs fail to deliver the expected outcome. According to Lindblom (1959), incremental change is obtained through an experience-based comparison of the performance of a few alternative options. If there are positive expectations to a marginally changed solution, it is tested and evaluated against the goals of the change process. If the positive expectations are confirmed, one might take another step in the same direction. In case of a negative evaluation, the course must be adjusted based on past experiences. Hence, instead of starting from scratch and evaluating the pros and cons of a broad range of more or less radical solutions, bureaucratic actors merely make small, step-by-step changes that are shaped by the evaluation of the last step they took. In short, change tends to be small and determined by what appears in the rearview mirror rather than what is glimpsed in any crystal ball.

According to the critics of public bureaucracy (Downs 1967), incremental change aiming to improve service quality while reducing costs is becoming increasingly difficult as public bureaucracies grow in size. Big public bureaucracies tend to spend more and more time and energy on internal coordination and fighting external turf-wars, and the resources available for the incremental improvement of goal attainment are dwindling. Advocates of NPM-style reforms recommend the import of management techniques such as total quality management (TQM) and LEAN from the private sector to improve service quality and cut costs. The functioning of these tools is to be enhanced by institutional reforms aiming to create a joint focus on goals rather than rules, develop new forms of leadership aiming to motivate and empower employees and introduce market-based competition that can help to identify user demands and put pressure on low performers (Hood 1991; Osborne & Gaebler 1993).

Attempts to strengthen the efforts to improve public sector outcomes tend to foster a lot of organizational innovation, but the organizational innovations in terms of performance management, managerialism, agentification, and marketization do not really translate into service innovation and policy innovation. There is hardly any focus on policy innovation beyond the continued neoliberal demand for increased reliance on private market forces, and service innovation is prevented by the overriding concern for efficiency that tends to reduce slack resources and risk-taking and by the strict implementation of performance management that seems to enhance the standardization of service production, ensure compliance with centrally defined goals, and drain local resources by increasing the time required to document local efforts (Ansell & Torfing 2014). While one might argue that innovation was never really the goal of NPM, which focused more on continuous service improvement (Hartley 2006), some research suggests that the impact of TQM and LEAN over time on service improvement and cost reduction has been waning. TQM did not really challenge the bureaucratic model for service delivery (Vinni 2007), and after the initial positive effects of the use of LEAN to cut slack, further cost reductions proved increasingly difficult (Radnor & Osborne 2013).

In sum, NPM helped to combat the increasing ossification of the public sector by stressing the need for incremental service improvement. The concrete efforts to ensure continuous improvement were supported by considerable organizational innovation, but public innovation of policy and service was never the goal of the public governance orthodoxy, and it was hampered by the combination of bureaucratic top-down control and fears that innovation failure would waste precious public resources at a time when economy, efficiency, and effectiveness were the main concerns.

RECOGNIZING THE NEED FOR PUBLIC INNOVATION AND THE INNOVATION CAPACITY OF THE PUBLIC SECTOR

Innovation is defined as the development and implementation of new and creative ideas and solutions that break with established practices and conventional thinking within a particular area (Torfing 2016). It may stem from the invention of entirely new and yet undiscovered solutions or emerge as a result of the adoption and adaptation of solutions invented and tested elsewhere. Hence, as long as something appears to be new to the context in which it is implemented, it counts as an innovation. Even a second move that uses a new idea from another country, sector, or municipality is considered an innovation if it has not been tried before in the new context where it is being implemented.

In the last two centuries, there has been much research on innovation in the private sector (Fagerberg et al. 2005). Political economists such as Smith, Marx, and Schumpeter have all stressed the importance of innovation for the ability of private firms to survive in cut-throat markets. Today, it is common knowledge that the key to enhanced profitability in private firms is innovation of the product, the production techniques, and the marketing strategy. Although Schumpeter (1942) paid considerable attention to social as well as political innovation, the ensuing research on private sector innovation was not matched by research addressing public sector innovation. Even when studies of organizational innovation blossomed in the 1960s and 1970s (Thompson 1965; Zaltman et al. 1973), hardly any attempts were made to carve out a special niche for public innovation (Kattel et al. 2015). Hence, the researchers who aimed to discover how organizational structures support innovation did not differentiate between public and private sector organizations. Recent pioneers who have aimed to reverse this trend by focusing on public innovation include Polsby (1984), who focused on innovative public reforms promoted by leading politicians; Kraemer and Perry (1989), who focused on the role of new digital technologies; Roberts and Bradley (1991), who focused on innovation through school reforms; Borins (2001), who focused on the drivers of public innovation; Mulgan and Albury (2003), who focused on the conditions for public innovation; and Koch and Hauknes (2005), who focused on the difference between public and private sector innovation.

There was real growth in the early twenty-first century in the research on public sector innovation, most of these studies being conducted in the Anglophone world (De Vries et al. 2016). Growing demands for public services from the affluent middle class, changing demographics featuring a growing proportion of elderly citizens, and the pervasiveness of complex societal problems with no standard solution combined to put pressure on the labor-intensive public sector, which struggled to enhance productivity and was hit by a series of economic crises. Public innovation was increasingly seen as the way out of this impasse. The new public innovation agenda was supported by international organizations such as the United Nations (UN) (2009), the Organisation for Economic Co-operation and Development (OECD) (2010) and the European Union (EU) (2013), which highlighted the need for public sector innovation and recommended the development of national initiatives for enhancing public innovation. In response, special government innovation labs mushroomed throughout the Western world and beyond (Dunleavy et al. 2006; Tõnurist et al. 2017), and public innovation was increasingly encouraged by the formation and use of national innovation award schemes (Rosenblatt 2011; Borins 2014).

The idea of a smart, innovation-led development of the public sector met a good deal of skepticism from those who were under the spell of the classic myth of the contrast between the dynamic and innovative private sector and the static and ossified public sector. This myth was effectively demolished by Mazzucato (2011, 2013, 2018), who demonstrated how the public sector is far more innovative than its reputation. The public sector is not only providing the conditions for private sector innovation, it is also proactively orchestrating mission-driven innovation by socializing risks and benefits. The entrepreneurial state is strategic, risk-taking and it pursues innovation both by itself and in a dynamic interplay with the private sector. In fact, many radical technical innovations (e.g., the World Wide Web, GPS, nanotechnology) that most people believe to be developed in the private sector have their roots in the public sector.

Mazzucato's work has helped to enhance the self-confidence of the public sector and convinced leading government officials that it is perfectly capable of fostering innovation with or without contributions from private actors. The many empirical examples of public innovation cited by Mazzucato and other researchers prompt us to reconsider the question of the barriers and drivers of innovation. The classical view has been that "public innovation" is close to being an oxymoron, since there is no competition in the public sector, no financial incentives, and too much red tape and centralized control. However, research has revealed how bottom-up innovation dominates despite the hierarchical structure of the public sector (Borins 2001). It has also pointed out that prohibitive red-tape rules tend to co-exist with green-tape rules encouraging public actors to improve and innovate public solutions when encountering problems and challenges (Hjelmar 2021). While there are few financial incentives beyond general cost-cutting in the public sector, there are other important motives for pursuing innovation, such as political missions, administrative ambitions, professional engagement, and pressure from citizens and stakeholders. Hence, public innovation tends to be more problem- and mission-driven and less incentive-driven. Finally, while it is true that there is hardly any competition in the public sector that is characterized by large integrated bureaucracies, this might be an advantage: the absence of cut-throat competition means that the conditions for knowledge-sharing are relatively good and there is no need for secrecy and protective patents that prevent innovation diffusion. Moreover, the lack of competition makes it easier to collaborate and co-create innovative solutions. Lastly, the large size of the public sector and its aggregate budget means that it is much easier to finance risky innovation projects, absorb the costs of failure and continue to revise innovative solutions until they work. In sum, while there are undoubtedly barriers to public innovation, we may have blinded ourselves to the fact that there are also strong drivers that make public innovation possible.

In sum, public innovation is both needed and possible. When successful, it may help to improve the effectiveness of public solutions, the efficiency of public administration and governance, user satisfaction, and democratic legitimacy. The outcome depends on the ability to consolidate the results and diffuse the innovative solutions within and across public organizations. Robust innovation is achieved when actors are capable of adapting innovative solutions to new developments and events and going in new directions to gain relevance and support.

PUBLIC INNOVATIONS AROUND THE WORLD

There has also been a fair amount of public innovation initiated by executive politicians, proactive civil servants, and local service providers brimming with public service motivation. We have not always called public innovation by its name, preferring instead to talk about public sector reform, creative problem-solving, and paradigmatic change. Now that public innovation has risen to the top of the public sector agenda, we can see the massive variety in public innovations that aspire to enhance public value creation. Let us consider a few examples of public innovation to appreciate its many different shapes and colors.

The first example focuses on service innovation that transforms the relation between street-level bureaucrats and their clients. The fear that passive social security systems create welfare dependency among benefit claimants led to a policy shift to workfare and activation systems (Torfing 1999; Lødemel &

Trickey 2001), where unemployed benefits were made conditional on participation in job counseling, educational activities and job training programs,
and unemployed individuals were made to document their job-seeking efforts
(quid pro quo). The introduction of welfare conditionality has been subject to
strong criticisms, not least for the possible mismatch between conditionality
as the primary instrument in employment support and the very heterogeneous
group of benefit claimants (Caswell et al. 2015; Van Berkel et al. 2017).
Hence, subjecting unemployment claimants with little education and an array
of social, physical, and/or mental problems to a strict and punitive workfare
scheme based on mandatory activation fails to bring them closer to the labor
market and merely produces poverty and marginalization. Even worse (but
not surprising), meeting vulnerable unemployed persons with harsh activation
requirements based on the assumption that they are unwilling to work tends to
create opposition, resentment, and strategies for escaping the "evil system." To
avoid the most vulnerable unemployed individuals being left behind as a result
of the form and content of the public services they receive, frontline workers
in Danish job centers have now been instructed to believe in the labor market
potentials of all clients and to begin with clients' own labor market goals when
planning their return to the labor market and how they can achieve a normal
life (STAR 2017). The basic idea of this remarkable service innovation is
that believing in their resources and taking their job interests seriously will
empower the unemployed clients to take ownership of their own lives and participate in the co-creation of service solutions that facilitate their labor market
integration. The service innovation in the Danish job centers transforms the
relationship between the frontline workers and the clients they are serving,
and it carries the potential of enhancing employment through the creation of
employment services that are efficient, fair, responsive, and respectful (Zacka
2017).

The second example concerns organizational innovation that is often
a precondition for improving service delivery. The health-care sector is highly
diverse and fragmented, and the work to provide seamless health-care services
is hampered by silo effects and a lack of coordination between public and
private health-care actors. As patients navigate the health-care system, they
meet general practitioners, in- and out-patient hospital wards, rehabilitation
centers, private insurance companies, patient associations, and so on. It is
important that these actors collaborate to avoid service gaps, overlaps and
mistreatment and to promote knowledge-sharing. The group of relevant and
affected actors is greatly enhanced by the new preventive health-care agenda,
which aims to combat lifestyle-related health problems and must therefore
intervene in the daily lives of citizens by mobilizing civil society organizations, local neighborhoods, schools, workplaces, sports clubs, and so on. The
persistent lack of communication, coordination, and collaboration has led

to the formation of health collaboratives: partnership arrangements bringing together two or more health actors in collaborative coordination based on shared objectives, such as preventing unwarranted variation and inequalities in the access to and outcomes of health-care services (Hearld et al. 2016). In the US, hundreds of health collaboratives are helping to provide chronic care for patients with diabetes. Research shows that innovative platforms for cross-boundary collaboratives tend to improve clinical processes of care over short-term (one- to two-year) periods, and clinical outcomes over longer (two- to four-year) periods. Most participants perceive these health collaboratives to be reaching their goals and worth the time and effort (Chin 2012).

The third example concerns innovations in public financing. Governments are facing growing demands to respond to social needs by launching costly preventive and early intervention programs while simultaneously facing fiscal pressures calling for the reduction of public social expenditure. This pinch is exacerbated by the fact that public investment in solving social problems is risky, as programs may fail to deliver on their promises; but, if successful, a long-term payoff is possible. In response to this dilemma, new forms of outcome-based commissioning, such as Social Impact Bonds (SIBs), have been introduced as a way to provide "more" social services for "less" public resources and with limited or no government risk (Olson et al. 2022). An SIB is an innovative financing mechanism whereby the government makes an agreement with a social enterprise or non-governmental organization and uses funding from private investors to cover the upfront capital required for the provider to set up a program and deliver a service or intervention that seeks to improve the prospects of a target group in need of public services (Mulgan et al. 2011).

Outcomes for the individuals enrolled in the program are measured, often compared to a baseline. The government body makes payments to the investors according to the outcomes. Since the investors are only repaid if the pre-determined outcomes are achieved, it is essentially a pay-for-success mechanism that limits the government risk while facilitating investment in social welfare solutions. Ultimately, SIBs may foster innovation by: (1) unlocking an untapped flow of social finance, (2) developing an evidence base for funded interventions, (3) encouraging experimentation, and (4) changing the role of government so that its focus is on defining and costing social priorities rather than bringing resources and expertise to bear (Social Finance 2009). Today, SIBs are used in many countries around the world, although most projects are found in the US. Where evidence of the impact of SIBs is available, it is rather mixed; at best, SIBs seem to present a new set of risks and opportunities in the field of social investment (Edmiston & Nicholls 2018).

The fourth example focuses on regulatory innovation. Fossil-fueled cars are a major source of CO_2 and thus a driver of climate change. While the ultimate solution is the transition to electric cars, the majority of cars still run on gasoline, hence the need to reduce the number of miles driven by each car and getting people to switch to public transport. Innovative forms of public regulation have aimed to do just that. London, Oslo, Singapore, and Stockholm have all introduced a new type of congestion charge aimed at discouraging drivers from driving their car into the city center. The system is simple: car drivers are charged if they drive into a congested zone in peak hours. The charge may be lower or nil in off-peak hours, and taxis, buses, service cars, and private automobiles with alternative powering systems are typically exempted. The revenue generated by these congestion charges can be used to expand collective transport and make it cheaper, thus creating an incentive to switch from individual to collective transport. After ten years with congestion charges, the Swedish experience is overwhelmingly positive: the innovative congestion charges have effectively reduced traffic in metropolitan areas, thereby helping to reduce emissions and enhancing the quality of life and social well-being. The technology of the charging systems has proven quite resilient, and the system operating costs have declined substantially over time. Finally, yet importantly, Swedish politicians and decision-makers have increasingly accepted the congestion charges despite their redistributive effects (Börjesson & Kristoffersson 2018).

The final example combines policy innovation with service innovation. Since the late 1970s, "tough-on-crime" policies in the US have increased the number of drug convictions and lengthened prison sentences, but recidivism is high because incarceration does not help to curb drug addiction (Hale 2011: 32–4). Since the establishment of the first so-called "Drug Court" in Miami in 1989, the number of such courts has exploded across the country. Drug Courts provide an innovative approach to drug-related crime by bringing a therapeutic element of treatment and rehabilitation into the judicial process for non-violent drug offenders (Hale 2011). The innovative approach to crime prevention combines efforts to protect public safety, provide public health services through treatment, and change the behavior of offenders through rehabilitation, counseling, and social intervention.

The new services that replace imprisonment are provided by an interdisciplinary team of professionals who are part of a nationwide network providing a persistent information flow that circulates new knowledge and concepts as well as concrete models and templates that facilitate the implementation of the new Drug Court policy and the design of the innovative services. Studies show that the introduction of these courts is associated with "reductions in recidivism that endure significantly beyond the duration of the individual's program participation" (Hale 2011: 84). The Drug Courts have also brought public interventions in the field of drug-related crime in line with a general shift in public opinion toward treatment and rehabilitation for drug offenders as opposed to simple incarceration and other forms of punishment (Hale 2011: 34).

This short cook's tour has presented how public innovation can assume many different forms and emerges in relation to public service, organization, financing, regulation, and policy. Although public innovation is pursued with the intention of outperforming existing practices, public innovation is not always successful; at least not immediately. If the examples above give a different impression, it is because the successful public innovations are more conspicuous and receive more attention from practitioners and researchers.

PUBLIC INNOVATION THROUGH COLLABORATION

Most of the research on private sector innovation makes the driver of innovation in competitive markets absolutely clear (Gilbert 2006; Vives 2008): competition between profit-seeking firms forces them to rely on individual entrepreneurs with equal measures of courage and genius or dedicated research and development departments when seeking to innovate their products, technology, and marketing strategy (Hagedorn 1996). Despite the indisputable success of the potent combination of competition and entrepreneurship, this innovation model has two crucial limitations. First, the intense inter-firm rivalry in the marketplace tends to be problematic because competing innovators waste valuable resources in bitter conflicts, including the duplication of efforts to develop and test new, innovative solutions, which creates a risk of resource depletion that prevents the winner from taking new innovative products to market (Teece 1992). Market competition also inhibits the exchange of ideas between innovators, since exclusive ownership is a condition for reaping an extra profit (Roberts 2000; Gilbert 2006). Frequently, the only way to promote knowledge-sharing in private markets is through industrial espionage and reverse-engineering at the risk of being caught and prosecuted. Second, the entrepreneurial model tends to rely solely on the knowledge, ideas, and resources found within the firm and fails to exploit the creative input from external actors. New research on swarm creativity (Gloor 2006) and collective wisdom (Landemore & Elster 2012) highlights the innovation potential found in crowds of different actors who deliberate about problems and possible solutions, but also warns against the trap of collective folly (Briskin & Erickson 2009). In response to these limitations, private sector innovation research has started to emphasize the role of collaborative networks and the need to open up for external inputs (Hervás-Oliver et al. 2021); hence, there is now a well-established literature on innovation systems (Lundvall 2007) and open innovation (Chesbrough 2006).

The innovation systems literature criticizes Schumpeter's supply-driven view of innovation, which too readily assumes that scientific research leads to new technology and that new technology satisfies market needs (Edquist & Hommen 1999). This criticism paves the way for the development of a system-oriented perspective emphasizing the existence of feedback loops from public and private consumers to business firms, from technical engineers to scientists and from scientists to the public authorities who fund scientific research. From this perspective, innovation can also be demand-driven. As such, innovation is increasingly seen as resulting from interaction between a broad range of public and private actors with different ideas and resources and who are collaborating within a complex and evolutionary system (Lundvall 2007).

The open innovation literature boldly asserts that companies must collaborate with other organizations to innovate effectively and remain competitive. They must look for creative input from outside the boundaries of their individual organization and pursue open innovation, defined as "the use of purposive inflows and outflows of knowledge to accelerate internal innovation, and expand the market for external use of innovation, respectively" (Chesbrough 2006: 1). Open innovation is a distributed innovation process wherein different firms, scientific experts, users, and public authorities interact in complex ways. While this may sound chaotic, the literature emphasizes how individual firms can manage the flow of knowledge, ideas, and resources to benefit from the inputs and pursue effective innovation (Chesbrough et al. 2014).

Inspired by these new literatures, public administration research tends to emphasize the role of collaboration in enhancing public sector innovation (Hartley 2005; Eggers & Singh 2009; Bommert 2010; Sørensen & Torfing 2011; Torfing 2016, 2019). A collaborative approach to innovation makes good sense in a public sector weak on competition but strong on collaboration. The open, transparent, and democratic structure of the public sector makes it relatively easy to convene relevant and affected actors and to engage them in discussions about how to solve pressing problems in new and innovative ways.

Collaboration is defined as the process through which a more or less diverse group of actors constructively manages their differences to find joint solutions to common problems (Gray 1989). Ideally, collaboration enhances innovation by: (1) developing a more precise and nuanced understanding of the problem at hand by studying it from different perspectives and vantage points; (2) bringing different solutions to the table and facilitating their revision, enrichment and integration; (3) stimulating mutual learning and fostering agreement about new and bold solutions while managing perceived risks; (4) developing, testing, evaluating, and revising prototypes based on agreed-upon success criteria; (5) constructing joint ownership of final solutions and facilitating coordinated implementation; and (6) ensuring negotiated adaptation to changing circumstances and supporting the diffusion of innovations that seem to work well.

It goes without saying that collaboration may not deliver all of this in real life, but it may still enhance innovation if only a few of these innovation potentials are realized. Much depends on the type of collaboration. Hence, if collaboration is ridden by interest conflicts, there is a risk of stalemate or agreement based on the least common denominator, which rarely results in innovative solutions (O'Toole 1997). If collaboration only includes the usual suspects who have worked together many times in the past and formed alliances around a common interest, there is a risk of the actors suffering from tunnel vision that prevents the pursuit of new ideas that might rock the boat (Skilton & Dooley 2010). These inherent risks point to an underlying dilemma: while collaboration thrives on the presence of strong similarities between the actors engaged in the collaborative process, innovation thrives on the presence of a diversity of experiences, views and ideas that can create disturbance, stimulate learning, and foster innovation (Torfing 2019). Hence, it is important to strike the right balance between similarity and diversity when recruiting participants for collaborative innovation processes.

There are many good examples of collaborative innovation addressing a wide range of problems, such as the revitalization of public parks (Fung 2008), watershed protection (Steelman 2010), crime prevention (Krogh & Torfing 2015), urban development (Ojasalo & Kauppinen 2016), homelessness (Crosby et al. 2017), and much more. In 2015, Gentofte Municipality in Denmark formed an innovation taskforce comprising five elected councilors, ten young people, and three administrators acting as facilitators. This diverse group of actors worked together over several months with regular meetings, excursions, and camps to develop a new youth policy. The collaborative process completely reframed the problem, prompting the development of a youth policy. The problem was not, as the politicians had originally thought, that a small proportion of a youth cohort failed to get an education and/or work and had problems with drug addiction and homelessness, but rather that most young people suffered from stress and anxiety caused by high expectations and performance pressure from their parents, friends, and society, and they seemed paralyzed by the wide range of choices between different education and job opportunities. The innovative policy response to this problem diagnosis called for improved counseling and the development of strong social communities, allowing the youth to share their problems and develop coping strategies. The innovation taskforce recommendations were submitted to the Municipal Council by two female high school students who, after the formal approval of the new youth policy, toured the municipality, describing the new policy to young people in schools, local associations, and culture and leisure facilities, the result being that the policy was being implemented before the municipality had even drawn up a plan to do so.

Despite best intentions, collaboration does not always foster innovative public solutions. There are many pitfalls. Motivating the relevant and affected actors to participate may prove difficult and there may be trust issues. Collaboration may be hampered by the lack of a clear sense of direction and the emergence of unforeseen conflicts. Finally, the participants may suffer from tunnel vision or be too risk-averse to try out new and bold solutions. To overcome these and other barriers, public leaders and managers may act as conveners, facilitators, and catalysts (Torfing 2016).

Well-designed and well-managed collaboration processes may be success-ful in enhancing public innovation, but collaborative innovation is not the only game in town. Innovative policy reforms are often driven by executive decision-makers at the apex of public hierarchies (Smith et al. 2019), and public agencies may also enhance innovation through the use of market forces, for example through green procurement (Rainville 2017). We need to develop a contingency theory that can specify the conditions for leaning on networks, hierarchies, or markets as the main innovation mechanism, and we must explore the conditions for developing hybrid forms of governance combining different mechanisms in pursuit of public innovation (Koppenjan et al. 2019).

ENHANCING PUBLIC SECTOR INNOVATION?

One of the key strengths of public bureaucracy is its capacity to deliver clear, transparent, and predictable services and regulatory solutions upon which citizens and corporate actors can depend. This strength relies on the presence of stable rules, standards, and policies that are only marginally modified when necessary. In a rapidly changing world, incremental change is enough to cater to the new and changing citizen demands. Responding to this problem, NPM set a new agenda for the public sector whereby organizational innovation was seen as a driver for the continuous incremental improvement of public ser-vices and persistent cost reductions. Hence, the public governance orthodoxy saw incremental improvement as a way of aligning the bureaucratic quest for stability with the need for continuous improvement. Service and policy innovation was off the table despite the growing appreciation of managerial entrepreneurship. The ossified public sector—with its centralized command structure, focus on rule-compliance, and lack of financial incentives—was deemed incapable of innovating. However, mounting fiscal, political, and popular pressures on the public sector, together with the discovery of the inno-vation capacities of the public sector, which had helped to transform public services, regulatory regimes, and public policies for decades, paved the way for a concerted effort to further enhance public innovation.

Seen from this perspective, the problem is not that the public sector is not innovative, but rather that public innovation is often accidental, infrequent, and driven by crisis or new technological opportunities. Hence, there is still some way to go before the public sector becomes a "serial innovator" that pursues innovation pervasively, systematically, and continuously. This observation begs the question of how we can spur public innovation, perhaps by stimulating collaboration, which seems to offer an important lever for public innovation.

First, we must open up the public sector for inputs from external actors. This can be achieved by creating collaborative platforms (Ansell & Gash 2018) that flag important problems, attract relevant and affected actors and reduce the transaction costs of collaborating by providing seed money, organizational templates, communication tools, professional advice, and factual knowledge about the problem in question. There seems to be huge potential in turning the public sector into a platform organization that—instead of aiming to solve problems merely by drawing on its own organization, budget, and employees—asks who can help to foster new and innovative solutions (Torfing et al. 2019). Collaborative platforms are institutional designs that help distributed actors to come together and collaborate to find innovative solutions to pressing problems without determining the form and content of the new solutions. They may be physical in the sense of fostering real-life interactions at a particular location or digital meeting places that allow distributed actors from different localities to engage in sustained interaction.

Second, innovation may be stimulated by creating flatter organizations with fewer hierarchical levels (Lundvall & Nielsen 2007). Flatter organizations may be more agile as they render the communication between the top and bottom of an organization easier and more direct. Bottom-up innovations may also have better chances of surviving as there are fewer higher-level instances to block, prevent, or defund innovative initiatives. The development of flatter and more agile organizations based on open dialogue up and down the chain of command may be facilitated by a shift from the classical principal–agent model to a new stewardship model that assumes that the top and bottom of public organizations more or less share the same goals (Schillemans 2013).

Third, drilling holes in the administrative silos to facilitate inter-organizational collaboration may spur innovation by bringing together different perspectives and ideas and stimulating learning. Administrative silos may be effective in solving specialized tasks based on professional knowledge and the learning taking place in communities of practice formed among those who are doing things together and are mutually engaged in work-related activities, the meanings of which they negotiate with one another (Wenger 1998). Administrative communities of practices may even become sources of innovation because their members constantly improvise and adapt their behavior to overcome limitations imposed either by the formal organization and its canonical practices or by changes in the environment (Brown & Duguid 1991). However, research shows that while the learning processes within a particular community of practice may facilitate incremental innovation, more radical innovations tend to rely on the integration of specialized and distributed knowledge that is possessed by a range of different actors working across different communities of practice (Swan et al. 2002). Hence, facilitating interagency collaboration, not by breaking down the administrative silos but rather by making it easy and less bureaucratic to contact employees in other public agencies to solve joint problems, may enhance the innovation capacity of public organizations.

Fourth, enhancing public innovation requires the development of a design-focused innovation culture in public organizations (Bason 2010, 2014). Innovation culture is a multidimensional phenomenon comprising the intention to innovation; the infrastructure to support innovation processes; the motivation, knowledge, and orientation of employees to support thought and action necessary for innovation; and the general ability to implement innovative solutions that manage risks and reward compromise (Wang & Ahmed 2004; Dobni 2008). Developing such a culture calls for strategic management focused on the long-term transformation of entire organizations (Ferlie & Ongaro 2015). It has been convincingly argued (Bason 2010, 2014, 2016; Lewis et al. 2020) that strategic managers should promote the use of design thinking as part of the innovation culture of their organization. Design thinking aims to respond to real-life problems by means of exploring problems based on an empathetic dialogue with users, questioning tacit assumptions through open discussion, experimentation and fast learning, and focusing on the production of outcomes that work in practice. To that end, design thinking uses heuristic devices, such as scenario-building, interdisciplinary workshops, prototyping, design experiments, and role-playing, to make new and emerging futures concrete and tangible.

Finally, public innovation and the collaboration needed to enhance it calls for new forms of public leadership and management. While direction and goal-setting are important for stimulating mission and problem-driven innovation, transformational leadership is insufficient to guide and manage collaborative innovation processes. Mobilizing middle managers and frontline staff and providing them with a license to innovate requires the exercise of distributional leadership whereby leadership responsibilities are decentered and dispersed throughout the individual organization (Bolden 2011). Involving external actors from the commercial or civic sectors requires integrative leadership aiming to foster collaboration between public and private actors based on early agreements about the problems to be solved and the kind of solutions to look for (Crosby & Bryson 2010). Leading cross-boundary innovation teams developing new designs calls for a facilitative leadership that encourages learning and experimentation and trusts the participants to anticipate and learn from failure (Bason 2010). Finally, the integration of new, bold solutions within entrenched institutional contexts necessitates adaptive leadership aimed at pragmatically aligning new and old designs (Heifetz et al. 2009).

The political and administrative endeavors to provide fertile conditions for public innovation require support from public innovation researchers who must provide further evidence of which antecedent conditions are necessary to promote innovation, how innovation processes unfold and gain momentum and what types of institutional design and leadership spur collaborative innovation in different contexts. Practitioners may also benefit from the development of new tools for assessing the innovation readiness of public organizations and new methods for making quick, research-based evaluations of innovation prototypes to produce fast learning. Looking further ahead, we need to study the barriers for professionally trained frontline staff to pursue collaborative innovation by engaging lay actors; for politicians to commit to and invest in radical policy innovation to solve complex problems, such as the climate crisis; and for administrative policy experts to experiment with regulatory reform in low-performance areas.

REFERENCES

Ansell, C. & Gash, A. (2018). Collaborative Platforms as a Governance Strategy. *Journal of Public Administration Research and Theory*, *28*(1), 16–32.
Ansell, C. & Torfing, J. (2014). *Public Innovation through Collaboration and Design*. London: Routledge.
Bason, C. (2010). *Leading Public Sector Innovation*. Bristol: The Policy Press.
Bason, C. (2014). Design Attitude as an Innovation Catalyst. In Ansell, C. & Torfing, J. (Eds.), *Public Innovation through Collaboration and Design* (209–28). London: Routledge.
Bason, C. (2016). *Design for Policy*. London: Routledge.
Bolden, R. (2011). Distributed Leadership in Organizations: A Review of Theory and Research. *International Journal of Management Reviews*, *13*(3), 251–69.
Bommert, B. (2010). Collaborative Innovation in the Public Sector. *International Public Management Review*, *11*(1), 15–33.
Borins, S. (2001). Encouraging Innovation in the Public Sector. *Journal of Intellectual Capital*, *2*(3), 310–19.
Borins, S. (2014). *The Persistence of Innovation in Government: A Guide for Public Servants*. Washington, DC: IBM Center for The Business of Government.
Börjesson, M. & Kristoffersson, I. (2018). The Swedish Congestion Charges: Ten Years On. *Transportation Research Part A: Policy and Practice*, *107*, 35–51.
Briskin, A. & Erickson, S. (2009). *The Power of Collective Wisdom: And the Trap of Collective Folly*. San Francisco, CA: Berrett-Koehler Publishers.
Brown, J. & Duguid, P. (1991). Organizational Learning and Communities of Practice: Toward a Unified View of Working, Learning and Innovation. *Organization Science*, *2*(1), 40–57.
Caswell, D., Larsen, J. E. & Sieling-Monas, S. M. (2015). Cash Benefit Recipients: Vulnerable or Villains? In Bengtsson, T. T., Frederiksen, M. & Larsen, J. E. (Eds.), *The Danish Welfare State* (217–31). New York: Palgrave Macmillan.

Chesbrough, H. (2006). *Open Business Models: How to Thrive in the New Innovation Landscape*. Boston, MA: Harvard Business Press.

Chesbrough, H., Vanhaverbeke, W. & West, J. (Eds.) (2014). *New Frontiers in Open Innovation*. Oxford: Oxford University Press.

Chin, M. H. (2012). Quality Improvement Implementation and Disparities: The Case of the Health Disparities Collaboratives. *Medical Care, 48*(8), 668–75.

Crosby, B. C. & Bryson, J. M. (2010). Integrative Leadership and the Creation and Maintenance of Cross-Sector Collaboration. *Leadership Quarterly, 21*(2), 211–30.

Crosby, B. C., 't Hart, P. & Torfing, J. (2017). Public Value Creation through Collaborative Innovation. *Public Management Review, 19*(5), 655–69.

Crozier, M. (1964). *The Bureaucratic Phenomenon*. Chicago, IL: University of Chicago Press.

De Vries, H., Bekkers, V. & Tummers, L. (2016). Innovation in the Public Sector: A Systematic Review and Future Research Agenda. *Public Administration, 94*(1), 146–66.

Dobni, C. B. (2008). Measuring Innovation Culture in Organizations. *European Journal of Innovation Management, 11*(4), 539–59.

Downs, A. (1967). *Inside Bureaucracy*. Boston, MA: Little, Brown and Company.

Dunleavy, P., Margetts, H., Bastow, S. & Tinkler, J. (2006). New Public Management Is Dead: Long Live Digital-Era Governance. *Journal of Public Administration Research and Theory, 16*(3), 467–94.

Edmiston, D. & Nicholls, A. (2018). Social Impact Bonds: The Role of Private Capital in Outcome-Based Commissioning. *Journal of Social Policy, 47*(1), 57–76.

Edquist, C. & Hommen, L. (1999). Systems of Innovation: Theory and Policy for the Demand Side. *Technology in Society, 21*, 63–79.

Eggers, B. & Singh, S. (2009). *The Public Innovators Playbook*. Washington, DC: Harvard Kennedy School of Government.

European Union (EU) (2013). *European Public Sector Scoreboard*. Brussels: The European Union.

Fagerberg, J., Mowery, D. C. & Nelson, R. R. (Eds.) (2005). *The Oxford Handbook of Innovation*. Oxford: Oxford University Press.

Ferlie, E. & Ongaro, E. (2015). *Strategic Management in Public Services Organizations: Concepts, Schools and Contemporary Issues*. New York: Routledge.

Fung, A. (2008). Civic Participation in Government Innovations. In Borins, S. (Ed.), *Innovations in Government* (52–70). Washington, DC: Brookings Institution Press.

Gilbert, R. (2006). Looking for Mr. Schumpeter: Where Are We in the Competition–Innovation Debate? *Innovation Policy and the Economy, 6*, 159–215.

Gloor, P. A. (2006). *Swarm Creativity: Competitive Advantage through Collaborative Innovation Networks*. Oxford: Oxford University Press.

Gray, B. (1989). *Collaborating: Finding Common Ground for Multiparty Problems*. San Francisco, CA: Jossey-Bass.

Hagedorn, J. (1996). Innovation and Entrepreneurship: Schumpeter Revisited. *Industrial and Corporate Change, 5*(3), 883–96.

Hale, K. (2011). *How Information Matters: Networks and Public Policy Innovation*. Washington, DC: Georgetown University Press.

Hartley, J. (2005). Innovation in Governance and Public Service: Past and Present. *Public Money and Management, 25*(1), 27–34.

Hartley, J. (2006). *Innovation and Its Contribution to Improvement*. London: Department for Communities and Local Government.

Hearld, L. R., Bleser, W. K., Alexander, J. A. & Wolf, L. J. (2016). A Systematic Review of the Literature on the Sustainability of Community Health Collaboratives. *Medical Care Research and Review*, *73*(2), 127–81.

Heifetz, R. A., Linsky, M. & Grashow, A. (2009). *The Practice of Adaptive Leadership: Tools and Tactics for Changing Your Organization and the World*. Cambridge, MA: Harvard Business Press.

Hervás-Oliver, J. L., Parrilli, M. D., Rodríguez-Pose, A. & Sempere-Ripoll, F. (2021). The Drivers of SME Innovation in the Regions of the EU. *Research Policy*, *50*(9), 104316.

Hjelmar, U. (2021). The Institutionalization of Public Sector Innovation. *Public Management Review*, *23*(1), 53–69.

Hood, C. (1991). A Public Administration for All Seasons? *Public Administration*, *69*(1), 1–19.

Kattel, R., Cepilovs, A., Kalvet, T., Lember, V. & Tõnurist, P. (2015). *Public Sector Innovation Indicators: Towards a New Evaluative Framework* (Vol. 6). LIPSE Research Report.

Koch, P. & Hauknes, J. (2005). *On Innovation in the Public Sector*. Oslo: NIFU.

Koppenjan, J., Karré, P. M. & Termeer, K. (Eds.) (2019). *Smart Hybridity: Potentials and Challenges of New Governance Arrangements*. The Hague: Eleven International Publishing.

Kraemer, K. L. & Perry, J. L. (1989). Innovation and Computing in the Public Sector: A Review of Research. *Knowledge in Society*, *2*(1), 72–87.

Krogh, A. H. & Torfing, J. (2015). Leading Collaborative Innovation: Developing Innovative Solutions to Wicked Gang Problems. In Agger, A., Damgaard, B., Krogh, A. H. & Sørensen, E. (Eds.), *Collaborative Governance and Public Innovation in Northern Europe* (91–110). Sharjah: Bentham Science Publishers.

Landemore, H. & Elster, J. (Eds.) (2012). *Collective Wisdom: Principles and Mechanisms*. Cambridge: Cambridge University Press.

Lewis, J. M., McGann, M. & Blomkamp, E. (2020). When Design Meets Power: Design Thinking, Public Sector Innovation and the Politics of Policymaking. *Policy & Politics*, *48*(1), 111–30.

Lindblom, C. (1959). The Science of "Muddling Through." *Public Administration Review*, *19*(2), 79–88.

Lødemel, I. & Trickey, H. (Eds.) (2001). *An Offer You Can't Refuse: Workfare in International Perspective*. Bristol: The Policy Press.

Lundvall, B. Å. (2007). National Innovation Systems: Analytical Concept and Development Tool. *Industry and Innovation*, *14*(1), 95–119.

Lundvall, B. Å. & Nielsen, P. (2007). Knowledge Management and Innovation Performance. *International Journal of Manpower*, *28*(3/4), 207–23.

Mazzucato, M. (2011). The Entrepreneurial State. *Soundings*, *49*(49), 131–42.

Mazzucato, M. (2013). *The Entrepreneurial State: Debunking Public vs. Private Sector Myths*. London: Anthem Press.

Mazzucato, M. (2018). Mission-Oriented Innovation Policies: Challenges and Opportunities. *Industrial and Corporate Change*, *27*(5), 803–15.

Mulgan, G. & Albury, D. (2003). Innovation in the Public Sector. *Working Paper*, Version 1.9, October, Strategy Unit, UK Cabinet Office.

Mulgan, G., Reeder, N., Aylott, M. & Bo'sher, L. (2011). *Social Impact Investment: The Challenge and Opportunity of Social Impact Bonds*. London: The Young Foundation.

Ojasalo, J. & Kauppinen, H. (2016). Collaborative Innovation with External Actors: An Empirical Study on Open Innovation Platforms in Smart Cities. *Technology Innovation Management Review, 6*(12), 49–60.

Olson, H., Painter, G., Albertson, K., Fox, C. & O'Leary, C. (2022). Are Social Impact Bonds an Innovation in Finance or Do They Help Finance Social Innovation? *Journal of Social Policy*, First View, 1–25.

Organisation for Economic Co-operation and Development (OECD) (2010). *The OECD Innovation Strategy: Getting a Head Start on Tomorrow*. Paris: OECD Publishing.

Osborne, D. & Gaebler, T. (1993). *Reinventing Government: How the Entrepreneurial Spirit Is Transforming the Public Sector*. Reading, MA: Addison-Wesley.

O'Toole, L. J. (1997). Implementing Public Innovations in Network Settings. *Administration & Society, 29*(2), 115–38.

Polsby, N. W. (1984). *Political Innovation in America: The Politics of Policy Initiation*. New Haven, CT: Yale University Press.

Radnor, Z. & Osborne, S. P. (2013). Lean: A Failed Theory for Public Services? *Public Management Review, 15*(2), 265–87.

Rainville, A. (2017). Standards in Green Public Procurement: A Framework to Enhance Innovation. *Journal of Cleaner Production, 167*, 1029–37.

Roberts, N. C. (2000). Wicked Problems and Network Approaches to Resolution. *International Public Management Review, 1*(1), 1–19.

Roberts, N. C. & Bradley, R. T. (1991). Stakeholder Collaboration and Innovation. *Journal of Applied Behavioural Science, 27*(2), 209–27.

Rosenblatt, M. (2011). The Use of Innovation Awards in the Public Sector: Individual and Organizational Perspectives. *Innovation, 13*(2), 207–19.

Schillemans, T. (2013). Moving beyond the Clash of Interests: On a Stewardship Theory and the Relationships between Central Government Departments and Public Agencies. *Public Management Review, 15*(4), 541–62.

Schumpeter, J. (1942). *Capitalism, Socialism and Democracy*. New York: Routledge.

Skilton, P. F. & Dooley, K. J. (2010). The Effects of Repeat Collaboration on Creative Abrasion. *Academy of Management Review, 35*(1), 118–34.

Smith, G., Sochor, J. & Karlsson, I. M. (2019). Public–Private Innovation: Barriers in the Case of Mobility as a Service in West Sweden. *Public Management Review, 21*(1), 116–37.

Social Finance (2009). *Social Impact Bonds: Rethinking Finance for Social Outcomes*. London: Social Finance.

Sørensen, E. & Torfing, J. (2011). Enhancing Collaborative Innovation in the Public Sector. *Administration & Society, 43*(8), 842–68.

STAR (2017). *Styrelsen for Arbejdsmarked og Rekruttering Årsrapport for 2017*. Copenhagen: STAR.

Steelman, T. A. (2010). *Implementing Innovation*. Washington, DC: Georgetown University Press.

Swan, J., Scarbrough, H. & Robertson, M. (2002). The Construction of Communities of Practice in the Management of Innovations. *Management and Learning, 33*(4), 477–96.

Teece, D. J. (1992). Competition, Cooperation, and Innovation. *Journal of Economic Behaviour and Organization, 18*(1), 1–25.

Thompson, V. (1965). Bureaucracy and Innovation. *Administrative Science Quarterly, 10*, 1–20.

Tõnurist, P., Kattel, R. & Lember, V. (2017). Innovation Labs in the Public Sector: What They Are and What They Do? *Public Management Review, 19*(10), 1455–79.

Torfing, J. (1999). Workfare with Welfare: Recent Reforms of the Danish Welfare State. *Journal of European Social Policy*, *9*(1), 5–28.

Torfing, J. (2016). *Collaborative Innovation in the Public Sector*. Washington, DC: Georgetown University Press.

Torfing, J. (2019). Collaborative Innovation in the Public Sector: The Argument. *Public Management Review*, *21*(1), 1–11.

Torfing, J., Sørensen, E. & Røiseland, A. (2019). Transforming the Public Sector into an Arena for Co-Creation: Barriers, Drivers, Benefits, and Ways Forward. *Administration & Society*, *51*(5), 795–825.

United Nations (UN) (2009). *Good Practices and Innovations in Public Governance*. New York: United Nations Publications.

Van Berkel, R., Caswell, D., Kupka, P. & Larsen, F. (Eds.) (2017). *Frontline Delivery of Welfare-to-Work Policies in Europe: Activating the Unemployed*. New York: Taylor & Francis.

Vinni, R. (2007). Total Quality Management and Paradigms of Public Administration. *International Public Management Review*, *8*(1), 103–31.

Vives, X. (2008). Innovation and Competitive Pressure. *The Journal of Industrial Economics*, *56*(3), 419–69.

Wang, C. L. & Ahmed, P. K. (2004). The Development and Validation of the Organizational Innovativeness Construct Using Confirmatory Factor Analysis. *European Journal of Innovation Management*, *7*(4), 303–13.

Weber, M. (1922). *Economy and Society*. New York: Simon and Schuster.

Wenger, E. (1998). *Communities of Practice: Learning, Meaning and Identity*. Cambridge: Cambridge University Press.

Zacka, B. (2017). *When the State Meets the Street: Public Service and Moral Agency*. Cambridge, MA: Harvard University Press.

Zaltman, G., Duncan, R. & Holbek, J. (1973). *Innovations and Organizations*. New York: Wiley.

12. From spectator and counter-democracy to interactive democracy

In representative democracies, citizens participate as voters in regular elections in which they may choose to run for office. This kind of participation is relatively thin as there is limited communication between the electorate and elected politicians, who often have little clue why they were elected, who they are supposed to represent and what they are expected to do as representatives of the people. The political parties, which are supposed to provide forums for political debate between party members and political representatives, have steadily declining memberships. Focus group interviews and social media interaction seem to be replacing face-to-face meetings with party members and potential voters, while increasing numbers of voters are being transformed into passive spectators of the political spectacle displayed in written and electronic media (Anderson & Hoff 2001).

The rising level of popular education and the anti-authoritarian cultural upheaval in the 1960s and 1970s raised the competence and desire among the citizenry for democratic participation. In response, affected citizens were allowed to comment on local development plans in townhall meetings. Service users became customers in new service markets in which they could vote with their feet and freely choose an alternative service provider, and they were given the option to join user boards overseeing and marginally influencing local service delivery. While clearly supplementing the thin and passive participation in regular elections with thicker forms of participation based on active participation in one- or two-way communication processes (Nabatchi & Leighninger 2015), these new forms of democracy tend to give rise to a "counter-democracy" that casts citizens in the role of critical veto actors who can criticize, oppose, and try to block public governance (Rosanvallon 2008). While the ability to go against the political and administrative elites is an important part of modern democracy, the problem is that the new forms of counter-democracy easily develop into an unproductive "citizens versus the public sector" struggle rather than a partnership between the actors with the greatest interest in improving governance and service delivery.

Interestingly, we have recently seen the emergence of dedicated attempts to replace the new counter-democracy with emerging forms of interactive democracy aimed at involving citizens and stakeholders in deliberative processes that can help to build joint responsibility for developing and improving public solutions (Rosanvallon 2011). One of the great challenges is to find ways to articulate the new forms of interactive democracy with the established forms of representative democracy, thus developing a kind of hybrid democracy combining the merits of the two forms of democracy while mitigating or overcoming their problems (Sørensen & Torfing 2019; Sørensen & Sandfort 2022). While this seems perfectly possible at the local level, it is more challenging to combine interactive and representative democracy at the national level, where government is subject to close scrutiny by the new forms of monitory democracy, and at the transnational level, where there is great distance between the political decision-makers and ordinary citizens. Building a robust hybrid democracy at these levels requires extensive experimentation.

This chapter aims to shed light on the current rethinking and transformation of democracy that tends to link citizens, public administrators, and elected politicians in new ways. First, it explains the basic attraction of representative democracy, accounts for its successful expansion and discusses the risk of representative democracy becoming a "spectator sport." Next, it considers how modern democracy has responded to the rise of competent, critical, and assertive citizens and discusses the features of the new counter-democracy, which seems to co-exist with (albeit largely uncoupled to) representative democracy. The third section examines the discovery of emerging forms of interactive democracy seeking to involve both citizens and elected politicians in the co-creation of public value outcomes. This recasts Arnstein's famous "ladder of participation," which had the self-government of the people as the zenith in the development of democratic participation. The fourth section argues that, ideally, interactive forms of democracy should be linked to representative forms of democracy, giving rise to a hybrid democracy combining the best of several forms of democracy. The final section discusses the prospect of expanding hybrid democracy at different levels of governance and sets out an agenda for further research.

THE EXPANSION OF REPRESENTATIVE DEMOCRACY AND THE RISK OF DEMOCRACY BECOMING A "SPECTATOR SPORT"

As the tax-financed public sector expanded, it was only natural for citizens to demand democratic influence on how tax revenues were spent and to protect themselves from the abuse of state power. In modern mass societies, democratic influence was facilitated through the appointment of political representatives through free, fair, and regular elections based on the egalitarian "one man, one vote" principle. The right to vote was gradually extended to wider sections of the population, and the democratic election procedures were complemented by the expansion of liberal individual rights, such as freedom of speech, freedom of the press, freedom of religion, and freedom to organize political parties. Democratic elections and liberal freedoms were the two main pillars in liberal democracy, which was accused of neglecting the socioeconomic inequalities in society that undermine the equal opportunities to influence democratic decisions (Macpherson 1977). In an attempt to solve this problem, the rights-based political and civic citizenship was gradually supplemented with a social citizenship based on the right to receive social welfare benefits that can help to reduce poverty and enhance social justice (Marshall 1981).

The strength of liberal democracy is that it provides a simple democratic procedure allowing the people to govern through its elected representatives, who make effective governance decisions based on majoritarian voting and are held to account for their deeds in the next election. Looking back, liberal representative democracy has been a tremendous global success that has expanded through consecutive waves of democratization. Until recently, there were more and more democratic regimes and more and more people in the world living in them. This positive development has now been halted by the growing number of despotic regimes, failed states, and "illiberal democracies" that continue to be governed by elected governments but lack the liberal freedoms that allow the opposition to challenge the incumbent government (Zakaria 2007).

As the storm on the US Congress demonstrated, the pressures on liberal democracies are not only found in the new democracies in central and eastern Europe. The core problem of liberal democracy is the thin relation between the elected representatives and the electorate. Voters cast their ballot for a particular party or candidate based on mediatized political debate and advertisement, but the elected political representatives do not receive a particular mandate from the voters; in fact, they often have little clue why they were elected, who they are supposed to represent, and what is expected of them. They may have made some key election pledges during the election campaign or referred to their party manifesto, but not only are these pledges soon forgotten, new political issues are constantly emerging and call for the formulation of new political opinions. Since there is virtually no access to sustained dialogue with the electorate to obtain input from different voter groups affected by different problems and decisions, the political representatives must trust their gut feeling or use more or less antiquated ideologies as signposts when formulating their opinion and taking a stance on new issues.

The relative insulation of the political elites from the people is much worse today than in the past. Election turnout, party membership, and party activity have all declined, and parties now hardly facilitate debate between political leaders and ordinary citizens (Mair 2013). Party strategists may use polling and focus group interviews with typical voters to adjust the political branding of the party and its candidates—but that's about it. Once they have cast their vote, citizens are reduced to passive spectators of the gladiatorial struggles between political leaders who use all of the available media platforms to spread their political ideas and criticize their political opponents. True, citizens can still write a letter to the editor and engage in political debates in national newspapers, radio, and television, but the number of politically engaged newspapers is decreasing and readership is dwindling, as is the number of public service TV channels. Alternatively, new social media, such as Twitter and Facebook, allow ordinary citizens to voice their opinion and comment on messages from the political elites, but this hardly qualifies as participation in political deliberation, as social media tends to favor the emergence of polarized echo chambers that reduce the exposure of the users to diverse information and spur the diffusion of so-called "fake news" (Iandoli et al. 2021).

In sum, representative democracy risks turning into a spectator democracy in which the citizens may be active in their social lives and seek information about political issues, but they have few opportunities to participate actively in the political and democratic process (Anderson & Hoff 2001). Hence, despite their interest in politics and society, citizens ultimately become relatively passive onlookers to a political spectacle in which elected politicians and government officials are the central actors who are governing through the performance of political rituals and symbolic actions (Edelman 1988) and with news presenters and political commentators as directors. Citizen input is limited in the new spectator democracy, decision-making is centralized and large-scale reforms are passed with little public debate.

Since Schumpeter, it has been claimed that citizens are not really interested in participating more actively in democratic decision-making and that attempts to involve the electorate in participation beyond the ballot box would run counter to their instincts and desires and merely further stoke popular resentment. This is very much the argument of Hibbing and Theiss-Morse (2002) in *Stealth Democracy*, their highly acclaimed book that contends that Americans dislike politics and prefer to leave public governance to authoritarian populists and administrative technocrats. When citizens do reluctantly participate in politics, it is typically more about defending public interests against corrupt politicians and less about being genuinely interested in politics.

Neblo et al. (2018) take issue with this pessimistic account of the apparent non-participation of US citizens, claiming that today's non-participation is rooted more in disaffection with the available participatory options than in any innate dislike of politics. Citizens are turned off by what they see as an unresponsive, distant, and corrupt system and bitterly partisan forms of politics—but that does not mean that they lack the motivation to participate more actively if they get a real chance to influence the political decisions affecting their daily quality of life. On the contrary, citizens seem to have become increasingly competent, critical, and assertive, and they demonstrate a growing appetite for more direct and active democratic participation (Dalton & Welzel 2014). While they may neither want to participate in political and democratic processes 24/7 nor be interested in fighting for big systemic changes, pragmatic ad hoc participation that enables them to affect relevant governance decisions about health, education, welfare, climate, and so on seems to be within reach for many citizens, although some deprived population groups continue to lack both competences and political efficacy.

THE DEVELOPMENT OF COUNTER-DEMOCRACY AND THE DANGER OF ANTIDEMOCRATIC RIGHTWING POPULISM

The growing ability and motivation of citizens to participate in democracy provide an important push factor driving the need for democratic renewal in Western democracies. Similarly, the need to strengthen democratic legitimacy that is persistently undermined by the lack of interaction between citizens and the increasingly distant and insulated political representatives provides a pull factor for democratic reform (see Beetham 2013). Fortunately, liberal democracy has proven rather robust and capable of transforming itself in the light of persistent problems and criticisms. Hence, elected politicians and their administrative aides have stimulated democratic innovation (Saward 2003; Smith 2009; Geissel & Newton 2012) aimed at changing constitutional, institutional, and operative rules, norms, and procedures.

The democratic innovation movement took place in the 1990s, when we saw a strengthening of the powers of political, judicial, and democratic oversight but also a series of attempts to give citizens new voice and exit options (Sørensen 1997; Warren 2011). Whereas "voice" gives citizens who are members of a particular organization, arena, or group the possibility to raise criticisms and suggest changes, "exit" allows people to "vote with their feet," expressing their dissatisfaction by leaving the organization, arena, or group. Stimulating voice and exit as democratic mechanisms is based on the assumption that citizens are competent, capable, and influence-seeking, but it also assumes that they are critical—possibly even distrustful—and therefore need a particular set of tools to influence public authorities and the policy, governance solutions, and services they provide. The latter assumption is well aligned with neoliberal ideas regarding the tyranny of government and the need to strengthen individual citizens vis-à-vis the state (see Hayek 1976).

Rosanvallon (2008) captures the democratic innovations that institutionalize the popular distrust in government solutions and government officials with his notion of "counter-democracy." Whereas the democracy of voting, elections, and parliamentary decision-making is a "democracy of proposition," the new counter-democracy is a "democracy of rejection" that gives citizens the right to oppose or even block public governance (Rosanvallon 2008: 15). In operational terms, counter-democracy finds its expression in the increased use of legal action or popular protests to prevent or stop government action. Legislation sometimes authorizes local groups of citizens or civic associations working on their behalf to make formal objections to new preservation acts. On top of the juridical possibilities to block public decisions, governments are increasingly organizing formal consultation or hearing processes in relation to new proposals that—despite their tokenistic form—may be used to orchestrate protests against government initiatives (Haughton et al. 2016). Townhall meetings in which citizens are informed about new initiatives and can voice their opinions have also become increasingly common, such meetings sometimes being held online (Moynihan 2008). In many countries, new legislation mandates local service organizations (e.g., nurseries, kindergartens, public schools, elderly care centers) to create elected boards in which users can voice their frustrations and marginally influence the daily operations (Pierre 2009). Finally, being able to choose freely among service providers provides citizens with the opportunity to penalize low-quality service providers by leaving them in favor of another service provider (Pierre & Røiseland 2016).

Many of these new ways of influencing public governance between elections are probably welcomed by the increasingly competent, critical, and assertive citizens, but the efforts to supplement spectator democracy with a new counter-democracy are coming at a high price. Citizens are re-cast as distrustful opponents of government action who use a variety of tools to criticize, oppose, or block governance initiatives. As such, counter-democracy carries a risk of stimulating the development of anti-government sentiments that feed the growth of rightwing populism aimed at confronting the corrupt, unresponsive, and technocratic political elites who are unconcerned with the needs of ordinary citizens and arrogantly pursue power and position to protect their own narrow interests. While this type of populism is partly justified in its criticism of self-seeking political and technocratic elites isolated from the people, it deepens the gulf between government and the people, presents a homogenizing view of a unified people that is opposed to democratic pluralism and claims that the interests of the people are best protected by a strong, charismatic leader who works for them, full of passion and commitment to make the nation great again (Stoker 2019). This type of populist discourse tends to undermine liberal democracy and strengthen autocratic rule by leaders claiming to know what the people want and need better than the people themselves. Hence, counter-democracy is not the solution to the severed relation between citizens and their political representatives, but rather a part of the problem as it aims to turn the citizens against the state, creating a situation of conflict and stalemate that will ultimately undermine liberal democracy.

THE EMERGENCE OF INTERACTIVE FORMS OF DEMOCRACY AND THE NEW LADDER OF DEMOCRATIC PARTICIPATION

The public governance orthodoxy has supplemented the representative spectator democracy with a new type of counter-democracy that gives citizens a more active role in relation to the public sector but casts them as obstinate veto actors rather than constructive collaborators bringing new ideas and additional resources to the table. Interestingly, the story does not end here. There is a growing tendency comprising many concrete examples that governments at different levels create networks, partnerships, and other collaborative arenas involving elected politicians, public administrators, and a range of private stakeholders, including citizens. While this is often intended to enhance efficient and effective governance by mobilizing resources from civil society and the economy, there is often also a democratic motive to building democratic legitimacy through enhanced and empowered participation and mutual exchange that lead to better solutions. We find these interactive governance arenas in all policy areas, including community policing, preventive health care, urban planning, and educational, environmental, and employment policy (Smith 2005; Sørensen & Triantafillou 2009; Torfing et al. 2012). In contrast to citizen juries, the interactive arenas for democratic deliberation and problem-solving have a mixed membership, meaning that both the participating politicians and citizens tend to develop a sense of ownership over the joint solutions, thus enhancing the chance that the solutions will be implemented. The Etorkizuna Eraikiz in the Basque province of the Provincial Council of Gipuzkoa offers a case in point: here, the provincial government is in the process of transforming itself into a platform organization that, instead of trying to solve all public tasks and problems by itself, creates participatory and collaborative governance arenas aimed at mobilizing a broad range of societal ideas and resources in an effort to boost policy innovation and deepen democracy (Murphy et al. 2020).

Collaborative governance arenas that include a diversity of actors and aim to link citizens and their political representatives have been described as a new type of "interactive democracy" in which citizens and private stakeholders are not merely supposed to comment, reject, or endorse public solutions devised and promoted by politicians or administrators but are invited to collaborate with public actors in defining the problems and challenges at hand, designing new solutions and frequently also implementing them in practice (Mayer et al. 2005; Rosanvallon 2011; Sørensen 2013). To illustrate: Gentofte Municipality in Denmark has made a dedicated effort to transcend the counter-democracy that expanded in the 1980s and 1990s in the field of urban planning by developing a more interactive approach to democratic participation in urban planning processes. Denmark was one of the first countries in the world to make citizen participation in hearings and consultations a mandatory part of the local municipal plans for neighborhood-level urban renewal. Gentofte had always taken mandatory citizen participation very seriously but found that the affluent and well-educated middle classes were becoming increasingly demanding, critical, and obstructive, thus acting as spoilsports who arrived at hearings with unrealistic demands and negative attitudes. To solve this problem, the whole procedure for participatory planning was redesigned, and citizens and local stakeholders are now involved in discussions with planners and elected politicians all the way from problem diagnosis and goal-setting, via scenario building, to solution design. The early involvement in the dialogue with planners and politicians means that citizens' needs and ideas inform the solutions, and citizens develop an understanding of the complexities in public planning processes. This has transformed the citizens from veto actors to partners in the co-creation of joint solutions with a broad democratic ownership. As explained earlier, the positive experiences with enhanced and early citizen participation resulted in the introduction of a new type of Task Committee in which politicians and citizens work together to solve the most pressing problems confronting the municipality (Sørensen & Torfing 2019). Similar experiences with more interactive forms of democracy that invite citizens into extended processes of dialogical policy development are found throughout Western societies (Klijn & Koppenjan 2000; Edelenbos & Klijn 2006; Geissel 2009; Esterling et al. 2011; Hendriks 2016), but also in countries such as Brazil, which spearheaded the development of participatory budgeting (Avritzer 2006; Wampler 2010), and India, where there are good examples of civil society-led deliberation between citizens and public leaders (Menon et al. 2021).

Interactive democracy is participatory but goes beyond the cries for participatory democracy in the 1960s and 1970s, as it is not merely a matter of letting citizens express their opinions more directly through participation in social movements, voluntary associations, and local community meetings. Citizens participate in collaborative processes that bring together state and civil society actors in a new way and contribute to public governance (Fung & Wright 2003). According to Rosanvallon (2011), interactive democracy creates a new proximity; that is, a new openness of government, an enhanced accessibility to questions and inputs and the capacity to engage with a diverse group of citizens who can both enforce and contest what government does.

Interactive democracy is also deliberative in the sense that the participants are voicing their views and opinions, presenting supportive arguments based on reason, passion and rhetorical ploys, listening to each other, and endorsing or problematizing what they have heard, and they are forced to revise their respective positions in the face of strong counterarguments (Gutmann & Thompson 2004). However, deliberative democratic theorists have either focused on deliberation among politicians within representative democratic institutions or within social movements and local citizen groups. By contrast, scant attention has been paid to deliberation between elected politicians and citizens, where the legitimacy of the participants, the possible knowledge discrepancies and the asymmetrical power relations become critical issues requiring careful attention (Rosanvallon 2011).

Finally, interactive democracy is a problem-solving democracy because it involves relevant and affected citizens in mutual learning processes based on critical reflection on experiences, ideas, and proposals in order to build consensus in a smaller public focused on a particular problem or challenge (Ansell 2011). Hence, democratic interaction is focusing neither on big, ideologically motivated transformations of society nor on the evaluation of established administrative routines and micro-level case processing. Instead, it focuses on pressing problems that are defined at the middle range between abstract norms, values, and principles together with concrete individual outcomes. The focus on common problems calling for public action is important as it ensures that both the political and civic participants are committed to the process. The motivation to participate and constructively manage emerging differences can be further stimulated by the production of small wins early in the process that may promise bigger wins further down the road (Ansell & Gash 2008).

Participation in problem-solving deliberation was also central to Arnstein (1969), who developed the famous "ladder of participation" that enables people to distinguish between forms of non-participation such as manipulation and therapy; tokenistic forms of participation such as consultation; placation and partnership in which the powerful remain in control; and ideal forms of participation, such as delegated power and self-determination, that facilitate citizen control. The embryonic emergence of interactive democracy problematizes the *telos* of the ladder of participation. In a complex and turbulent world in which the power to act is distributed across levels, sectors, and actors, it makes little sense to insist on citizen control based on self-government as the ultimate goal of democratic participation. Rather, the goal should be that both citizens and politicians can initiate the creation of a collaborative arena for problem-focused interaction leading to new and well-informed solutions. The formation of reusable institutional platforms that make it easy to form such arenas will help to scaffold interactive democracy (Ansell & Gash 2018).

THE HARD ROAD TO DEMOCRATIC RENEWAL

The development of platforms and arenas for interactive democracy will help to provide a more direct and active involvement of citizens as constructive discussion partners in democratic processes aiming to advance effective public governance. The new proximity provides valuable information and ideas to elected politicians, thus strengthening their ability to jointly explore and properly define policy problems and to design new and feasible solutions. This also allows citizens to better understand the conflicting demands and complex conditions that constrain and complicate democratic decision-making in turbulent times. Most importantly, however, it may help to overcome the implementation resistance nurtured by the growing distance between leaders and led.

There are important push and pull factors driving us down the road of interactive democracy, but also a number of roadblocks (see Ansell & Torfing 2017). The first obstacle is institutional inertia (Núñez et al. 2016). Our current democracy is locked in a particular pattern that is supported by a fine-grained system of institutional norms, rules, and procedures that, in most Western countries, appear to be relatively robust vis-à-vis recent attacks. In comparison with the uncertain and flimsy ideas about democratic reform, thicker citizen participation and interactive policymaking, the institutions of representative democracy seem rock solid despite the declining participation in political parties and regular elections, the failure to solve complex societal problems and the dwindling trust in government in some countries. "We know what we have got"—and we have great difficulty seeing what new and more interactive forms of democracy will look like in practice. Democratic experimentation may help us to make the future of democracy concrete, but we lack beacons of interactive democracy that can show us the way. They are often found at the local level and often go unnoticed, meaning that they fail to diffuse and upscale.

The second obstacle is the potential lack of participant legitimacy (Nissen 2014; Ansell et al. 2020). Transforming citizens from relatively passive voters and slightly more active veto actors into constructive and responsible co-creators of democratic decisions requires the recruitment of scores of citizens into collaborative arenas where they can exchange information, views, and ideas with elected politicians. The legitimacy of the solutions resulting from joint deliberation hinges on the legitimacy of the selected citizen group participating in the deliberative process. While an open call for interested citizen participants will tend to create a selective participation bias favoring the white, retired middle classes, random selection may result in the recruitment of disinterested citizens who may quit halfway. Hence, we must develop a new set of procedures targeting relevant and affected citizens while ensuring the inclusion of a diverse group of citizens. A possible solution is for public leaders to draw up different competence profiles of the relevant and affected actors they want to involve in policy interaction, broadcast the profiles together with an account of the pressing problem to be addressed via all of the available communication channels and finally let citizens register their interest to become involved and have the elected politicians match them against the competence profiles, thus taking responsibility for ensuring diversity.

The third roadblock is the perfectly legitimate concern of many elected politicians: that their democratic responsibility for authoritative decision-making is undermined by the formal and informal interaction with citizens, which tends to influence and bind their political decisions, thus undermining their democratic mandate (Klijn & Koppenjan 2000). But might the time have come to rethink what a democratic mandate is? Instead of defining the democratic mandate bestowed on elected politicians on Election Day as the right to govern on behalf of the citizenry, we may want to define it as a right to govern and make binding political decisions based on a continuous dialogue with a diverse group of citizens.

A fourth potential obstacle is the fear of "ungovernability" if small batches of elected politicians are each tied to their respective arenas for democratic interaction with relevant and affected citizens. Ensuring holistic coordination and prioritization across myriad interactive arenas may be difficult, and the result may be a Balkanization of democratic politics and the loss of a sense of political direction (Pellizzoni 2003). Hence, it is important for the elected assemblies to assume responsibility for metagoverning the democratic interaction in collaborative arenas to ensure a clear political framing of the deliberations, monitor and evaluate the interaction processes based on continuous reporting, and finally evaluate the emerging policy proposals based on overall political goals (Sørensen & Torfing 2016). Ideally, interactive democracy should begin and end with decisions made by elected politicians.

Finally, yet importantly, involving non-elected participants in non-majoritarian institutions of interactive democracy creates severe accountability problems, as it is uncertain who took which decisions how, when, why, and with what effects (Sørensen & Torfing 2021). The appointed citizen participants cannot be held to account for failing to reach a joint decision or for decisions with problematic outcomes. Moreover, it is difficult to hold elected politicians to account for decisions that they were not alone in making. Thus, accountability may become fuzzy and difficult to ensure if the arenas for democratic interaction are not forced to submit regular accounts of how they perceive the problem at hand and how they think it should be solved so as to facilitate public scrutiny, the posing of questions and the passing of judgment.

Besides the roadblocks that may hamper the development of interactive democracy, we should bear in mind that the involvement of citizens and private stakeholders in a structured exchange with elected politicians and their administrative aides may not always be possible or optimal. Issues pertaining to national security, crisis situations with an extreme time pressure, and politically contentious matters may not be amenable to interactive democracy, as the orchestration of deliberative processes through which experiences, views, and ideas are trustfully exchanged takes time, and major political conflicts may be too difficult to manage when taking place in a fishbowl.

LINKING REPRESENTATIVE AND INTERACTIVE DEMOCRACY IN HYBRID FORMS OF DEMOCRACY

The last three of the obstacles to the development of interactive democracy can be solved by linking representative democracy in hybrid democracy that combines representative democracy with interactive arenas where citizens are participating directly and actively in political deliberation that leads to new policy and governance solutions. A simple design principle would be to maintain that representative democratic assemblies should *both* mandate the formation of interactive democratic arenas with mixed membership *and* debate, amending and endorsing the ensuing proposals before they are implemented. While the co-creation of new joint proposals means that citizens are not reduced to external advisers, the dual role of the representative assemblies as both initiators and endorsers helps to keep the elected politicians in the driver's seat, facilitates holistic political coordination and prioritization and ensures accountability, since all of the policies are ultimately endorsed by politicians who can be ousted in the next election. Linking representative democracy and interactive democracy in this manner invokes the idea of elected politicians assuming the role of political metagovernors who are orchestrating, participating in, and concluding interactive processes of democratic decision-making (Sørensen & Torfing 2016).

The idea of creating compound or hybrid forms of democracy that combine representative democracy with a mixture of participatory and deliberative democracy is controversial but interesting: controversial because democratic theorists have spent decades advocating for either representative democracy or some form of participatory and deliberative democracy, and interesting because, as indicated in Table 12.1, the representative model of democracy and the participatory and deliberative models seem to complement each other as the problems of representative democracy are countered by the merits of participatory and deliberative democracy and vice versa. This discovery begs the question of how the two models could be integrated to achieve their combined merits while limiting their respective problems.

Thus far, there have only been scant attempts at integrating the two models of democracy. Parliamentary assemblies and their permanent committees

Table 12.1   *The two models of democracy—complementary merits and problems*

	Representative democracy	Participatory and deliberative democracy
Merits	Ensures formal participatory equality based on the "one man, one vote" maxim	Helps to construct a "we" and thus to counteract individualistic atomization and group-based fragmentation
	Comprises a widely accepted procedure for conflict resolution (majority voting)	Enables policymakers to elicit relevant information, experiences, and ideas through the inclusion of relevant and affected actors in joint deliberation
	Produces relatively clear and determinate outcomes of the decision-making process	Spurs the production of innovative solutions by stimulating processes of mutual and transformative learning
	Contains an efficient mechanism for holding political decision-makers to account for their doings (regular elections)	Builds joint ownership over new and bold solutions that help to ensure their implementation
Problems	By taking existing or minimally corrected preferences as given, it risks reinforcing existing distributions of power	Fosters biased and unjust outcomes if participation is low and selective and power asymmetries among the participants are large
	By excluding large segments of the population from the actual decision-making process, it turns citizens into passive spectators	Leads to paralysis if destructive conflicts persist in the face of attempts to overcome or mediate conflicts
	Lacks an efficient mechanism for transmitting relevant information, views and ideas to the actual decision-makers and mobilizing resources in the implementation phase	Results in non-implementable outcomes when deliberation leads to unclear and muddy compromises
	Fails to produce a sense of broad ownership over new solutions and thus hampers implementation	Has no clear method for holding decision-makers accountable for their decisions and the impact they have

Source: Sørensen & Torfing (2019).

provide considerable room for deliberation (Bächtiger 2014), but citizens are seldom part of these deliberations. Representative democracy is sometimes combined with direct democracy based on mass participation, as exemplified by the use of referendums in Switzerland (Trechsel & Kriesi 1996) and California (Bowler & Glazer 2008), but decision-making in referendums is based on majority rule rather than deliberation. In sum, while representative democracy is frequently combined with elements of either deliberation or direct participation, it is rarely combined with both elements, although there are important exceptions, such as the Oregon Citizens Initiative Review and the European Citizen Consultation, both of which allow elected politicians to engage with and take advice from citizens who are participating directly and actively in deliberative policymaking.

The integration of the two models of democracy through the creation of an institutional linkage between representative democracy and interactive democracy can be carried out in several ways. The way described above gives the elected politicians in representative democracy a privileged role in initiating and concluding processes of democratic interaction with citizens, which may clash with an ambition to enable politicians as well as administrators and citizens to prompt the formation of problem-focused arenas for interactive democracy. However, executive public administrators tend to have ample opportunity to persuade elected politicians to form interactive arenas when they can help to spur alignment, knowledge-sharing, and innovation, and is not difficult to imagine setting up procedures to allow citizens to suggest topics for joint deliberation or initiating processes of deliberation and inviting politicians and administrators to participate. To illustrate, Gentofte Municipality in Denmark organizes an annual political festival in which citizens can suggest topics for joint deliberation in new Task Committees and openly discuss problems and the need for new political solutions with local councilors and administrators.

TOWARD A MULTI-LEVEL HYBRID DEMOCRACY?

In the version presented above, hybrid democracy creates an institutional linkage between traditional forms of representative democracy and new forms of interactive democracy aimed at bringing citizens and politicians closer together in an effort to bridge the gulf of mistrust that nurtures right- and left-wing populism, which in turn constitutes an acute danger of authoritarianism, as seen with Trump in the US and Chávez in Venezuela. Obviously, the new proximity between elected politicians and citizens is easier to establish at the level of local government, where problems calling for public action are clearly visible to everyone, the physical distances are small, and it is easy to meet in person and exchange views and ideas about problems and possible solutions. However, digital tools supporting the use of online meetings can facilitate interaction across huge distances and may therefore allow national-level politicians to interact regularly with local constituencies of relevant and affected actors (see Esterling et al. 2011). If contact with local citizens is informal and organized individually by each politician, it might be difficult to link it to the institutions of representative democracy, although the politicians may carry valuable knowledge and ideas into the political deliberations in political committees and the democratic assembly. Hence, it is necessary to organize problem-focused meetings between groups of politicians and citizens who possess relevant experience and possibly even suggestions about which solutions might work. Excursions into real life, with visits to local institutions, open discussions with affected groups and the collection of expert assessments, may help elected politicians to improve the quality of political decisions while improving their democratic anchorage in local constituencies (see Ercan 2014).

Interestingly, attempts at connecting local, regional, national, and supranational government officials with local constituencies of citizens can also be organized bottom-up. In a fascinating book, *Mending Democracy*, Hendriks et al. (2020) describe several empirical cases of how local citizens have strived to connect with their political representatives to facilitate sustained democratic interaction. We need much more of this kind of democratic repair work and persistent efforts to link bottom-up and top-down initiatives if we are to build hybrid democracy based on an institutional linkage of representative and interactive democracy at all levels.

Ideally, elected politicians at all levels of government should have regular and sustained interaction with relevant constituencies of citizens from different localities in order to improve democratic input and output legitimacy. To prevent the interactive arenas being captured by a particular group of citizens acting as a pressure group on government, participation should be pluralistic, and the elected politicians should have both the first and final word in the sense of being able to frame and shape the interactive arenas and to make the final assessment of joint ideas or policy proposals. Rather than merely relying on the aggregation of political and democratic decisions from the local, regional, and national levels and to the supranational level, we must find ways to facilitate problem-focused dialogue between political representatives at different levels of government and groups of relevant and affected citizens, preferably through a two-stage process in which local, regional, and national politicians first engage a diverse group of citizens and then continue the discussion with elected politicians at the supranational level and a cross-national sounding board of specially invited citizens. The current experiments along these lines within the European Union must be expanded to produce a multi-level hybrid democracy.

New research must support practical efforts to expand democratic repair work aimed at connecting citizens with their political representatives. Three key areas of research require special attention: first, we must identify, describe, and assess different procedures for recruiting a diverse group of relevant and affected citizens to participate in arenas of interactive democracy in order to find ways of optimizing the legitimacy of selected groups of citizen participants. Second, we must explore the conditions for fruitful interaction between citizens and their representatives, as we have limited knowledge about how best to create a common knowledge base, how to level the playing field between citizens and their elected politicians, and how to formulate joint solutions that reflect the needs and wants of the citizens, the political commitments of the politicians, and the economic constraints of the public budget. Finally, we must analyze the different institutional designs aimed at linking interactive arenas with established democratic institutions to find new ways of balancing the need for bottom-up input and top-down political steering. Ideally, these pertinent research tasks should be addressed at different levels of government and within multi-level governance systems.

REFERENCES

Anderson, J. & Hoff, J. (2001). *Democracy and Citizenship in Scandinavia*. Basingstoke: Palgrave.

Ansell, C. (2011). *Pragmatist Democracy: Evolutionary Learning as Public Philosophy*. Oxford: Oxford University Press.

Ansell, C. & Gash, A. (2008). Collaborative Governance in Theory and Practice. *Journal of Public Administration Research and Theory*, *18*(4), 543–71.

Ansell, C. & Gash, A. (2018). Collaborative Platforms as a Governance Strategy. *Journal of Public Administration Research and Theory*, *28*(1), 16–32.

Ansell, C. & Torfing, J. (2017). Strengthening Political Leadership and Policy Innovation through the Expansion of Collaborative Forms of Governance. *Public Management Review*, *19*(1), 37–54.

Ansell, C., Doberstein, C., Henderson, H., Siddiki, S. & 't Hart, P. (2020). Understanding Inclusion in Collaborative Governance: A Mixed Methods Approach. *Policy and Society*, *39*(4), 570–91.

Arnstein, S. R. (1969). A Ladder of Citizen Participation. *Journal of the American Institute of Planners*, *35*(4), 216–24.

Avritzer, L. (2006). New Public Spheres in Brazil: Local Democracy and Deliberative Politics. *International Journal of Urban and Regional Research*, *30*(3), 623–37.

Bächtiger, A. (2014). Debate and Deliberation in Legislatures. In Martin, S., Saalfeld, T. & Strøm, K. (Eds.), *The Oxford Handbook of Legislative Studies* (145–66). Oxford: Oxford University Press.

Beetham, D. (2013). *The Legitimation of Power*. New York: Bloomsbury Publishing.

Bowler, S. & Glazer, A. (2008). *Direct Democracy's Impact on American Political Institutions*. New York: Palgrave Macmillan.

Dalton, R. J. & Welzel, C. (Eds.) (2014). *The Civic Culture Transformed: From Allegiant to Assertive Citizens*. Cambridge: Cambridge University Press.

Edelenbos, J. & Klijn, E. H. (2006). Managing Stakeholder Involvement in Decision Making: A Comparative Analysis of Six Interactive Processes in the Netherlands. *Journal of Public Administration Research and Theory*, *16*(3), 417–46.

Edelman, M. (1988). *Constructing the Political Spectacle*. Chicago, IL: University of Chicago Press.

Ercan, S. A. (2014). Same Problem, Different Solutions. In Gill, A. K., Strange, C. & Roberts, K. (Eds.), *Honor Killing and Violence* (199–217). Basingstoke: Palgrave Macmillan.

Esterling, K. M., Neblo, M. A. & Lazer, D. M. (2011). Means, Motive, and Opportunity in Becoming Informed about Politics: A Deliberative Field Experiment with Members of Congress and Their Constituents. *Public Opinion Quarterly*, *75*(3), 483–503.

Fung, A. & Wright, E. O. (2003). *Deepening Democracy: Institutional Innovations in Empowered Participatory Governance.* London: Verso.

Geissel, B. (2009). Participatory Governance: Hope or Danger for Democracy? A Case Study of Local Agenda 21. *Local Government Studies*, *35*(4), 401–14.

Geissel, B. & Newton, K. (2012). *Evaluating Democratic Innovations*: *Curing the Democratic Malaise?* London: Routledge.

Gutmann, A. & Thompson, D. (2004). *Why Deliberative Democracy?* Princeton, NJ: Princeton University Press.

Haughton, G., Gilchrist, A. & Swyngedouw, E. (2016). Rise Like Lions after Slumber: Dissent, Protest and (Post-)Politics in Manchester. *Territory, Politics, Governance*, *4*(4), 472–91.

Hayek, F. A. (1976). *The Road to Serfdom.* London: Routledge.

Hendriks, C. M. (2016). Coupling Citizens and Elites in Deliberative Systems: The Role of Institutional Design. *European Journal of Political Research*, *55*(1), 43–60.

Hendriks, C. M., Ercan, S. A. & Boswell, J. (2020). *Mending Democracy: Democratic Repair in Disconnected Times.* Oxford: Oxford University Press.

Hibbing, J. R. & Theiss-Morse, E. (2002). *Stealth Democracy: Americans' Beliefs about How Government Should Work.* Cambridge: Cambridge University Press.

Iandoli, L., Primario, S. & Zollo, G. (2021). The Impact of Group Polarization on the Quality of Online Debate in Social Media: A Systematic Literature Review. *Technological Forecasting and Social Change*, *170*(C), 120924.

Klijn, E. H. & Koppenjan, J. F. M. (2000). Public Management and Policy Networks: Foundations of a Network Approach to Governance. *Public Management*, *2*(2), 135–58.

MacPherson, C. B. (1977). *The Life and Times of Liberal Democracy.* Oxford: Oxford University Press.

Mair, P. (2013). *Ruling the World: The Hollowing of Western Democracy.* London: Verso.

Marshall, T. H. (1981). *The Right to Welfare.* London: Heinemann.

Mayer, I., Edelenbos, J. & Monnikhof, R. (2005). Interactive Policy Development: Undermining or Sustaining Democracy? *Public Administration*, *83*(1), 179–99.

Menon, S., Hartz-Karp, J. & Marinova, D. (2021). Can Deliberative Democracy Work in Urban India? *Urban Science*, *5*(2), 39.

Moynihan, D. P. (2008). *The Dynamics of Performance Management: Constructing Information and Reform.* Washington, DC: Georgetown University Press.

Murphy, A., Canel, M. J. & Barandiarán, X. (2020). How Do Public Leaders Learn from Society? A Reflexive Analysis of Action Learners. *Action Learning: Research and Practice*, *17*(2), 172–85.

Nabatchi, T. & Leighninger, M. (2015). *Public Participation for 21st Century Democracy.* San Francisco, CA: Jossey-Bass.

Neblo, M. A., Esterling, K. M. & Lazer, D. M. (2018). *Politics with the People: Building a Directly Representative Democracy* (vol. 555). Cambridge: Cambridge University Press.

Nissen, S. (2014). Who's in and Who's Out? Inclusion and Exclusion in C. Anterbury's Freshwater Governance. *New Zealand Geographer*, *70*(1), 33–46.

Núñez, L., Close, C. & Bedock, C. (2016). Changing Democracy? Why Inertia Is Winning over Innovation. *Representation*, *52*(4), 341–57.

Pellizzoni, L. (2003). Uncertainty and Participatory Democracy. *Environmental Values*, *12*(2), 195–224.

Pierre, J. (2009). Thematic Review: Reinventing Governance, Reinventing Democracy? *Policy & Politics, 37*(4), 591–609.

Pierre, J. & Røiseland, A. (2016). Exit and Voice in Local Government Reconsidered: A "Choice Revolution"? *Public Administration, 94*(3), 738–53.

Rosanvallon, P. (2008). *Counter-Democracy*. Cambridge: Cambridge University Press.

Rosanvallon, P. (2011). *Democratic Legitimacy: Impartiality, Reflexivity, Proximity.* Princeton, NJ: Princeton University Press.

Saward, M. (Ed.) (2003). *Democratic Innovation: Deliberation, Representation and Association.* Abingdon: Routledge.

Smith, G. (2005). *Power beyond the Ballot: 57 Democratic Innovations from around the World.* London: The Power Inquiry.

Smith, G. (2009). *Democratic Innovations: Designing Institutions for Citizen Participation.* Cambridge: Cambridge University Press.

Sørensen, E. (1997). Democracy and Empowerment. *Public Administration, 75*(3), 553–67.

Sørensen, E. (2013). Institutionalizing Interactive Governance for Democracy. *Critical Policy Studies, 7*(1), 72–86.

Sørensen, E. & Sandfort, J. R. (2022). Towards Hybrid Democracy and Interactive Political Leadership. In Krogh, A. H., Agger, A. & Triantafillou, P. (Eds.), *Public Governance in Denmark* (93–110). Bingley: Emerald Publishing Limited.

Sørensen, E. & Torfing, J. (2016). Political Leadership in the Age of Interactive Governance: Reflections on the Political Aspects of Metagovernance. In Edelenbos, J. & Meerkerk, I. (Eds.), *Critical Reflections on Interactive Governance: Self-Organization and Participation in Public Governance* (444–66). Cheltenham: Edward Elgar Publishing.

Sørensen, E. & Torfing, J. (2019). Towards Robust Hybrid Democracy in Scandinavian Municipalities? *Scandinavian Political Studies, 42*(1), 25–49.

Sørensen, E. & Torfing, J. (2021). Accountable Government through Collaborative Governance? *Administrative Sciences, 11*(4), 127.

Sørensen, E. & Triantafillou, P. (Eds.) (2009). *The Politics of Self-Governance.* London: Ashgate.

Stoker, G. (2019). Can the Governance Paradigm Survive the Rise of Populism? *Policy & Politics, 47*(1), 3–18.

Torfing, J., Peters, B. G., Pierre, J. & Sørensen, E. (2012). *Interactive Governance: Advancing the Paradigm.* Oxford: Oxford University Press.

Trechsel, A. H. & Kriesi, H. (1996). Switzerland: The Referendum System and Initiative as a Centrepiece of the Political System. In Gallagher, M. & Uleri, P. V. (Eds.), *The Referendum Experience in Europe* (185–208). Basingstoke: Palgrave Macmillan.

Wampler, B. (2010). *Participatory Budgeting in Brazil: Contestation, Cooperation, and Accountability.* University Park, PA: Pennsylvania State University Press.

Warren, M. E. (2011). Voting with Your Feet: Exit-Based Empowerment in Democratic Theory. *American Political Science Review, 105*(4), 683–701.

Zakaria, F. (2007). *The Future of Freedom: Illiberal Democracy at Home and Abroad* (revised edn.). New York: W. W. Norton & Company.

13. Reinvigorating public governance studies

This book has aimed to show how the ideas and practice of public governance are changing rapidly and profoundly in response to new demands, events, and opportunities. The changes are far from global and have a different pace in different parts of the world. Some of them are still only embryonic, whereas others are more consolidated and part of the new normal. However, it seems clear that the public governance orthodoxy, which seeks to combine elements of public bureaucracy with elements of New Public Management (NPM), is being challenged by the development of new forms of governance that are both supplementing and supplanting existing ideas and practices.

This concluding chapter aims to assess the transformations of public governance in a more holistic perspective and to discuss how the new and old forms of public governance can be combined in the real world. The chapter also raises the question of whether public governance and administration research are geared toward the analysis of the new and emerging trends that are part of the practical rethinking and redesign of governance that is currently unfolding. Finally, it sets out a research agenda for further studies of the changing forms of public governance.

RETHINKING AND REORGANIZING PUBLIC GOVERNANCE

The current transformations of public governance are surprising in the light of the deep-seated understanding of the public sector as being characterized by institutional inertia, structural path dependencies, and political resistance to change. However, the pervasiveness of complex problems, increasing societal turbulence, organizational learning from positive and negative governance experiences, new technological opportunities, and new demands from citizens and private stakeholders combine to drive public governance reforms that vary from disruptive changes to incremental shifts.

There are countless transformations in public governance. Some of the key transformations discussed in this book include:

- An emerging shift from sovereign to a more interactive political leadership whereby elected politicians aim to solicit inputs from citizens that enable them to better understand the problems at hand and to design new and better solutions that hit the target;
- A clear and notable shift from an inward focus on the compliant implementation of policy programs to a more outward-looking focus on creating public value for users, citizens, and society at large;
- A growing embrace of trust-based governance and management that spurs dialogue up and down the chain of command and provides a welcome alternative to control-based governance and management, which tends to produce unwanted rigidities and to demotivate public employees;
- A strategic reorientation of the public sector from a one-sided focus on the efficient use of existing resources to the mobilization of new ones through a growing emphasis on co-production and co-creation;
- A gradual transition from unicentric coordination based on centralized imposition and market-led multicentric coordination to pluricentric coordination based on negotiations between a plurality of actors;
- A shift from the predominance of the national governance of economic regulation and social policies to a growing embrace of multi-level governance involving public and private actors at the local, regional, national, and perhaps even international or supranational levels in relative self-organized interactions;
- The gradual erosion of the foundation for the use of hard power based on legal and political coercion and the complementary expansion of new forms of soft power based on voluntary norms and standards, ongoing dialogue, and jointly formulated discourses;
- A transition from an almost exclusive focus on intra-organizational leadership to a growing emphasis on inter-organizational leadership in networks and partnerships that provides arenas for collaborative innovation;
- A repurposing of public organizations from a fundamental preference for stability and incremental improvement to the embrace of disruptive forms of innovation aimed at step change designed to solve wicked problems in turbulent times;
- A rethinking of democracy through the development of a new interactive democracy based on direct and active participation in policy deliberation as a supplement to the classic spectator and counter-democracy in which citizens play a more passive role as voters and/or customers.

Extrapolating the ongoing attempts to rethink and reorganize public governance helps to paint a broad picture of where we are heading. While this book
has described and analyzed the new trends in public governance one by one and
in isolation from one another, there are clear affinities and spillovers that seem
to combine to form a relatively coherent pattern. Public governance appears
to be becoming more relational, interactive, and collaborative while simultaneously opening itself to the outside world, which is seen both as a resource
and a goal for public value creation. Political leadership and the practices of
democracy are becoming more interactive in a dual attempt to provide input
to public policymaking and to cater to citizen demand for more active and
direct influence on democratic decisions. Coordination increasingly involves
horizontal collaboration between multiple agencies and actors, and the formulation and implementation of public governance initiatives increasingly
include actors from different levels in collaborative efforts to produce effective
solutions and needs-based outcomes. Horizontal and vertical collaboration
is supported by the turn to trust-based governance and inter-organizational
leadership. The latter is also a key factor in mobilizing external resources from
the economy and civil society through the formation of networks, partnerships,
and other forms of participatory and collaborative arenas. In the new world of
interaction, collaboration, and networking, soft power plays an increasingly
important role vis-à-vis hard power, and the mobilization of the ideas and
resources of manifold public and private actors helps to enhance innovation
and produce important public value outcomes.

The current rethinking of public governance is motivated by problems
associated with classic forms of bureaucracy and the recent reforms associated
with NPM, and it squares in many ways with ideas promoted under the banner
of New Public Governance and to a lesser extent Digital Era Governance and
Public Value Management (see Torfing et al. 2020). Looking at the current
transformation from a different angle, we can compare the pattern emerging
from the rethinking of public governance described in this book with the
four scenarios for the future of public governance advanced by Peters (1996)
more than a quarter of a century ago. Here, Peters compares four emerging
visions of public governance: (1) market governance aimed at breaking
the public monopoly on policy, regulation, and service production through
decentralized governance based on market mechanisms in order to lower
public expenditure; (2) participatory governance that seeks to dismantle the
bureaucratic hierarchy by creating flatter organizations based on teamwork,
negotiations, and involvement in order to enhance public consultation; (3)
flexible governance that aims to counter the dysfunctionalities of permanent
governance institutions by creating virtual organizations with temporary staff
and to focus on experimentation in order to enhance effectiveness; and (4)
deregulated governance aimed at removing bureaucratic regulations by reduc-

ing control and giving managers and employees more freedom, thus fostering a more entrepreneurial government that pursues creativity and innovation. Interestingly, the pattern of governance transformation unearthed in this book suggests that participative and deregulated governance go hand in hand—and they would appear to have had greater impact than market governance and flexible governance. This might not be too surprising, as market governance and flexible governance are both anti-government scenarios, whereas participatory governance aiming to enhance collaboration and democratic legitimacy and deregulated governance aiming to diminish the impact of bureaucratic control and command mechanisms both aim to reform government to make it more democratic and effective.

COMBINING OLD AND NEW FORMS OF PUBLIC GOVERNANCE

This book has studied new trends in public governance that become visible when compared to the public governance orthodoxy that is a hybrid governance regime combining highly entrenched forms of public bureaucracy with elements of NPM, such as the introduction of quasi-markets, free service choice, performance management, and a focus on cost efficiency. While most of the recent attempts to rethink public governance have emerged in response to negative experiences with and criticisms of particular aspects of the public governance orthodoxy—and can therefore be seen as oppositional—it is more likely that we will see different combinations of old and new forms of public governance, as the old is seldom disappearing because new ideas and practices are coming to the fore.

The combination of old and new forms of public governance can assume many different forms. One possibility is that the new forms of governance become subject to repressive tolerance on the part of the old and established governance paradigm. Hence, the new forms of governance are given a limited space and influence, and they are generally seen as a necessary but somewhat problematic supplement to the old forms of governance. This may be the fate of interactive political leadership in places where elected politicians are reluctant to share the power bestowed on them through elections with the citizens and stakeholders engaged in interactive policymaking.

Another possibility is that the new takes over and becomes predominant within the public sector, thus relegating the old to a marginalized position and viewing it as a remnant of the past. This may occur with the new focus on resource mobilization, since the old idea that the public sector can solve all problems on its own and merely by using its own budget and staff seems less and less tenable in a cash-strapped public sector facing growing service demands that are increasing expectations to its problem-solving capacity.

A third possibility is conflict: the old and new forms of governance may both have a strong group of supporters in the public sector who tend to believe that there is a zero-sum game between the old and new and that one can only grow at the expense of the other. In some public organizations, this is the situation in relation to the control–trust nexus, as some public managers think that trust-based governance will erode the much-needed control with public employee performance, while others think that the expansion of trust-based management presupposes the elimination of top-down control.

A fourth option is cohabitation based on some kind of contingency approach recognizing the strengths and weaknesses of both old and new forms of governance and making a selective choice between them pending a careful analysis of the context and situation. Hence, both old and new forms of governance co-exist as tools in a toolbox that are used when deemed appropriate. To illustrate, hard and soft governance can be seen as tools that can be used in different measures in different contexts and situations.

A final option is hybridization, where particular aspects of old and new forms of governance are merged and integrated either deliberately or by a slow grafting process. This might be the case both with the attempt to integrate intra- and inter-organizational leadership and with the attempt to create hybrid forms of democracy combining representative democracy with more interactive forms of democracy.

Hybridization may be taken to the next level by strategic managers who carefully analyze their organization and the threats and opportunities it faces and then try to form a dream team consisting of the best and most relevant of the old and new forms of governance. Such an exercise may help executive public managers to adjust their public governance toolbox flexibly and without throwing the baby out with the bathwater in the name of agility and radical change. As such, dynamic conservatism may be the prudent way forward (Ansell et al. 2015).

THE STATE OF PUBLIC GOVERNANCE AND ADMINISTRATION RESEARCH AND THE NEED FOR CHANGE

The introduction of NPM beginning in the late 1970s was the first major challenge to the hitherto undisputed rule of representative democracy and public bureaucracy, and a new hegemonic combination of old and new governance elements materialized a decade or more later. After years of stable predominance, the new public governance orthodoxy has been challenged and problematized; and this time, the criticisms and attempts to rethink governance came from many different quarters. The result is the proliferation of a broad range of new ideas and practices, some of which have been discussed in this book.

Public governance and administration research is struggling to keep track of the empirical transformation of public governance and its manifold implications. As indicated in the chapters above, new theories are being developed to conceptualize, understand, explain, and assess the current rethinking of governance. But many of these new theories are ad hoc, tentative, and incomplete, and it goes without saying that they are short on precise concepts, well-tested arguments, and well-informed predictions. This is not necessarily a problem, since all new research in the social sciences must necessarily begin by exploring and interpreting important phenomena before proceeding to more rigorous comparative, qualitative, and quantitative analysis that can falsify new propositions. What is clear, however, is that we need more research and more critical contestations of new provisional insights to produce more solid conclusions.

The research on the rethinking of public governance that lies before us may benefit from three reorientations in how we are conducting public governance and administration research. The first reorientation calls for a stronger embrace of what is currently referred to as "positive public administration" (Douglas et al. 2021). Science is by definition critical, as it aims to scrutinize existing knowledge, insights, and assumptions. The attempt to falsify hypotheses rather than trying to verify and confirm them bears witness to the critical aspirations of science. However, in the field of public governance and administration, an enormous amount of energy is being directed at pinpointing and dissecting instances in which governments fail our expectations by delivering public governance that is inefficient, wasteful, failing, and bad. By contrast, public governance and administration researchers are not as attuned to spotting and naming successes in public administration and governance as they are to finding faults and blaming public officials and agencies for them (Luetjens & 't Hart 2019). This inherent bias impairs the ability to identify new and emerging forms of governance that have a demonstrably positive effect on the provision of fair, effective, efficient, robust, and democratic outcomes for citizens and society at large. To solve this problem, a group of academic researchers has launched a research program that, instead of narrowly focusing on the dark side of governance, also aims to walk on the bright side by seeking to uncover what works in practice, why it does so and how it can be scaled. Such a program will help to answer the pertinent question of why some new and emerging policies, programs, strategies, organizations, services, networks, and so on emerge and manage to perform better than others to produce widely valued societal outcomes (Douglas et al. 2021).

The second reorientation calls for an improvement of our capacity to work closely with practitioners and to apply an interactive research strategy when analyzing how public governance is transforming. Continuous interaction with practitioners in and around the public sector can help public administration researchers to detect new trends and innovations early on, and it may start a conversation about the problems that are being addressed and the solutions that are provided through emerging innovations in public governance. Identifying new and promising practices may spark research-based evaluations that can test the initial conjectures about the benefits accruing from governance innovation. Practitioners may help to provide access to data and critical feedback to preliminary conclusions. Discussing the results of the evaluation with practitioners at different levels and in different localities may help to explore the potential for scaling and diffusing new public governance solutions that enhance the production of public value.

The third reorientation calls for deliberate effort to bring political science back into public governance and administration research. As the above analysis of the empirical transformations of public governance shows, political and administrative logics are intertwined and almost inseparable (Peters et al. 2022). However, while politics, power, and democracy pervade the efforts of elected politicians and public administrators to govern society and the economy, there is an unfortunate bifurcation between political science and public administration research that hampers the quality and relevance of much of the public administration research, which frequently fails to address questions concerning the political foundation of administrative practices, the power struggles within and around public administration, and the administrative efforts to protect democracy and democratize public governance. Hence, we must break down the institutional and academic lines of demarcation separating the two adjacent disciplinary sub-fields and focus on how political logics structure public governance and administration and, *mutatis mutandis*, how administration serves as a vehicle for politics, power, and democracy.

Changing how academics are conducting their research is difficult, but the combined effect of a more interactive and interdisciplinary research approach and greater appreciation of new positive experiences with public governance solutions that combine administrative and political logic may be considerable. Hopefully, then, new generations can be persuaded to widen their perspective, engage with practitioners, and help to identify and critically evaluate novel forms of public governance in order to identify and enlarge what works, thereby improving public value creation.

FURTHER RESEARCH ON THE RETHINKING OF GOVERNANCE

This book has considered different examples of how public governance is being rethought and redesigned in some Western countries. The governance transformations are cutting-edge in the sense that they are pioneering, and they are not found everywhere. Little is known, however, about their empirical prevalence in Western and non-Western countries—so here lies a massive task for future research. We need to know much more about how these and other innovations in public governance, administration, and management are diffused across the globe. Further research is also required to address the specific drivers of the many different governance transformations and further analysis of the emerging patterns is needed.

Moreover, while this book has offered insights into how new and emerging forms of governance can be conceptualized and theorized, we need to further explore the interaction between new empirical forms of governance and new theories of governance (see Ansell 2023).

Finally, we need to test whether the current rethinking of governance and the ensuing governance transformations are sufficient to solve the many challenges to the provision of fair, efficient, effective, democratic, and robust governance. If they are not, we must ask ourselves how public governance research can support the development of an experimentalist strategy capable of providing the solutions we need. In some respects, the European Union has served as a governance laboratory (Sabel & Zeitlin 2010), but the experimentalist approach to public governance must be extended upwards, downwards, and outwards.

REFERENCES

Ansell, C. (2023). *Rethinking Theories of Governance*. Cheltenham: Edward Elgar Publishing.

Ansell, C., Boin, A. & Farjoun, M. (2015). Dynamic Conservatism: How Institutions Change to Remain the Same. In Kraatz, M. S. (Ed.), *Institutions and Ideals: Philip Selznick's Legacy for Organizational Studies* (89–119). Bingley: Emerald.

Douglas, S., Schillemans, T., 't Hart, P., Ansell, C., Bøgh Andersen, L., Flinders, M., … & Torfing, J. (2021). Rising to Ostrom's Challenge: An Invitation to Walk on the Bright Side of Public Governance and Public Service. *Policy Design and Practice*, 4(4), 441–51.

Luetjens, J. C. & 't Hart, P. (2019). *Governing by Looking Back: Learning from Successes and Failures*. An ANZSOG research paper for the Australian Public Service Review Panel.

Peters, B. G. (1996). Political Institutions, Old and New. In Goodin, R. E. & Klingemann, H. (Eds.), *A New Handbook of Political Science* (205–20). Oxford: Oxford University Press.

Peters, B. G., Pierre, J., Sørensen, E. & Torfing, J. (2022). Bringing Political Science Back into Public Administration Research. *Governance: An International Journal of Policy, Administration, and Institutions*, 35(4), 962–82.

Sabel, C. F. & Zeitlin, J. (2010). *Experimentalist Governance in the European Union: Towards a New Architecture*. Oxford: Oxford University Press.

Torfing, J., Andersen, L. B., Greve, C. & Klausen, K. K. (2020). *Public Governance Paradigms: Competing and Co-Existing*. Cheltenham: Edward Elgar Publishing.

Index